WRITER'S MARKET® FAQs

Peter Rubie

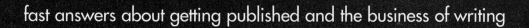
fast answers about getting published and the business of writing

WRITER'S DIGEST BOOKS
Cincinnati, Ohio
http://www.writersdigest.com

Writer's Market® FAQs: Fast Answers About Getting Published and the Business of Writing. Copyright © 2002 by Peter Rubie. Manufactured in the United States of America. All rights reserved. No part of this book may be reproduced in any form or by any electronic or mechanical means including information storage and retrieval systems without permission in writing from the publisher, except by a reviewer, who may quote brief passages in a review. Published by Writer's Digest Books, an imprint of F&W Publications, Inc., 1507 Dana Avenue, Cincinnati, Ohio 45207. (800) 289-0963. First edition.

Visit our Web site at www.writersdigest.com for information on more resources for writers.

To receive a free weekly e-mail newsletter delivering tips and updates about writing and about Writer's Digest products, register directly at our Web site at http://newsletters.fwpublications.com.

06   05   04   03   02   5   4   3   2   1

Library of Congress Cataloging-in-Publication Data

Rubie, Peter
   Writer's market FAQs: fast answers about getting published and the business of writing / by Peter Rubie.—1st ed.
      p.   cm.
   Includes index.
   ISBN 1-58297-071-8 (alk. paper)
      1. Authorship—Marketing. 2. Authorship. I. Title.

PN161.R83   2002
808'.02—dc21
                                                              2001046880
                                                              CIP

Edited by Jack Heffron and Meg Leder
Designed by Mary Barnes Clark
Cover design by Tin Box Studio, Inc./Cincinnati, Ohio
Production coordinated by Kristen Heller

Dedication

For Mel, who has taught me so much

Acknowledgments

Thanks to Jack Heffron and Meg Leder
at Writer's Digest for their
guidance and patience

About the Author

   Peter Rubie grew up in the United Kingdom before coming to America in the early 1980s and is currently the president of The Peter Rubie Literary Agency in New York City. Prior to becoming an agent, he was an editor whose authors won prizes and critical acclaim. He has also been the editor-in-chief of a Manhattan local newspaper and a freelance editor and book doctor for major publishers. In England he worked for BBC Radio and in Fleet Street as a journalist, and he is also currently the director of the New York University (NYU) Summer Publishing Institute. He is a member of the NYU faculty Center for Publishing, where he teaches the only university-level course in the country on how to become a literary agent. He was a regular reviewer for the international trade magazine *Publishers Weekly* and is a published author of two novels and several books of nonfiction, including the *Everything Guitar Book: From Buying the Right Guitar to Mastering Your Favorite Songs* (with Jack Wilkins), *Everything Shakespeare, Hispanics in Hollywood: An Encyclopedia of 100 Years in Film and Television*, the well-received *The Elements of Storytelling: How to Write Compelling Fiction* and *How to Tell a Story: The Secrets of Writing Captivating Tales* (with Gary Provost). He regularly lectures and writes on publishing and the craft of writing and is a jazz musician. A new novel about jazz and a thriller are in the pipeline.

Table of Contents

Annotated Table of Contents

Chapter 3: AGENTS, EDITORS AND OTHER PUBLISHING PEOPLE. 42

Chapter 4: MARKETING YOUR WORK: FROM
IDEA TO BOOKSTORE 82

Chapter 7: READING THE CONTRACT 155

Chapter 8: SUBRIGHTS AND ROYALTIES 196

Chapter 9: E-PUBLISHING AND OTHER ROUTES 211

Chapter 10: WRITING AND EDITING TIPS 226

 **Introduction**

Why bother to write yet another book about publishing?

The best answer to that question actually starts with the poem "Infant Innocence" by Ogden Nash:

> The grizzly bear is huge and wild,
> He has devoured the infant child.
> The infant child is not aware
> He has been eaten by the bear.

With the proliferation of computers and word-processing programs and a growing cult of "personality" authors making big bucks, it is tempting to think that publishing has become an easy avenue for making quick money while at the same time satisfying some latent creative urge. This is a bit like deciding, "I think I'll make a movie. After all, I've watched lots of them on TV and in movie houses," and then buying a video camera and some digital tape and thinking that's all you need.

Rather like Ogden Nash's infant child, "young" writers sometimes innocently believe that studying writing and honing their talent is all they need to do in order to get published, rather than treating those things as necessary first steps. One of the major traps of all the arts (whether it's writing, music, painting or whatever) is the mistaken belief that technique, which is so hard come by for so many artists, is an end in itself, and the artist should be rewarded for proficiency. Alas, technique is only a path, not an end. The end should be powerful, emotive storytelling. The great jazz guitarist Wes Montgomery was once asked how much technique a jazz musician needed to master in order to consider himself a real jazz musician. Wes's answer was, "You need as much technique as you have ideas to play."

And so, rather than learn how to manipulate the system to their advantage, young writers mistakenly approach the publishing industry as though it were an ogre that must be slain, wielding their talent like a cudgel, trying to fell all obstacles before them as they attempt to bludgeon their way to fame and literary success.

More experienced writers often face the same kinds of issues: They have mastered their craft to some degree, perhaps even published a book or two, but they have not really come to grips with the marketing and business ends of writing, feeling that talent and effort will conquer all. Alas, for most of us it doesn't.

Writers (and other artists as well) often fail to appreciate that in the twenty-first century economy, coming to terms with marketing and sales tactics and realistically understanding the audience is a huge part of becoming a successful writer. It's not just about creating the art: It's also about honing and clarifying the message until it is easy to grasp and disseminate to an audience that is brutally overwhelmed by the noise of thousands of other artists all clamoring for their attention at the same time. These days it is not the loudest but the most focused who win.

Publishing is an industry that is almost schizophrenic—in its obsessions with marketing and promotion as well as an eagerness to fall in love with a writer's achievements and ability. Gaining as much intimate knowledge as possible about publishing is a decided edge to any writer's ambitions to become well published.

Getting published is not just about being a good writer—it's about (1) *thinking*, that is, exploring new ideas in an entertaining way; and (2) learning how best to present yourself and your work to publishing industry professionals so that they in turn can help you reach your core audience and become someone who consistently makes money (if not always a living) using graceful, exciting language to put down on paper those interesting ideas.

Publishing has changed—and is changing—radically. New words are entering the lexicon—Web page, digital audio, e-publishing—joining old ones such as proposal, query, sell through, reserve against returns, etc.

Today, publishing is more corporate than ever and more focused on the bottom line. It is much less concerned with "art" and creativity (though it's something of a myth to think it ever was); yet it is a mistake to think that both "art" and "creativity" don't matter. Paradoxically, they count more than ever before.

While more books are being published overall, fewer books are being published by individual publishers. However, independent publishers like Running Press, Andrews McMeel, Ten Speed, Soho Press or Sourcebooks are flourishing like mushrooms in the shadows of the corporate takeovers and mergers of the "biggies."

The trick for a new writer is to discover *what* kinds of books particular publishers are looking for and *who* is publishing what authors are writing. In other words, pay attention to your audience. Cynicism, particularly "writing just for the money," gives little advantage to the beginning writer because the road one must travel as a writer is too tough for anyone but the pure of heart and purpose.

These days, sales of mass-market paperback books are falling off. Meanwhile, the hardcover book, whether fiction or nonfiction, is making a strong comeback because potential profit margins on these books are much more attractive to publishers. Indeed, more hardcovers are being printed and sold than ever before, either by big-name houses such as Random House or small publishers like Walker & Co. or Algonquin.

But hardcover books have always been the province of the more elegant and accomplished writer and the writer who can sell big numbers on his or her reputation. It's tough for a writer to come out of the gate first time out with a "winner," though this is being demanded from the bigger publishers more and more. It used to be you could "cut your teeth" on writing and publishing a few paperback books. This is harder to do, even in the fields of mystery, science fiction and romance. The bar of expected accomplishment is being raised on the new writer. In other words, it's tougher to get published than it used to be.

There are lots of books about writing, but the editors at Writer's Digest and I realized that few books address the metamorphosing business of publishing. And there are questions galore to ask about what's happening and what you should do about it.

Whenever I teach, the most productive, informative and enjoyable part of the session is invariably the Question and Answer section. This could be a reflection of being a frustrated "ham actor" (When I was sixteen, I confided to an older, relatively successful professional actor friend, "I'm thinking about becoming an actor." He said, "If you're *thinking* about it, don't do it."), but it's also partly connected to my earlier days as an improvising musician. I love the give-and-take of the classroom and the challenge of answering a pointed, well-thought-out question because it makes me think about familiar things in new ways. That in turn improves me as both a writer and as a publishing industry professional.

What we intend to do in this book is use a question and answer format to trace a few typical writing projects and hopefully introduce novice writers to some important information they should possess to successfully get themselves in print.

So, to the question "Why should I bother to read your book?", I answer, "Why not? You've nothing to lose, and it might even be fun."

chapter one

The Basics

How do I go about getting started in the business of writing?

First, if you want to be taken seriously as a writer, run, don't walk, to your nearest bookstore and buy a copy of William Strunk Jr. and E.B. White's *The Elements of Style*. Take it home and read it from cover to cover.

This little book is fantastic and should be compulsory reading for every writer of *anything*, regardless of how often he or she has been published. After you've read it, wait a few months, and then read it again. Read it often.

It is a model of the very advice and guidance it offers, and it discusses language, style and grammar—the tools of our trade—in ways that may be revelatory or at least intriguing to you if you intend to be considered a serious writer.

You should also have the following reference books: *Merriam-Webster's Collegiate Dictionary, Tenth Edition*; *Roget's Thesaurus*; *Bartlett's Familiar Quotations*; an atlas; a library card.

What about things like talent, discipline and determination? How do they affect my goals?

Talent is a really tricky subject to tackle. It's like trying to define "love." Perhaps talent can be considered the speed with which someone learns something, but that's probably not a satisfactory answer. It does mean that it may take you longer than others to reach your goal as a writer, but you can get there in the end if you apply yourself appropriately.

Reaching your goal requires the other elements in the question, of course: determination and discipline. If you don't have determination—and at the beginning of your writing career the line between determination and obsession may be razor thin—you won't get anywhere without extraordinary luck.

Discipline is about stamina, organization and a realization that you only get better by working on the weakest parts of your technique, not continually reveling in your abilities to do this or that well. Writing is not about an ability to do dialogue, exposition, description or any of a myriad of other things; it's about how you integrate them as a whole to the service of your imagination and the clarity of your thinking.

What equipment do I need?

All good writers are also thinkers and most are well read. A writer's most important tool (after his brain) is some sort of word processor. Its ease of use and innate organizational abilities, plus a deskjet or laser jet printer for neat printouts, are really a must. The computer and printer don't have to be the latest, cutting-edge equipment; when all is said and done, all you need is a way to get words (that is, your thoughts) down on paper and then correct them later. (If you don't have a computer, explore the possibility of using one at your local public library.)

One of the great tools at a writer's service is the ability to research. Buy some books on how best to organize yourself and your work. Get yourself a library card.

Apart from the library, which is still the best place for you to do some research, buy yourself a modem for your computer so that you can use the Internet for *initial* research that you can finish in the local library. Many new computers come already equipped with a 56K internal modem and software that will allow you to connect to the Internet. Though harder to find these days, there are still some free ISPs (that is, gateways to the Internet), such as BlueLight.com from Kmart; free e-mail services are still plentiful. You're better off with MSN, Earthlink, AOL or some such ISP if you're a novice in this field, though, because they make e-mail easier to use initially.

If you use the library for computer-based research, rather than printing what you discover and paying a per page fee to the library, you can often e-mail the information to yourself for free.

Also, subscribe to some magazines, including a writing magazine like *Writer's Digest* or *Writer*, and get a couple of good books on writing. These will help you become familiar with issues in the field of publishing.

But I don't have any of this stuff yet. Can't I just handwrite my stuff and send it to an editor or agent?

If you want to handwrite drafts of your work, that, of course, is entirely a matter for you and the speed with which you are comfortable working. However, handwriting *anything* that is to be sent to an editor or agent is an absolute no-no. Most editors or agents won't even bother to read what you've handwritten. In fact, many editors even look skeptically at manuscripts produced on a typewriter, although they are accepted if formatted correctly and neatly produced.

Remember, your manuscript will create a first impression that can encourage an editor or agent to read your manuscript next or make them groan at the sight of it, only to be placed on a pile to be looked at later, if you're lucky. Editors and agents read a lot; therefore, it's in your best interest to make their reading experience as pleasurable as possible. Don't cram words on the page or use narrow margins; don't use single spacing (except in letters) or tiny fonts. Have mercy on our tired eyes and some thought for the person on the receiving end of your material. It will work in your favor, trust me.

What are the titles of some good books on writing?

There are zillions of books on writing, and their quality varies widely. Here's a list of some good nonfiction books about writing and publishing that helped me. (I've also shamelessly included several I've written, too.) They will hopefully start you off on the right track by providing advice and inspiration.

The Elements of Storytelling: How to Write Compelling Fiction—Peter Rubie

This gives you the basics of what to look for when you start writing fiction or narrative nonfiction.

You Can Write a Novel—James V. Smith

An introduction to the basics of writing fiction.

Novelist's Essential Guide to Creating Plot—J. Madison Davis

I confess: Jim is one of my clients, and this is one of the best books on plotting (a tricky subject to master) that I've read.

How to Tell a Story: The Secrets of Writing Captivating Tales—Peter Rubie and Gary Provost

If you can find it, a book that will help you with the concepts of line editing your manuscript.

The Tyranny of Words—Stuart Chase

Brilliant in the way it tackles how we use language and the pitfalls that befall the unwary writer.

The Elements of Style—William Strunk Jr. and E.B. White

Enough said. *The* book on language and style. Don't call yourself a writer if you haven't read it.

The Hero With a Thousand Faces—Joseph Campbell

Despite becoming a somewhat trendy interpreter of myths for the Hollywood set because of his association with George Lucas, Campbell wrote one of the definitive books on mythology, which is in turn one of the basic elements of writing any kind of narrative.

Character Analysis—**Wilhelm Reich**

What is fiction if not stories about dysfunctional people or people with problems? One of the major psychological tracts on character and how it manifests itself in a physical way. After reading this you'll be able to "see" neurotic people with much greater ease. It's a real eye-opener.

Memories, Dreams, Reflections—**C.G. Jung and Aniela Jaffe**

Jung's definitive work on what makes us tick. It can help you with developing your characters.

The Art of Fiction: Notes on Craft for Young Writers—**John Gardner**

One of the best books on writing fiction ever published, in my opinion. It will make you think about writing in challenging ways that will improve your technique.

On Becoming a Novelist—**John Gardner (Foreword by Raymond Carver)**
On Moral Fiction—**John Gardner**

Both books develop ideas raised in the first book.

The Screenwriter's Workbook—**Syd Field**
The Screenwriter's Problem Solver: How to Recognize, Identify, and Define Screenwriting Problems—**Syd Field**

Screenwriting is about structure, and these are among the best books on screenwriting on the market. Modify these ideas to narrative writing. It will be an eye-opener for you.

Aspects of the Novel—**E.M. Forster**

One of the more interesting and thoughtful books on writing (actually, a collection of lectures given at Cambridge University) by one of England's premier writers (*A Passage to India*, etc.) during the early part of the twentieth century.

Make Your Words Work—Gary Provost

Gary treasured words and the use of language, and this discusses how to use words as tools better than many books and does so in Gary's distinctive and deceptively graceful prose. It seems so easy to write like this—until you try to do it yourself.

What If?: Writing Exercises for Fiction Writers—Anne Bernays and Pamela Painter

Exercises and thought-provoking ideas about writing fiction.

Starting From Scratch: A Different Kind of Writers' Manual—Rita Mae Brown

An idiosyncratic view of writing that is entertaining and thought provoking.

Bird by Bird: Some Instructions on Writing and Life—Anne Lamott
I'd Rather Be Writing—Marcia Golub

Two more entertaining and idiosyncratic explorations of the writer's journey and craft.

Editors on Editing: What Writers Need to Know About What Editors Do—Gerald Gross

Interviews with several leading editors on what they look for in manuscripts and what they think constitutes good writing and publishable material.

Writing for Story: Craft Secrets of Dramatic Nonfiction by a Two-Time Pulitzer Prize Winner—Jon Franklin

An interesting book on writing nonfiction by a prize-winning author that will show you how to follow a true story, draft an outline and make factual pieces come alive.

The Art of Creative Nonfiction: Writing and Selling the Literature of Reality—
Lee Gutkind
An award-winning author and editor gives concise, specific advice on writing
and selling your work.

The Insider's Guide to Getting an Agent—Lori Perkins
A unique insider's approach to how some literary agents think and what they do.

I've never really done any real writing before. Should I go to school or take lessons or something?

Absolutely. Read some books on writing aimed at senior high students. This is
an excellent audience to imagine as you develop and write your nonfiction
book. The reason? To be successful as a writer, you need to be able to explain
complex ideas in a simple yet focused way that doesn't talk down to your
audience and yet entertains and grips them.

Writing classes will remind you of all the things you thought you knew from
high school but had forgotten. You'll mix with people who are like-minded.

Writing is usually such a solitary pursuit that if you get an opportunity to
mix with others who think and talk writing just like you do, take advantage
of it. A writing class will provide you with your first audience; then you can
judge whether or not your ideas or the way you are presenting them is working.

It will also provide you with discipline and techniques for developing stamina
so that you use your time and effort effectively. Take advantage of what people
have already worked out and see if it will work for you; if you reject it, you'll
be rejecting it in favor of something that will work for you. How do you know
if it's working? You'll get published.

Writing to be published may seem easy, but it's not. Most people who do it
seriously have been at it a long, long time. The key to writing is to continually
read what you've written and ask yourself two basic questions: (1) Do I really
mean what I've written? In other words, carefully examine the literal meaning
of your words; and, (2) When the words and sentences start to spin their sticky

spider's web around you, ask yourself, "What, exactly, am I trying to say?" Once you've answered that question for yourself, just write it down.

What about writers conferences? Are they worth attending?

Once you have the writing bug and you've been working at it for a little while, consider attending a writing conference. This will allow you to listen, meet and talk to others like yourself.

Conferences also provide the opportunity to mingle with and occasionally meet published authors, editors and agents. Listen to what they have to say. Just remember: Every published author was in exactly your position sometime in their life.

I hear a lot about writers groups? Are they worthwhile?

One of the best ways to start writing is to join a local writers group or workshop. Failing that, form your own small group with a few other like-minded souls. Advertise your group in the local paper or on the bulletin board of your local bookstore and see if you get favorable responses. Check out writers forums on the Web and post your work on those.

If ever a medium seems divinely designed for one group of people, it's the Internet and people with writing aspirations. If you have a computer with Internet access, search for some sites about writing.

There are many online writing groups of varying quality and friendliness. Some of the best places to start are forums on America Online, Compuserve, DejaNews or About.Com, to mention only a few.

Writing workshops and groups are an excellent way of working out your writing muscles. Listening to what others do and the problems they are having can be instructive guides to your own bad writing habits and weaknesses. You'll mix with people with whom you have much in common. Writing is a solitary enough pursuit; if you get an opportunity to mix with others who think and talk writing just like you do, take advantage of it.

What's so great about joining a writers group? I hate being a member of something.

Yeah, yeah, we all know the Groucho Marx quote about never joining a club that would have him as a member. But, engaging in serious and positive critiques of the works of others is as important as the time you spend putting down words on the page. Why? Because it affords you the objectivity to see what works—or doesn't work—and why. And once you see mistakes in the work of others, you inevitably start seeing similar things in your own work.

Writers groups are also about reaffirming one's creativity, getting reassurance and feedback on your work and developing confidence and individuality when it comes to putting down words on paper. Guaranteed, there will be someone in the group whose literary talent or skills you envy. But the joke is, that person probably envies something in your writing.

Toni Morrison, Karen Joy Fowler and Amy Tan, for example, all began their writing careers as members of different writers groups. I joined a writers group in the early 1980s, though I must confess after twelve plus years as a professional journalist, I was something of a skeptic at first. What could I learn? It turned out to be fun to meet every week and take turns reading and listening, watching other people's books (as well as your own) grow like acorns into slender oak trees. Out of the regular six or so members who attended every week, three of us ended up working full time in the publishing industry, and all but one ended up with published books under our belts.

I seem to stare at a blank computer screen for ages, sometimes days. How do I get started?

There are a number of camps on how to deal with this problem. Some say just sit down and start writing. That's fine if something comes. The thing to avoid is a sort of "Mexican standoff" between you and your computer, where you sit there determined to write, nothing comes, and you refuse to get up and do something else until you've written your requisite number of words or pages.

There are several good books for help with this problem: Anne Bernays's

What If? is a good one to start with. Jack Heffron's *The Writer's Idea Book* or James V. Smith's *Fiction Writer's Brainstormer* are others.

Here's my advice: Know what you want to say before you sit down to say it. If you don't know what to say, do something mundane and think out your writing problem while you're doing, say, the laundry or gardening. Writing takes place first in your mind, not your fingers.

Second, come up with a writing routine, something that gets you in the mood. Ernest Hemingway reportedly sharpened lots of pencils. I share Thomas Wolfe's liking for walks. Remember, writing is about *thinking*, so you can write while you're doing the laundry, the ironing, cooking, mowing the lawn . . . get the idea?

Unless you're going to do a stream-of-consciousness exercise, where you write down everything that pops into your head as it happens, try to develop an idea of what you want to write about before you sit down to do it so that you avoid staring at a blank computer screen for hours.

Is keeping a journal a good idea?

Hang this up in a prominent place in your home: *Writers write.*

Regardless of what they write, writers are plagued by a need to put down words on paper. Do it regularly, and do it often. Keeping a journal is one way.

It provides a certain discipline; you can always find something to write about, even if it's only a shopping list or a piece about doing the laundry, and the regular habit of writing every day is invaluable for growing writers.

It may also provide you with some material from which to draw one day. That shouldn't be a primary concern, however. Write in your journal for the sake of keeping the journal. Journal writing will help you refine your ability to put down your thoughts and feelings in a clear, concise way. Read a good book about journal writing such as *Keeping a Journal You Love* by Sheila Bender, *The Book of Myself: A Do-It-Yourself Autobiography in 201 Questions* by Carl and David Marshall, *All About Me* by Philipp Keel, and *Leaving a Trace: On Keeping a Journal* by Alexandra Johnson.

What's *Publishers Weekly,* and should I get a subscription?

Publishers Weekly is the industry magazine. It's read avidly by everyone in publishing and a few weeks' worth of issues will help you gain a focus on the business of publishing and bookselling and why they are the way they are. It's also worth subscribing to Michael Cader's e-mail newsletter PublishersLunch .com, which is both witty and informative.

The more you keep in touch with what's going on and why it's happening, the more likely you will be to write something of merit that's publishable.

What are some basic things I need to know about publishing?

Publishing is first and foremost a *business,* and decisions are made not on how well written a book is, but on how much money it will earn the publishing company. Name the last prize-winning literary novel to make the bestseller lists. Did you buy a copy? Did you pay full price at a small local bookstore or get it at a discount at a big national chain? Did you at least borrow a copy from the library and read it? How long was *The Celestine Prophecy* or *The Bridges of Madison County* on the lists? A lot longer than anything by literary greats such as Cheever, Irving, Beckett or even Tom Wolfe, rest assured.

The great lure of publishing a book is that you can wander into any bookstore in the world, look around and see that someone else has managed to achieve what you dream about. Not just one "someone" but thousands of them. On average, fifty thousand books a year are published in the United States. So why not yours?

Let's start by defining the two types of books that publishers publish:

• **Fiction.** This is an invention, usually in the form of a story. There are broadly three types of fiction formats: short stories—usually no longer than 30 double-spaced manuscript pages and often much shorter; novellas—which range from 30 pages up to 150 manuscript pages; and novels—which start at about 250 manuscript pages and go up. In reality, a good length to aim for in a novel is between 250 and 450 manuscript pages. Usually novels are the only thing that publishers are interested in looking at as far as fiction is concerned.

• **Nonfiction.** This is exactly what it means—anything that is *not* fiction. That is, it's all true and based on research and/or expert opinion. Pay attention to that last part—*expert* opinion, not just your opinion on something into which you think you have an insight. This obviously includes narrative nonfiction, which uses fictive techniques to tell a true story. The modern examples of *The Perfect Storm: A True Story of Men Against the Sea* and *Into Thin Air: A Personal Account of the Mount Everest Disaster* have their origins in the style set by the classic *In Cold Blood* by Truman Capote.

What if I'm writing a piece based on a true story or real people?

In nonfiction you are drawing word portraits of real people; therefore, you must be as accurate and as factual as you can. You shouldn't make up information, or elaborate, even though some experienced writers try to do so on occasion. Two examples that spring to mind are *Dutch*, a biography of Ronald Reagan in which the author created himself as a character to tell the story, and *The Last Brother: The Rise and Fall of Teddy Kennedy* by Joe McGinniss, a biography of Teddy Kennedy where McGinniss invented thoughts in the very much alive mind of Senator Kennedy without interviewing him or checking to see if it was even remotely verifiable. Both authors were roundly condemned for their cavalier approach to the truth and veracity in general, and the books did not sell particularly well either.

Composing fiction about real people is somewhat easier because the truth you're after is often a "spiritual" truth, or a character truth, not an actual truth. It's worth remembering, though, that real people who are still alive and not particularly famous can sue you for libel if you take too much dramatic license.

Why aren't more people published?

OK, let's be honest; we all fantasize about getting paid a ton of money for a book we've written. Hollywood falls at our feet and makes an obscenely large offer of cash for the movie rights, and before you know it, you're hanging out with Arnold and Maria and George "Dubya" and Laura at society dinner parties. What's seductive about publishing is that you can hang out in any bookstore in the world, look around and see that thousands of others have managed to achieve what you dream about.

The irony is that even when you *are* eventually published, the experience may end up being so frustrating and poorly paid that you will wonder why you bothered.

The horrid truth is that many unpublished writers will remain so because they have more ego than skills and they approach the business with a self-absorbed mind-set.

Don't handicap yourself with ideological notions about how publishing *ought to work*. Deal with how it *does* work. If you can do that, you'll more than double your chances of getting published. Once you develop a professional attitude and an understanding of what everyone does in the industry, you'll be able to target your submissions with far greater precision and success.

Why does it sometimes feel like everyone in publishing is conspiring to stop me from getting published?

Publishing is first and foremost a *business*, and decisions are made not just on how well written a book is (*gasp!*), but on *how much money* it will earn a publishing company. What holds back many unpublished writers is a fancy that everyone in publishing is out to "get" them. The truth is, editors don't even get to see a lot of what is sent to them unsolicited. Editorial assistants and secretaries with ambitions to become editors go through the slush pile, trawling for appropriate material for the editor they work for, rejecting 95 percent of the material sent to the editor.

It may seem as though there is some conspiracy afoot, a phantom blacklist with your name on it. Editors and agents have secretly determined that *your* work will never see the light of day if they have anything to say about it.

It's nonsense, of course. The trick to getting published is to get the right idea in front of the right editor. That's essentially what agents do. They aren't really salespeople; they're much closer to matchmakers who manage author's careers.

Nine out of ten editors are keen to find new talent and get it into print when they find it. But the idea that editors sit around discussing manuscripts and saying things like, "It's quite a *nice* idea really, and he is such a *nice* fellow. Let's help him fix his book," is—and pretty much always has been—a myth.

The best way for aspiring authors to begin to come to grips with publishing is to start acting like publishing companies are businesses; and writing, however artful, is also a business.

You need to be specific and creative in targeting your audience. Then help the publishing company understand what a money-making opportunity publishing your book will be. When I say help them understand, I mean provide facts and figures that will make sales and marketing types start to drool with delight, not just offer your unvarnished opinion that this "is destined for the best-seller lists." Trust me, we've heard it all before.

As a would-be author, your job is to learn your craft; gain real understanding of how publishing works; come up with a salable, focused idea; and present it in the most effective way.

As you read through this book, hopefully you'll get advice on how to achieve this and suggestions as to where to go for further reading.

Should I start my fiction-writing career publishing short stories rather than a novel?

The short answer is: Publish anything you can to build a track record.

The honest answer is that it's pretty tough to get short story collections published unless you have a literary mentor of some fame or some connections in publishing. Even then, a lot of the short stories have probably been published first in magazines like *The New Yorker*.

Better you should work on a novel in the first place if you can.

Is there a format I should know in order to submit my material to an editor or agent?

I'll go into specifics about proposal formats and such in chapter five. However, it's worth noting here that in general your manuscript should conform to these guidelines:

It should be in a 12-point clean pica, elite or Times Roman typeface, double-spaced with inch margins all the way around. Better to have more pages and fewer words on the page, which is easier on the eyes, than to cram many small-sized words on one page in an effort to make the proposal look shorter than it is.

There should be a header on every page, with a catchword and your name in the top left-hand corner and consecutive and continuous page numbering in the top right-hand corner.

Don't bind or staple your proposal. If you want to keep it together, use a clip and/or slip it into a folder, or take a piece of cardboard as a backing and slip a large rubber band around everything. Remember, if you manage to get an agent or if an editor picks up on your proposal, they're going to need to make copies for colleagues, editorial meetings, submissions, etc. They don't want to be bothered unstapling copies that could rip in the process.

How do I know if my manuscript is ready to be published?

The honest answer is that unless you've been published before, what you think is ready is really only a polished first draft nine times out of ten. The only sure way to answer this question is to submit your work and see what the professionals say about it.

Genres

What is a genre? Is it really so important?

Readers gravitate toward a certain kind of reading experience. If you stop and think about it, every time you go to the library or the bookstore, you have some idea of what you want to read before you start browsing the book stacks.

One of the first questions an editor asks of a manuscript is, "What genre is it?" Without knowing that, how is the editor or bookstore owner going to know where to place the book in the bookstore? And how will the editor be able to convince colleagues that a book she wants to buy is a commercially viable project?

On average, some fifty thousand books are published yearly in the United States. Some are hardcover (sometimes called cloth); many more are paperback, both mass market (the small-sized books that fit in your pocket) and trade (the larger-sized ones that almost look like hardcovers). All can be categorized in some fashion.

Category and genre are marketing terms that mean, more or less, the same thing. Basically they help you more easily find what you're looking for. They are also *guidelines* that let you know, generally, what you can expect to find in a certain type of book.

Genres developed as a way of marketing and selling mass-market paperbacks. As a result, even mainstream novels, when reprinted as mass-market paperbacks, need to be slotted into a genre of some sort.

A common mistake inexperienced writers make is to assume that because, say, a crime takes place in their romance, then the book must also be a mystery. That's why, when you ask such writers what their book is about, they often give you a list as long as your arm about the various categories into which their book fits and why as a result it should be a best-seller because it has wide appeal.

If the story focuses on the trials and tribulations of a nineteenth-century wagon train of women on their way to California from Arkansas, you are writing a Western, even if one or several of the women fall in love along the way. If the thrust of the story is the love affair between one of the women on the wagon train and, say, the Indian scout leading them to the promised land, it's a romance. *The genre is determined by the main focus of the story. If it is squarely centered on the romance between two characters, then it's a romance.*

Bottom line is that knowing your genre will help you place your manuscript in the marketplace and allow you to introduce it to the best audience in a more focused way, rather than a scattershot approach that may or may not be effective.

How many genres are there, and what are they?

There are basically four overall categories: adult fiction, adult nonfiction, children's fiction and children's nonfiction.

Within these groupings, the subgroupings or genres evolve with each generation of reader, reflecting changes in reading tastes. However, the main categories are listed on page 41. Think of the main categories as primary colors, with the variations of genre being different shades of these colors.

Why do I have to be concerned with genre?

Readers (and editors) are looking for books that reflect contemporary tastes (even if the story being told is a historical story of some kind) because they want to relate emotionally to the story. Readers also expect a certain category of story to have predictable elements in it.

Although genres are being constantly reinvented, familiarize yourself with the classic of the genre, then read the latest published books in the genre to understand what readers expect now.

Genre thinking is more and more a critical aspect of modern publishing. One of the first questions an editor asks of a manuscript is, "What is it?" What they mean, of course, is what genre is it? Once that's determined the manuscript will be judged by the standards of that genre. For instance, if you've written an extremely intelligent Western, intelligence, while admirable, is not the point. What the editor is interested in is your ability to create convincing characters that speak to the readership. How well and accurately do you work in historical detail in an unobtrusive manner? How do you keep the reader involved and turning the page? To be successful, you must not just read but study the books in the genre and define for yourself those qualities that helped make the genre so special.

Do all books fit a category? Why must we think like this about books?

Probably 98 percent of books written fall into some category, so the answer to the question, "Why must we think like this about books?" is that readers gravitate toward a certain kind of reading experience. It could be broadly fiction or nonfiction or more precisely a book about the intricacies of a computer program or maybe a biography of Warren Buffet, the financial advisor and stock market wizard.

Maybe you've had this experience: After reading a lot of Westerns, you started reading science fiction. Or you read quite a number of romances, then Jackie Collins, some mysteries, moving on to *Devil in a Blue Dress* by Walter Mosley, and before you knew it, you were reading *The Kitchen God's Wife* by Amy Tan and then novels by Alice Hoffman and Toni Morrison. But every time you went to the library or the bookstore, you had some idea of what you wanted before you got there.

There are millions of people who love to read science fiction, for example, and while they're looking for a certain type of science fiction, say "space opera" a la *Star Wars*, or more heady stuff such as Arthur C. Clarke's brilliant *Childhood's End*, they have no interest at all in reading, say, a romance or a Western.

On the other hand, if the last book you enjoyed was a romance, then you'll probably go back to the store looking for that author's next book or one like it. So it's important for an author to understand what genre is and how her work fits into this scheme of things so that she can find her readership and not disappoint the audience's expectations.

Does writing a genre book mean I have to write formulaic stories or write poorly?

Absolutely not. There are no formulas for writing category or genre fiction because formulaic writing doesn't have the zing and pizzazz needed to get published these days. However, genres do have conventions to which a writer must pay attention in order to write a successful book. For example: In a crime novel, there must always be a crime to solve.

What are the fiction genres?

Romance

Romance is a huge field earning nearly $1 billion a year and accounting for at least 50 percent of all mass-market paperback books sold. Romance fiction has a strict form, usually a variation on girl meets boy, girl loses boy, girl finds boy again.

The variations on this are many, however. There are gothic romances, traditional Harlequin romances (published by Canadian publisher Harlequin, who once dominated this genre), Native American romances, Western romances, historical romances, time travel romances, futuristic romances, fantasy romances, even vampire and paranormal romances. The biggest evolution in romances since the 1960s has been the expansion of a genre that exclusively featured "virginal" heroines such as those of Barbara Cartland to include the raunchy, sexy (sometimes promiscuous) heroines of Rosemary Rogers and others that developed in the 1990s.

If you write to the publishers of romance fiction, they'll send you guidelines that will tell you how they like their books to be structured, how long they should be and so forth.

At the heart of every romance is how a relationship between a woman and a man develops into love and the problems that men and women have communicating with each other and negotiating their roles in a relationship.

The reader of romance fiction expects that both the hero and heroine will be alive and well and thoroughly in love with each other by the end of the story. They also shouldn't be separated for long periods of the book, and the story should end at a point in their story where there is the most hope for their relationship.

Mysteries and Crime Novels

After romance, or perhaps keeping pace alongside it, the other money-making major fiction genre is the mystery or crime novel. It's so popular that confederations of independent mystery bookstores in the United States and around the world, such as the IMBA (Independent Mystery Bookstore Association), have grown up to promote and sell the genre. Such groups specialize in "hand-selling" mystery authors and promoting them with signings, readings and so forth.

The mystery can be traced back to the August Dupin proto-Sherlock Holmes-type stories of Edgar Allan Poe (hence the annual Edgar Awards for the best in mystery fiction) written in the 1840s. The first mystery novel is often said to be *The Woman in White* by Wilkie Collins, written in England in the 1860s. Undoubtedly, the most famous of the early mystery novelists was Sir Arthur Conan Doyle and his creation, Sherlock Holmes.

If you consider that in many cases the books are still readily available, some of the biggest selling authors of the twentieth century have been mystery writers: Agatha Christie, Sir Arthur Conan Doyle and Erle Stanley Gardner.

Soft mysteries, sometimes called "cozys," usually feature an amateur sleuth and are typically along the lines of an Agatha Christie, John Dickson Carr or *Murder She Wrote* kind of puzzle story.

Mysteries can also be like the novels of Mickey Spillane, who is famous for writing archetypal "tough guy" or "hard-boiled" mysteries that feature a cynical private investigator or PI. Others include Raymond Chandler, Dashiell Hammett, Richard Stark (aka Donald Westlake) and John D. MacDonald.

Then there are police procedurals, where the usually gritty detail of what cops do to bring a criminal to justice is more prominent than the puzzle. This genre was pretty much invented by Ed McBain (aka Evan Hunter) in his 87th Precinct series, now numbering some fifty novels. His books paved the way for TV shows like *Hill Street Blues* and later *NYPD Blue*.

Intriguingly, one of the more interesting elements of the rise of the mystery novel has been the growing prominence of women writers and characters. While women were always present in crime fiction, from Dorothy L. Sayers onward, there can be no ignoring the importance of the organization Sisters in Crime. Formed in the mid-1980s by women writers who felt that they were being ignored by book reviewers in favor of male writers, the group decided not just to complain about the inequality they felt, but went out of their way to empower women writers (and the men who support them and join as Brothers in Crime).

Most mystery novels are conceived (or should be, anyway) as the start of a series, although the books should be able to stand alone.

What most mystery editors agree they're looking for are writers who have a unique "voice" and interesting characters and setting, rather than just an intriguing puzzle.

Thrillers and Suspense Novels

Thrillers and suspense novels share this element: The protagonist is constantly in danger. In a suspense novel it can be more localized and emotional, such as in *Sleeping With the Enemy*, about an abused wife who fakes her own death to avoid her abusive husband who tracks her down regardless. Or, it can be more overt, harder edged and "bigger," with the fate of the world or a city or a group at stake in what Stephen King calls "get out of that" storytelling. Every time the protagonist solves one problem, the solution leads him to another crisis, like going from the frying pan into the fire. The hero manages to rescue the girl from the clutches of the villain, but in doing so causes the car to go over the edge of the cliff. Real "Indiana Jones" kind of stuff.

Thriller readers expect this type of convention, and if you don't provide it, you're going to aggravate them. Think how disappointed you'd feel.

A number of romance writers, most recently Kay Hooper, have begun to move away from straight romance to write romantic suspense and women-in-jeopardy fiction—suspense novels that can be thought of as "soft" thrillers by any other name.

A more hard-boiled kind of thriller is Ken Follett's *Eye of the Needle*. Time was, in America anyway, the thriller was synonymous with WWII, the spy story and the Cold War. The leading writers included Jack Higgins, Ken Follett and John le Carré. The fall of Communism and the Berlin Wall played havoc with these and a lot of other writers' careers, and since 1989 the search has been on for a new "global villain."

What has risen in the thrillers' place, at least temporarily it seems, is a twenty-first-century reinvention of the Jack London-esque man-against-nature story, particularly in the nonfiction genre, such as *The Perfect Storm* and *Into Thin Air*.

But the thriller is still searching for a good villain to take the place of Cold War commies and WWII Nazis. The techno-thriller, a la Tom Clancy, makes an appearance every now and then, but it is really a "tomorrow" type of science fiction novel in disguise or a variation of the action adventure category like the novels of Richard Marcinko. Meanwhile, nearly every lawyer in the world who wants to write fiction is hoping that he or she can write a legal thriller that will knock John Grisham from his pedestal, ignoring the fierceness of the competition.

Classic thrillers with which you should be familiar include John Buchan's *The Thirty-Nine Steps*, Richard Condon's *The Manchurian Candidate*, Frederick Forsyth's *The Day of the Jackal* and John Gilstrap's *Nathan's Run*.

The problem with the thriller is that the writer has to really convince us of the danger and the high stakes and sustain it to the end. Not an easy task, but one worth trying if you can manage it.

Horror

While the thriller aims to scare us with villains like a rampaging virus (such as in *The Andromeda Strain* or the nonfiction *The Hot Zone*) or a homicidal genius like Hannibal Lecter (*Silence of the Lambs*), the horror genre is more preoccupied with making us confront our fears either personally or societally. Is *Hannibal* (the sequel to *Silence of the Lambs*) still a thriller, or has it become a horror novel?

Who is the biggest selling novelist of the last decade? Stephen King, of course, followed closely by Anne Rice, Clive Barker and Dean Koontz. Horror fiction, once a part of science fiction and fantasy, has grown up to become a major genre in its own right.

Horror fiction has been best described by author Peter Straub as "the thin ice of life." While it was a strong selling genre for authors to break into a couple of years ago, currently most horror novels being published are from well-established writers.

What is horror's appeal? To take everyday things and magnify them, exposing our fears so that we can examine them safely. Ultimately, horror is about confronting and dealing with our fear of death and disaster.

Science Fiction and Fantasy

By the early 1990s, science fiction and fantasy books were multibillion dollar generators of profit for publishing houses. Sci-fi (or SF, for short) and fantasy, while around for a long time, took off as a genre after the striking success of the movie *Star Wars* in 1977. In many ways SF has also paved the way for how publishing in general developed in the 1990s.

SF and fantasy, like romance and mystery, are "author-driven" genres, which simply means that readers pay attention to who wrote the book they last read and enjoyed and make efforts to find something else by that author. However, unlike romance titles, which sell mainly in supermarkets and drugstores, SF is largely sold through bookstores. It has also been a benefactor of advertising and "word of mouth" sales on the Internet—a pretty obvious place to market such books when you stop to think about it.

Author-driven material overcomes one of corporate publishing's biggest problems, how to mass market a commodity (that is, a book) in an industry that for most of its existence has been defined by its idiosyncratic nature. The idea of selling books by turning authors into personalities, which now dominates publishing, first developed in the SF and fantasy genre.

SF and fantasy is a genre of contradictions: When anything is possible, and the phrase "cutting edge" is applied to almost every new writer of SF, there is, nevertheless, a powerful force of conservatism among SF and fantasy editors. Many of the people involved in publishing SF and fantasy cling to the notion that aping the success of others is more important, because of potential financial rewards, than encouraging what one executive editor at HarperCollins once called "the literature of revolution."

There are all kinds of science fiction, from the hard science type of story, "space operas," like *Star Wars* and *Star Trek*, cyberpunk written by authors such as William Gibson and K.W. Jeter, to what can be called "head" science fiction or speculative fiction of Robert A. Heinlein, where the science may be almost nonexistent.

A point worth remembering, however, is that a growing portion of SF is devoted to tie-in books. These are novels, written by professional, published writers, that are based on SF movies, TV shows, comics or games. The chances of an unknown unpublished writer getting one of these work-for-hire jobs is small; yet *The X-Files* fan or the *Star Trek* fan still feels it's worth his while to have a go.

Among the most famous fantasy novels are the Lord of the Rings trilogy by J.R.R. Tolkien, the Thomas Covenant series by Stephen R. Donaldson and the witty Belgariad series by David Eddings. Then there are the sci-fi/fantasy novels of Arthur C. Clarke, Stephen Chambers, Louise Marley and Anne McCaffrey among many, many others. For the moment, fantasy, especially "high" or "epic" fantasy seems to be more in vogue and open to newcomers than SF. But things change, so read *Locus* magazine or *Asimov's Science Fiction* magazine or one of the other SF/fantasy genre magazines and keep your eyes open for industry news.

Westerns

Until recently, the Western was considered a dead-end genre with little prospects of resurrection. But just as everyone was ready to pack up and move on, lo and behold the genre found new blood in stories about women in the West, an expanded definition of what a "Western" should be, and revisionist stories about Hispanics, Native Americans and African Americans. *Shane* by Jack Schaefer, *The Virginian* by Owen Wister or *Hombre* by Elmore Leonard have given way to *Sarah Canary* and *Blood Kin* about women in the West or *Hanta Yo*, an epic Western about Native Americans.

Covers are reflecting this change. Instead of cowboys with sidearms on rearing horses, the images are nineteenth-century photographs or paintings by famous artists like Charles Schreyvogel or Frederick Remington.

The Western is a peculiar brand of story that is partly gritty, partly historical, partly mythological in its stories about the western frontier of America. The Western is about the opening of the frontier, the perils and tribulations of creating something from nothing and those who gambled, often with their lives and their fortunes, in order to establish themselves and their dreams. There is a natural conflict at the heart of every Western, be it man against man, man against nature or man against himself. These conflicts are concerned with morality and the challenges of survival. The stories are filled with concepts such as sacrifice, self-denial, unwavering commitment to a goal or an ideal that have a direction and clarity contemporary stories sometimes lack, for whatever reason.

Furthermore, they are (or should be), on one level, historical novels about people who existed in a specific time and place. The novels should reflect just enough accurate historical detail to convince a reader she is in eighteenth- or nineteenth-century America.

Westerns are not an easy genre to break into, though, because there are only a handful of editors working in the field, and their lists are already full with established writers.

Historical Novels

To succeed as a historical novelist, you must be able to pick a period of history that seems to speak to our contemporary senses and weave a fictional plot into real historical events without distorting the historical characters who appear.

The appeal of the historical novel is very often the chance to meet real people as they really were. The historical writer also strives to maintain the customs, culture and knowledge of the period. In a time of political correctness, it is sometimes difficult to maintain the integrity of portraying cruelty, ignorance and hardship that clash heavily with contemporary values. Perhaps for that reason historical novels are more difficult to write and sell now than previously. Like the biography, the historical novel has relevance because of what the past has to tell us about the present. Arthur Miller's play *The Crucible*, about the Salem witch trials, was written in the early 1950s, but is also an allegory about the McCarthy House Un-American Activities Committee witchhunt for Communists. Most historical novels are best slanted to other genres, such as historical romance or historical mystery, to make them more commercial these days.

The Literary Novel

Literary or mainstream is a genre like any other. Some practitioners of this genre, though, believe that story is not important and that writing and atmosphere is all. Such writers forget that plot is merely what characters do next. Stories with no plot are stories that feature passive characters, and characters like that are often boring to read about. Characters usually need to *do* something to be worthy of a story about them.

The literary genre is a tough nut to crack for first-time writers. What do we mean by this? Can you really write well, not just in terms of language, but in terms of perception of the world? How do you establish this? Well, by having a well-regarded literary mentor who will speak up for you. Have you won prizes or awards for your work? Has it been published in prestigious small presses or *The New Yorker*? Have you studied at places such as the Iowa Workshop and come out with accolades? Without some or all of these factors on your side, getting your literary novel published will be very tough.

Your competition is *The Shipping News* by E. Annie Proulx, *Portrait of the Artist as a Young Man* by James Joyce, *For Whom the Bell Tolls* by Ernest Hemingway, Umberto Eco's *The Name of the Rose, Jazz* by Toni Morrison, *The Joy Luck Club* by Amy Tan, *White Teeth* by Zadie Smith. Is that fair? No. But who said writing and publishing had to be fair?

Some people confuse literate with literary, but they're not the same things. All books, whether fiction or nonfiction, should be literate, that is, gracefully well written.

The literary novel thrives on the reputation and consummate skill of the writer, on book reviews and blurbs from other more famous writers and on word of mouth. If you're a beginner, you often don't have much of that going for you. There are plenty of exceptions to this rule, of course, but then the authors are probably not reading this book and almost certainly are not making a living writing fiction exclusively.

The best advice I can offer is to remind you what James Joyce said about writing fiction: All stories should begin, "Once Upon a Time . . ."

What are the nonfiction genres?

The Narrative Nonfiction Book

Narrative nonfiction is character-driven nonfiction having a structure that echoes fiction. It can be divided into many subgenres and should have a narrative spine that either gives us the "why" of a situation (such as *Into Thin Air*) or frames a question and then provides the answer encompassing a debate on a topic of national interest (like Rachel Carson's *Silent Spring*). You can scare people (just read Truman Capote's *In Cold Blood*), but you should also find a positive spin on even the most negative topic. Readers don't want to plunk down twenty-five dollars for a book only to be told that life stinks. While that approach can work effectively in a magazine or newspaper because it is balanced by other more upbeat pieces in the same issue, it's a hard sell as a book.

A book of nonfiction must contain much information and should not be used as a soapbox for you to spout your pet grievance. Carefully and honestly recount in a strongly written narrative infused with much emotional content what it was like to go through the experience. People must trust you as an informed guide to the topic you're writing about before they'll bother to read what you have to say. That's why most successful nonfiction is written by either journalists or experts of one sort or another.

True Crime and Current Events

The model for true crime books—and the book that still defines the genre—is *In Cold Blood* by Truman Capote. Is it nonfiction or fiction? It's a true story, after all, though it was the first one to extensively use fictional techniques to tell a true story. The experts who write true crime successfully are or have been lawyers, cops, investigators, journalists, forensic specialists and so forth.

True crime and current events books allow us to peer into the mind of the demented, though it is also very influenced by how much of a gripping story can be woven, who the characters are, where the story takes place and so on. One of the elements of narrative nonfiction that many writers do not consider carefully enough is that it takes the techniques and skills of a journalist *and* a novelist to write a compelling story. *How* the story is told is as important as *what* happened.

There are two basic types of true crime book: the gut story, that is, one that affects us on a primal level (such as Anne Rule's *Small Sacrifices*, about a mother murdering her children), and the glamour story, set in the world of the rich and famous (such as William Wright's *The Von Bulow Affair* about the murder trial of Claus Von Bulow, accused of killing his socialite wife, Sunny.

Beyond powerful—and, of course, accurate—characterization with identifiable villains and heroes, the narrative nonfiction book should have some sort of unraveling investigation.

Biography

Biography is a very popular nonfiction category if you can find a suitable subject; but to carry it off, the writer must be an expert on the subject. The same kind of investigative, analytical attention to detail used in true crime is foremost in biographies such as A. Scott Berg's *Max Perkins: Editor of Genius*, Diane Wood Middlebrook's *Anne Sexton: A Biography* and Gerald Clarke's *Capote*, about writer Truman Capote.

Biographies take several forms. Some use the work and life of the biographical subject as an indicator of the subject's inner world. Others are more literary in nature, placing more emphasis on how and why the biography subject structured and crafted their books.

The different types of biography all try to reveal the essence of the subject: interpretive, where the events of a subject's life lead us to a better understanding of the inner person and how they fit in with their world; objective, which gathers facts and document how the subject lived; and dramatic, which uses fictional techniques to recreate the subject and his or her times.

Dramatic biographies such as *Eleanor of Aquitaine: A Life* or *Elizabeth I* use known facts about the subject and her time, which are interpreted by the biographer's imagination, in an effort to reveal the intimate qualities of the subject. The controversial Ronald Reagan biography *Dutch* broadly falls into this category. Edmund Morris's biography of ex-President Reagan involved the author creating himself as a fictional character in order to tell the former president's story and attracted a lot of criticism for its approach.

In general, a biography has to have a theme, and its subject has to fit into the context of the times in which the subject lived. More than that, the subject of a biography should also be a symbol of some sort for the spirit of their age. The book should bring out some thematic element of that culture. Broadly, a good biography is one that illuminates and shows the times as much as the person. Historian Doris Kearns Goodwin said, "The past is not simply the past, but a prism through which the subject [of a biography] filters his own changing self-image."

The subject's life should have had a profound effect not only on the people who came into contact with him or her, but some shadow of it should also touch the biography's reader.

The dangers of biography are inaccuracy and hero worship. The biographer needs to cultivate an objective eye that fits his subject into the world with compassion. Most biographies treat their subjects as one of three things: an example, a victim or a source of wisdom.

Research for writing a biography depends on two things: public and personal papers and sources, and living witnesses. Of course, in the case of the long dead, you're stuck with only one of the two.

It's also a demanding form of writing, requiring that the author know her subject intimately, live with them for a long time, somehow make peace with their flaws yet obtain necessary permissions from those relevant people who are living and ensure any quotes are accurately related and sourced.

The biographer must have the skills of a storyteller to construct an insightful, compelling narrative, the skills of a diplomat to deal with the many witnesses who can shed light on the subject's life, and the skills of a detective in order to dig out facts and research on the subject. Biographers must also be devoted to their subject and yet be objective enough to explore the dark nooks and crannies of the life in question. They must have the literary and psychological brilliance to create a book that the subject could honestly admit was an accurate portrayal of who they are and what they are. Unless you are a skilled writer and someone with a strong analytical background, biography is going to be a tough genre to use to break into publishing.

Memoirs

This is another demanding genre to write well. A big fuss was made of Kathryn Harrison's book about incest, *The Kiss*, and of Frank McCourt's *Angela's Ashes*, a memoir of a childhood cursed with drink, violence and poverty, because both were so intimate and revealing of these terrible experiences. But they also "upped the ante" for the average writer of memoir because not only were the books well written, they had a salacious quality that has set the bar higher for writers of commercial memoirs.

Nowadays, commercially successful memoirs are about traumatic events in a writer's life that a writer of exquisite skill can *transform into a universal experience we can all share*. It is the nearest thing to poetry a writer of prose can write. Read Isabel Allende's moving book, *Paula*, about the sickness and coma her daughter suffered.

Memoirs are about a child's sickness, a father's death, a loss of honor or career. We read another's pain because the writer's sensibility allows her to extract from her dreadful experience powerful universal emotions that illuminate our lives. Editors who buy memoirs do so because the writer has successfully transferred the experience to the page in a strong, emotional way and in so doing, like the alchemists of old, has transmuted the experience from base lead into gold.

When a memoir such as *A Year in Provence* by Peter Mayle succeeds, which is not about personal pain but a growing and learning experience, it often edges into another genre. In this case, the travel section.

How-To Books

How-to books are one of the best nonfiction genres to write to break into publishing. It's probably the largest and one of the most successful nonfiction genres. How-to books embrace knitting and hobbies, health, finance, sports and parenting. Although your book may well fall under the broad category of how-to, be as specific as you can about who your audience is and what your book on the subject covers that other books have yet to mention or tackle.

Reference Books

I'm not just talking about dictionaries and encyclopedias here, but also lighter books such as *The 85 Ways to Tie a Tie: The Science and Aesthetics of Tie Knots* by Thomas Fink and Yong Mao or David Feldman's *Why Do Dogs Have Wet Noses?*

Mostly, these kinds of books are sold to libraries and schools, as well as bookstores.

Cookbooks

Most cookbooks are written by people who own restaurants, have become famous as chefs, have their own TV show or are in the public eye already in some fashion as food writers. The publishing company then cashes in on the author's name recognition. Opportunity in this field will start with some success at the regional or local level, and the book will echo this success in some way.

Travel Books

These break down into narratives of adventures getting from point A to point B, travel guides and destination guides. The books provide information on hotels, restaurants, places to go, interesting sights to see and so forth.

A travelogue will often have lyrical descriptions of faraway places and is aimed at an audience known as the "armchair traveler."

Travel guides are nondestination books that tell you how to travel in a particular way, such as traveling by donkey across Tibet or by train across China as in Paul Theroux's *Riding the Iron Rooster*.

A destination guide is an informative guide like *The Everything Guide to Washington, D.C. Book* or *Fodor's Paris*.

Pop Culture

Pop culture books have become very popular as we start the new millennium and try to understand who we are, what cultural forces are shaping our identity and what messages the mass media is sending us. To write this successfully, you must have some expertise, often reflected by a passion for a subject that has made you something of an expert. The trick becomes parlaying that passion (let us not call it an obsession, please) into a book that others will read and enjoy and from which they will derive some entertainment and new knowledge. Examples might range from an unofficial biography of the actor/producer Michael Douglas, to classic TV commentary such as *Total Television*, to more culture-based quiz books like *Disco Nixon* or *Rambo Reagan*.

Humor

Cartoon books like *Dilbert* or Gary Larson's *Far Side* and books with humorous observations on life like *Dave Barry on Computers* or Paul Reiser's *Babyhood* are lumped together as humor.

You're on your own here. Do others think you're funny? Can you make an overworked editor smile enough to see the commercial potential in your scribblings? It's probably easier doing stand-up comedy in a comedy club, though not by much.

Humor is possibly the most subjective category of any in publishing, so good luck hunting for your humor soul mate in editorial. If you're really funny and can put it down on paper, you'll do very well. The best place to start is in newspapers and magazines. If you can regularly produce your writings for an audience, particularly a sophisticated one like *The New Yorker*, you'll do very well as a humorist.

Children's Books and Young Adult

Children's books broadly fall into picture books for the very young, chapbooks for middle grade audiences—roughly ages 7 to 12—and young adult or YA for teenagers.

Many beginning writers think children's books are easy to write—but they're wrong. It's actually one of the most skillful and demanding of genres. Such inexperienced writers often assume that tales for children should be "good for them" and write simplistic morality tales. Kids are a rough audience, and they're not easily fooled. They want stories that speak *to* them, not *at* them, and they loathe blatant moralizing.

In general, kids love books that afford an escape into fantasy. What were the biggest selling children's books on both sides of the Atlantic at the turn of century? The Harry Potter series.

YA books also deal seriously and candidly with issues that face teens today.

These issues are very important, from incest and teen violence to alienation and loss of innocence, and they need to be handled with great sensitivity and insight.

What about other genres?

The other genres not mentioned here can be learned about by studying the bookshelves of bookstores and libraries. You can also consult books like the *Writer's Market* or the *Literary Market Place* (aka LMP).

Most writers are successful in a genre because they already know it and have been reading in it for years. Is there a magazine devoted to your topic? More than one? How many readers does it have? What genre is hip-hop, for example? Music or pop culture? Only by carefully studying the market can you answer these questions. (The answer to the above question is probably both, depending on the slant of the book.)

Are there "fashions" in genres?

Genre popularity goes in phases. While once very popular, for example, true crime, horror and traditional Westerns are now harder to break into because fewer copies are sold in each genre. A genre can be "hot," and then it is over-bought and becomes hard to sell into for a while. The genre becomes dormant until a book comes along that reinvigorates the category beyond the work of the few established authors who have continued to write and sell in that area, keeping it "ticking over."

How do I find my genre?

If you understand what a reader's expectations are, you can make your book that much stronger and that much more likely to be sold to a publisher.

Of course, the reader's anticipation of something in the book can be spoiled by a poorly chosen title or cover artwork (which you usually can't control), but if you call your Western *Sexy Cyber Girls*, you're not likely to attract readers who are looking for the type of experience you're providing.

So, be careful with titles and with the language you use, making sure they're similar to other books in the category in which you've chosen to write.

Study the category. Familiarize yourself with various genres, then read a lot of books in the genre that appeals to you. In fact, if you're not reading the genre, you probably shouldn't be writing in it. Your first successfully published book, will, almost inevitably, be centered around some category that you really love. You don't "write what you know," as the old saw has it; you draw upon what you know, but you write what you read.

Why does genre really matter?

Genres really help publishers and bookstore owners know where to place your book in the bookstore.

When your novel comes out you're not really competing with all the other books in the store; you're competing with the other books in your genre. So, without diverging too much from what's expected, think about how you're going to make your book different from others like it. That difference comes from knowing your genre well enough that you can spot a "hole," or good idea.

What do you mean, "Meet the reader's expectations"?

Know your audience. Authors who know their target, core audience do much better than those who pay no attention to who is likely to buy their books.

Books are written with specific audiences in mind. Self-help books, for example, have a strong female readership; while adventure travel books, such as man against nature (e.g., *Into Thin Air* or *The Perfect Storm*), are largely bought and read by men. Only books that become big sellers transcend those general limitations.

What do people mean when they talk about "cross-genre" books?

You can mix genres, coming up with what is called a "cross-genre." However, publishers do not encourage authors to do this. The argument many novice writers put forward for cross-genre novels is that by combining two genres, they'll double their audience. Optimistic thought, but alas, not true.

Experimentation is well worth it, but know that's what you're doing—experimenting. For every time travel romance, there is an unsellable sci-fi Western. The audience for cross-genre books tends to be a small, usually inquisitive overlap group with wide-ranging tastes. Unfortunately, the majority of the book-buying public seems to have voted with their hard-earned dollars (or in some cases voted by not buying) for classifiable and predictable categories. The best advice is to push the envelope of an accepted genre, but don't try to bestride two; it can prove career slowing, if not wrecking.

So, what to do? Go for a really strong story that in the end may be true to another genre entirely. Is it horror? Is it romance? Perhaps, instead, it's a dark fantasy? See what I mean?

Help the publisher, help the bookstore owner and help yourself earn cash by putting your book in the right spot in the bookstore. Seriously think about your audience, categories and genres when you revise. The right marketing strategy might just get you published.

Does it make sense to use different names for the different genres I write in?

Yes, it does. When you develop an audience for your romances, some of that audience may be taken with you to a nearby genre, say, a cozy mystery. However, it's unlikely they'll go for a literary novel, a horror novel or something gritty and realistic.

If you want to write in different styles, it's worth considering developing different personas, each of whom has his or her own audience and identity. The audience for Donald Westlake's witty novels is a far cry from the hard-bitten Richard Stark novels he writes. Similarly, Ed McBain's 87th Precinct cop novels are very different from Evan Hunter's more literate commercial novels such as *The Blackboard Jungle.*

Will you give me a list of all the genres?

But of course. The following aren't all the genres and categories, but they probably cover most of the important ones. For a more complete list, check out the *Literary Market Place* (LMP) or *Writer's Market.*

Nonfiction

Academic, adventure, biography, business/finance, computers, cooking/food, current events, dance, education, entertainment, ethnic, film/TV, gay/lesbian, gift books, health/medicine, history, how-to, humor, illustrated books/coffee table, Judaica, literary criticism, memoir, military/war, motivational, music, narrative nonfiction, nature/environment, New Age, parenting, pets and animals, philosophy, politics, pop culture, psychology, reference/scholarly, religion/spirituality, romance/relationships, science/technology, self-help/personal improvement, sports, textbooks, theater, travel, true crime, women's issues

Fiction

Adventure, commercial, crime, erotic, ethnic, fantasy/SF, gay/lesbian, historical, horror, humor, literary, military, mystery/suspense, romance, thriller, Western, women's fiction, comic books, plays, poetry, screenplays

Children

Adventure, fantasy/SF, mystery/crime, literary, picture books, early readers, pop-up/chapbooks, middle grade, young adult

chapter three

Agents, Editors and Other Publishing People

OK, now I know something about genres and categorizing books. What's next?

This is probably a good time to introduce you to the people in publishing with whom you're going to be dealing.

I believe, ideally, the first person in publishing you should contact once you have something ready is an agent.

Being one myself, I'm partial to good agents because they can do wonders for your writing career. Business decisions are best made by the author and his business advisors, usually an agent or manager who handles the business and legal aspects upon instructions from the author.

Why should I bother with a literary agent? They're impossible to get, anyway. Why shouldn't I just go straight to an editor and save myself the 15 percent commission?

Unless you're a really capable entrepreneur like the authors of *Chicken Soup for the Soul*, the rule of thumb should be: Writers write, editors edit and agents agent. It's not wise to mix these elements and it's rarely successful. However well you think you do on your own, you'll do even better with the right agent.

The wrong agent or a poor agent will not help you at all and may even hinder you. They'll offer bad advice, make you work hard at the wrong things because they don't have the proper editorial skills and then not get your work to the right editors.

The right agent can suggest the best audience for your work and advise you on how to polish your submission to appeal to that audience. He'll know the editors who are looking for the kind of material you've written, and his reputation will definitely carry some weight with editors when it comes to looking at the material both seriously and quickly.

If an editor contacts you and says she wants to buy your book, the chances are high that you'll get the agent of your choice to represent you if you contact them and say that Editor X at a certain publishing house wants to buy your book. Would you please negotiate the deal for me?

In the fields of magazines, children's books and small or university presses, the odds are greater that you will be able to get a book deal without involving an agent, partly because these areas don't pay enough money to attract an agent's attention when you compare the effort spent submitting the project to the income earned when you successfully place it.

I can do just as good a job as any agent. Lots of people do it, don't they?

People you know may *say* they've done it, but most successful writers use either an agent, a literary lawyer or some sort of manager to help on the business end.

I've been writing professionally since I was nineteen. I've worked in newspapers, on radio, on TV, as a publishing house editor, a book doctor and a literary agent, plus I've published both fiction and nonfiction. However, once upon a time . . . my former agent was going through a personal crisis and was not focused on work. This didn't mean that my career should be on hold, however. I signed a small book deal with an editor, Ms. A, with whom I thought I had a good relationship. Over the course of the next few months, I learned to my horror that I was being edited not only by Ms. A, an elderly but experienced editor, but also by Ms. B, a woman in her forties, and Ms. C, who was both opinionated and not long out of college. Someone would request a change, I'd make it and a couple of weeks later the manuscript would come back with different handwriting asking why I'd made the change.

"I don't care if I'm edited by Attila the Hun," I cried, "just pick one person for me to work with and let me get on with it!"

My relationship with the publishing company rapidly deteriorated. I embraced Zen Buddhism, chanting the mantra "Better published than not published" before I went to sleep at night.

Thankfully, at this point my agent came back into the picture. One of the things an agent spends a lot of time doing is solving problems with and for clients. We call it "putting out fires." At this point I had a nice "three-alarm" raging.

My agent spoke with Editor A, and when my agent realized what a nightmare the company was putting me through, she helped me move the book to another company. She even got the original publishers to let me keep the royalty advance.

The new publisher, John Wiley & Sons, paid me a better royalty advance, changed barely a word of what I'd written, and *The Elements of Storytelling* was published to good reviews. You can still buy it in the stores, and twice a year I get a royalty check with my royalty statement. All's well that ends well—but without my agent, none of this would have been possible. Let this be a lesson to you—it certainly was for me.

A good agent knows which editor to go to at the various houses, and those editors will be particularly receptive to the agent's material because of the relationship that has developed between the agent and the editor over the years. Editors change jobs and move from house to house, but they will often still deal with the same agents who make it a point to know their likes and dislikes.

That doesn't mean that the agent isn't an advocate for the author, and nowhere does that become more apparent than when an agent negotiates a contract for her author. She will argue and fight for the best deal for that author. Perhaps, because the author and the agent lack leverage, that is, good commercial reasons to get what they want from a publisher, the deal won't be a great deal because it favors the publisher too much. Nevertheless, it will still be the best deal that agent could get for that client under those circumstances and almost certainly it will be a better deal than the client could secure for herself without the aid of the agent.

I know I should research what agents handle particular types of books so that I can target my work appropriately. Where do I find this information?

There are a variety of sources. If you are enthusiastic about a particular genre, then presumably you read books in that field. Check the acknowledgments to see if an editor or agent is mentioned.

Read *Publishers Weekly* and publisherslunch.com for the latest news and gossip.

Finally, consult books like Writer's Digest *Guide to Literary Agents*, Jeff Herman's *Writer's Guide to Book Editors, Publishers, and Literary Agents* and the *Literary Market Place* (LMP), which can be found in any reference library.

I know it's possible to submit to an editor without an agent. How do I do that?

Know the areas in which you're likely to succeed. Many children's literature authors are unagented at first, for example.

Another area is nonfiction science, an area that may be covered by imprints of larger houses, university or small press publishers. Editors in this field make it their business to attend professional conferences of all sorts, whether historical, medical, engineering, scientific or whatever, and they know who the top dogs are in a particular field. These editors cultivate relationships with leading academics and in some cases actively help these academics create and write books on subjects in which the authors are considered to be experts. In such cases, editors find you rather than the other way around.

To catch an editor's attention, have an outstanding resume in your field of expertise and make sure you have already published articles on the subject. It's also advisable to have lectured on the subject.

A growing field for previously unpublished writers (whether agented or not) who are working in what could be considered a niche area with a limited but specific audience is the small press arena. If you have a seminar or strong regional presence, exploit it regionally.

Niche publishing, or publishing with a specific focus, has become more and more important in the modern publishing landscape. There are medium-sized companies such as Prima in California, or Sourcebooks and Adams Media in Connecticut, Andrews McMeel in Kansas City, Walker & Co. and Four Walls, Four Windows in New York. Running Press, for example, was started for—you guessed it—runners. Sierra Club Books publishes environmental guides, while Harvard Common Press is interested in books focusing on New England and the Northeast.

All are interested in seeing proposals and books from authors willing to accept modest advances for being published well. An added advantage to this route is that with some luck and careful work, you can establish a track record of escalating sales (what we call giving a book "legs") that will attract the attention of major publishers and perhaps eventually get you a contract with them.

Small press publishing companies are springing up all over with experienced editorial staff and very specific philosophies about the kinds of books they want to publish and can publish well. For example, one of the most successful books in the 1990s didn't come from a major conglomerate; it was an unagented manuscript that was picked up by a small publisher in Florida called Health Communications. The book? *Chicken Soup for the Soul* and the many sequels it spawned.

To catch an editor's attention read chapter five on submitting book proposals. In short, find out an editor's name, write a dynamite query letter and proposal, mail the material, then sit back and wait for a response.

If a small press makes you an offer, you could negotiate it on your own. It's a wise writer who, with an offer in hand, returns to her search for an agent, this time telling potential agents that she has an offer from Publisher X. Almost certainly an agent will respond quickly and positively to you. How do you find these small publishers and university presses? Again, do some research—look in the *LMP* or the Jeff Herman and Writer's Digest guides.

What do I do if I'm able to actually speak with an editor?

Be prepared: If you're lucky enough to be put through to the editor, pitch your book idea succinctly and intelligently.

OK, you don't have an agent, but you're convinced you have a strong seller on your hands. First, do some research to make sure you are submitting to the right publisher. Use books and Web sites to discover this information, then find out if the publisher you're contracting has published other books like yours.

Next, get the name of the editor who specializes in the kind of book you want to write. Call the publisher and ask to speak to the editor or his assistant.

The editor will soon enough tell you whether or not he is interested in seeing your project. If he says yes, then say thank you, confirm the correct spelling of his name and politely ask how long he thinks it will take him to read it.

If you haven't heard by the date the editor suggested, wait a few days, then call again and politely ask how things are progressing.

What should I know about an agent before I approach one?

There's a common misconception that agents spend all their time developing new material and new clients for publishers. Unpublished writers think that if you just take your place in line, they'll eventually get to you. Alas, it's not really true. You have to really catch an agent's attention with good writing and strong ideas.

Agents spend some of their time in the evenings and on weekends reading unsolicited or "slush" mail, but only after they've finished reading the latest material sent to them by their clients. Most agents have a full complement of clients, varying from fifty to one hundred writers. Although they're always on the lookout for good new material by talented writers, they have plenty to do just keeping on top of their existing workload.

That means your new material has to be really special. If it is, you will attract the attention of agents and editors.

Unagented writers don't seem to realize that when an agent takes on a new client, the agent is taking on a negative asset. The client will actually cost the agent money in time, energy, mailing fees, telephone calls, photocopying proposals and so forth before the agent ever sees a dime of the commission they earn from a sale.

There are basically three types of literary agents: First, there are former editors and editorial types who develop and shape projects with writers. Then, there are agents who prefer selling to editorial work and are into the "gavotte," as a friend of mine calls it, the "dance of hard bargaining" that can take place during a book deal negotiation. These agents prefer to represent "one-off" projects (often nonfiction and high-profile writer-based) that look like commercial successes and then move on to the next author and the next deal, rather than concern themselves with developing a writer's career. Finally, there are entertainment lawyers who basically just do the deal for the writer.

Very successful authors sometimes use lawyers because it's cheaper for them to pay an hourly rate than a 15 percent commission. That does not work well for less well paid authors for obvious reasons.

OK, so what does an agent do?

Agents spend a lot of time developing new contacts with editors and publishers and renewing old ones. They pitch projects by clients, write query letters on behalf of the client and the project, check up on royalty statements, pursue outstanding royalty advances, go through the fine print of contracts, put out "fires," negotiate deals, come up with career plans and tactics to get their clients well published . . . the list is exhaustive.

Agents also take lunch meetings, attend book parties, speak at writers conferences and make it their business to meet and get to know as many publishing house acquiring editors as they can. The essence of the job is matchmaking—putting the right project with the right editor at the best house. One of the definitions of a good agent is someone who knows who the right editors are for a project and what their likes and dislikes are.

Each publishing house has its own personality and specialties and is continually reinventing itself in order to gain as large a share of the market as possible. These days editors also move around a lot. Then there are all the mergers and acquisitions that have taken place in the last couple of years and the reshaping of giant companies such as Bantam, Doubleday, Dell and its imprints with Random House and all its imprints.

You can guarantee that in the next few years, publishing won't resemble what it looked like a few years ago. In the face of all this industrial volatility, agents provide a font of cutting-edge knowledge and a haven of stability for authors.

Agents make it their job to keep up with where editors are currently working, what they like and what they are looking for (not necessarily always the same thing), and in certain circumstances they actually help to create books for their authors that editors seem keen to try and acquire.

Is it better to have an agent before I sell my book or to obtain one after I've sold a book?

Ideally you should approach an agent before you approach a publisher. If you aren't having any luck catching an agent's eye, there's no reason you shouldn't approach editors. If they say they want to see your material and you reach the stage where they want to make you an offer on your book, put the deal on hold briefly and tell the editor you are in the process of finalizing your relationship with a new agent. Then try to get the agent you want. With a contract in hand, you should have little trouble this time around.

How can I tell a good agent from a bad one?

One of the best indicators of a good agent is: Does the agent make a living solely from commissions on sales?

If an agent charges a reading fee, my advice is: Don't go near him. Reputable agents, with one or two notable exceptions, don't charge reading fees, nor do they provide reader's reports. The whole concept of charging for reading is questionable. How can you give someone an unbiased opinion on her work if you're interested in representing it but also charge for editorial advice? It's a conflict of interest that leads to authors buying their agent's time and attention with very likely little to show for their money at the end of the project except hard lessons learned.

Agents look for writers who have put together a terrific project, have "got their act together" as writers and are ready to be published. They then help them polish their project and sell it, thus beginning, hopefully, a wonderful and enduring partnership.

The hard truth is that if you can't get an agent interested in your work without paying for some sort of service, you're almost certainly not ready to be published yet, and you'll have a hard time getting a publisher interested.

Agents are not in the business of teaching writers how to write or helping unpublished writers find a publisher or even earn a living. Their job is to get you the best deal possible for a book.

Best advice: Don't spend your money on these services, but spend it instead on taking writing classes or working with a reputable book doctor who will teach you how to fix your project. A good place to start if you're looking for a book doctor is the Editorial Freelance Association [(212) 929-5400)], or on their Web site at www.the-efa.org.

I'm told that agents who charge reading fees should be avoided. Is that true?

Agents should make their living from the commissions they earn on selling an author's work. If the agent has to earn his living by charging the author for such things as reading fees and editorial services, there is an inherent conflict of interest.

What does it matter whether or not the client is publishable, as long as she can come up with the money to get advice on how to get published? The advice becomes more important than the publication process to such an agent. If a project needs that much work before it is ready to be submitted, then it's not ready and a reputable agent will tell you so. He may recommend a freelance editor for you to work with, but the financial arrangement would be strictly between you and the freelance book doctor, and the agent would have nothing to do with it.

You could end up spending a lot of money, and perhaps learning a lot about writing, but without producing a publishable manuscript. By paying an agent for services other than selling the book, the implication is that the project will be published at the end of the day. That is a promise no agent can honestly make. An agent accepting payment for such services is about taking advantage of a writer or massaging the egos of the unpublishably mediocre.

What's the difference between an agent and an author's representative and what is AAR?

They're really the same thing. In fact, the agent's guild is called the Association of Authors' Representatives, or AAR. The best agents help to manage their clients' careers. AAR has a canon of ethics, imposing qualifications a new agent has to meet before her name is put to a vote for acceptance into the association. If the agent does something unethical, they'll throw her out on her ear.

Publishing is a small industry, and stories about unethical behavior by agents can be very damaging. In some cases, it can mean that editors won't take their phone calls or buy books from them. Anyone can hang out a shingle and call themselves an agent, take on clients, charge them money for this and that, make outrageously optimistic claims ("I'll make you a star, baby!") and never get anyone published.

AAR was formed to set a standard and distinguish good agents from bad. It is a not-for-profit trade organization of literary and dramatic agents. It was formed in 1991 through the merger of the Society of Authors' Representatives founded in 1928 and the Independent Literary Agents Association founded in 1977. The association's objectives include keeping agents informed about conditions in publishing, the theater, the motion picture and television industries and related fields; encouraging cooperation among literary organizations; and assisting agents in representing and defending their authors' interests.

Membership in the AAR is restricted to agents whose primary professional activity for the two years preceding application for membership has been as an authors' representative or a playwrights' representative.

To qualify for membership, an applicant must have sold ten different literary properties during the eighteen-month period preceding application. Member agents must adhere to the AAR's Canon of Ethics, and associate members are full-time employees of a sponsoring agent member.

For the most up-to-date AAR membership list, send seven dollars (as of this writing, Fall 2001) either by check or money order made payable to AAR. *Do not send cash*. Include a self-addressed, business size #10 envelope, and write to AAR, 10 Astor Place, Third Floor, New York NY 10003. Alternatively, visit the Web site at www.aar-online.org for free information, though it won't necessarily be the most up-to-date member list.

What is the AAR Code of Ethics?

(The following is reprinted by permission of the Association of Authors' Representatives.)

Association of Authors' Representatives Canon of Ethics

1. The members of the Association of Authors' Representatives, Inc. are committed to the highest standard of conduct in the performance of their professional activities. While affirming the necessity and desirability of maintaining their full individuality and freedom of action, the members pledge themselves to loyal service to their clients' business and

artistic needs, and will allow no conflicts of interest that would interfere with such service. They pledge their support to the Association itself and to the principles of honorable coexistence, directness, and honesty in their relationships with their co-members. They undertake never to mislead, deceive, dupe, defraud, or victimize their clients, other members of the Association, the general public, or any person with whom they do business as a member of the Association.

(Translation: The client comes first, and we won't lie to him, steal from him or cheat him.)

2. Members shall take responsible measures to protect the security and integrity of clients' funds. Members must maintain separate bank accounts for money due their clients so that there is no commingling of clients' and members' funds. Members shall deposit funds received on behalf of clients promptly upon receipt, and shall make payments of domestic earnings due clients promptly, but in no event later than ten business days after clearance. Revenues from foreign rights over $50 shall be paid to clients within ten business days after clearance. Sums under $50 shall be paid within a reasonable time of clearance. However, on stock and similar rights, statements of royalties and payments shall be made not later than the month following the member's receipt, each statement and payment to cover all royalties received to the 25th day of the previous calendar month. Payments for amateur rights shall be made not less frequently than every six months. A member's books of account must be open to the client at all times with respect to transactions concerning the client.

(Translation: We'll make sure a client's money is treated with respect and efficiently forwarded to her once the agent's commission has been deducted. Any money or information about earnings from the book will be sent to the client within a month of the agent receiving them.)

3. In addition to the compensation for agency services that is agreed upon between a member and a client, a member may, subject to the approval of the client, pass along charges incurred by the member on the client's behalf, such as copyright fees, manuscript

retyping, photocopies, copies of books for use in the sale of other rights, long distance calls, special messenger fees, etc. Such charges shall be made only if the client has agreed to reimburse such expenses.

(Translation: Agents can charge reasonable expenses for representing and submitting a work as long as it is agreed upon by the client.)

4. A member shall keep each client apprized of matters entrusted to the member and shall promptly furnish such information as the client may reasonably request.

(Translation: Agents will call as soon as they have any information to pass along.)

5. Members shall not represent both buyer and seller in the same transaction. Except as provided in the next sentence, a member who represents a client in the grant of rights in any property owned or controlled by the client may not accept any compensation or other payment from the acquirer of such rights, including but not limited to so-called "packaging fees," it being understood that the member's compensation, if any, shall be derived solely from the client. Notwithstanding the foregoing, a member may accept (or participate in) a so-called "packaging fee" paid by an acquirer of television rights to a property owned or controlled by a client if the member: a) fully discloses to the client at the earliest practical time the possibility that the member may be offered such a "packaging fee" which the member may choose to accept; b) delivers to the clients at such time a copy of the Association's statement regarding packaging and packaging fees; and c) offers the client at such time the opportunity to arrange for other representation in the transaction. In no event shall the member accept (or participate in) both a packaging fee and compensation from the client with respect to the transaction. For transactions subject to the Writers Guild of America (WGA) jurisdiction, the regulation of the WGA shall take precedence over the requirements of this paragraph.

(Translation: An agent can't represent a client and the publisher who is going to publish that client's work at the same time because it's a conflict of interest.)

6. Members may not receive a secret profit in connection with any transaction involving a client. If such profit is received, the member must promptly pay over the entire amount to the client. Members may not solicit or accept any payment or other thing of value in connection with their referral of any author to any third party for any purpose, provided that the foregoing does not apply to arrangements made with a third party in connection with the disposition of rights in the work of a client of the member.

(Translation: Agents can't ask for or take "under the table" payments for their efforts to get an author published.)

7. Members shall treat their clients' financial affairs as private and confidential, except for information customarily disclosed to interested parties as part of the process of placing rights, as required by law, or, if agreed with the client, for other purposes.

(Translation: Your financial information is private, between you and your agent and no one else.)

8. The AAR believes that the practice of literary agents charging clients or potential clients for reading and evaluating literary works (including outlines, proposals, and partial or complete manuscripts) is subject to serious abuse that reflects adversely on our profession. For that reason, members may not charge clients or potential clients for reading and evaluating literary works and may not benefit, directly or indirectly, from the charging for such services by any other person or entity. The term "charge" in the previous sentence includes any request for payment other than to cover the actual cost of returning materials.

(Translation: Members of AAR can only earn money through commission on sales of authors' works and not by charging reading fees.)

What should I expect from a potential agent?

First, has the agent actually *read* your book or book proposal? Can he talk about it intelligently? Undoubtedly he will have suggestions to either make something clearer, more focused or more commercially viable, but does he really understand what you're trying to do and sympathize with your efforts? Is he enthusiastic?

Sometimes an agent is just starting out, and in many cases new agents are the best bet for new writers. New agents are not always new to the publishing business. Many are former editors or publishing house employees who may not yet have placed many books, but they do know the business, how it's conducted and a lot of the people in it.

Get an agent with a strong reputation who will give you some attention when you need it. That doesn't necessarily mean that she'll call you back immediately, but she should certainly respond within a few days. If you make repeated calls to an agent and don't get a reply, that's a clue something's going sour in the relationship.

Your agent will often be someone you like, but he or she is not your friend, nor is that a good basis for a business relationship. They are not shrinks, sources of emotional or psychological support or even personal editors. A good agent may exhibit some or all of these abilities because the job involves nurturing, but don't expect it and don't ask for it. If you have problems, figure them out before you get together with your agent. Her job, remember, is to sell your work. If you have nothing to sell, there isn't much she can do for you.

What should I ask a potential agent?

AAR publishes a list of questions that you may wish to pose to a new agent when the two of you are contemplating establishing a business relationship. Remember that most agents are *not* going to bother to take the time to answer these questions unless they've decided to represent you.

The following is reprinted by permission of AAR (the Association of Authors' Representatives, Inc.):

• Are you a member of the AAR?

• How long have you been in business as an agent?

• Do you have specialists at your agency who handle movie and television rights? Foreign rights?

• Do you have subagents or corresponding agents in Hollywood and overseas?

• Who in your agency will actually be handling my work? Will the other staff members be familiar with my work and the status of my business at your agency? Will you oversee or at least keep me apprized of the work that your agency is doing on my behalf?

• Do you issue an agent-author agreement? May I review the language of the agency clause that appears in contracts you negotiate for your clients?

• How do you keep your clients informed of your activities on their behalf?

• Do you consult with your clients on any and all offers?

• What are your commission rates? What are your procedures and time-frames for processing and disbursing client funds? Do you keep different bank accounts separating author funds from agency revenue? What are your policies about charging clients for expenses incurred by your agency?

• When you issue 1099 tax forms at the end of each year, do you also furnish clients upon request with a detailed account of their financial activity, such as gross income, commissions and other deductions, and net income, for the past year?

• In the event of your death or disability, what provisions exist for my continued representation?

• If we should part company, what is your policy about handling any unsold subsidiary rights in my work?

What's an author/agent agreement and should I sign one?

There is a debate among agents as to whether or not to have letters of agreements with authors, but they are becoming more common.

Every agent has an Agency Clause that is inserted into a successful publishing contract. The clause basically says that the agent is the agent of record for that book and that all the money will be funneled through the agent, who will take an agreed-upon commission from the gross amount before remitting the rest to the client. In rare cases, the agreement will state that the publisher will send the commission to the agent and separately send the client the rest of the money due after the agent's commission is deducted.

The basis of any successful agent/author relationship, just like a marriage, is trust. Although authors often insist upon it, in fact a letter of agreement is in the agent's interest a lot more than the client's. It protects the agent from many things, including doing all the work and having the client waltz away at the last moment and reap the rewards without the agent earning any money. It can also tie up an author to working exclusively with an agent when the agent is not the best person to represent a certain project. As in romance, once the marriage is over, regardless of the piece of paper legalizing the union, the author/agent relationship has nowhere good to go if it continues when neither party trusts or can work with each other anymore.

How can I be sure the publisher is giving me the best deal and that they'll honor the contract?

The best way to secure the best deal is to use a reputable agent who has examined and negotiated the best deal for you, the writer. This may not be a great deal compared to what others may have been offered, but it will be the best deal for that author and that book at that moment in time.

Similarly, an agent is in a position to ensure that a contract is honored, saving the writer from pestering the publisher if a problem comes up.

Tell me about publishing lunches. Why is it so hard to get hold of an agent or editor between 12 P.M. and 3 P.M.?

Publishing lunches are important because, rather like platonic dating, it is an opportunity for agent and editor to get to know each other's tastes and styles without the phone ringing or someone barging into your office with something to sign, a crisis to solve or a reminder you're late for yet another meeting.

Publishers value agents so highly that editors usually pay for lunch. Why? Because just as writers can't effectively concentrate on writing and selling at the same time, editors have to rely on agents to bring them hot new properties and help fix problems that may be on the horizon with authors' books the agent represents.

Editors can't edit a book, look after a variety of projects at various stages of completion in the publishing process and also screen unknown new properties all at once, so they rely on agents to do some of the screening for them. Ensuring that the agent keeps the editor in the loop and sends the editor his most exciting new projects and authors is worth at least the price of a lunch.

Agents also commonly submit a project to more than one editor at the same time, and the editors know this and accept it, though they don't much like authors trying to do the same thing. It's hard for an editor to discuss how much she loves a book editorially with an unagented writer and then have to switch gears and tell that same writer in harsh terms all the book's weaknesses in order to try and negotiate as small a royalty advance as possible for the book. Cool heads and objectivity are needed to do that job. It's not personal, it's about business, and that's one of the things an agent does for an author—takes care of business.

Suppose an editor wants to buy my book. What does my agent do next?

Once an editor makes an offer on a book, the agent informs everyone else who has it that she and the author have an offer. If they're lucky, they can get an auction going, with editors bidding against each other to buy the book. If every editor but one drops out, the agent sometimes has a number of persuasive arguments she can make to get the editor to increase the proposed royalty advance.

Most deals operate from the guiding principles that the editor really wants to buy the book and the author really wants to be published by that house and ideally by that editor. In an effort to get the best deal for his house, an editor may make the argument to an agent that the book he wants to buy may well not be a success, despite a belief in the author's talent. The editor will argue that he's going out on a limb for an untried author, he has colleagues he must convince, and because of this risk, he needs to get as many rights as possible to maximize the opportunities to earn back a royalty advance.

The agent will argue that first novelists are a better bet in some cases than previously published writers because there are no sales records to impact how many books a bookseller will order. Besides, people know when they are being "screwed," and it is not a wise move to treat an author poorly from the outset but to give them some respect so that the relationship can grow in a healthy manner to many books with that editor. The principle that an author should be allowed to reap the benefits of the work if the book performs well is one that good editors have no problem honoring. The success of a book should be everyone's success. Give us this; show some good faith so that the author will really know how important she is to the company, etc. Of course, if there is a good sales track record, then an agent will argue that very strongly as well. The author has proven herself already and should be treated accordingly.

Having negotiated the deal in broad measure, once the publishing contract arrives, the agent now turns into a paralegal and examines the contract closely. She'll discuss technical details with the editor as well as the publishing company's contract staff in an effort to get the client the best deal possible, taking care of contingency disasters that almost certainly will never happen but nevertheless need to be prepared for.

Does my agent have to be based in New York City?

Manhattan is still the heart of American publishing, and most of the publishing industry is based there. However, there are many good agents based outside of the city. Those not based in New York usually make regular trips into the city to meet with editors. However, most of the work is done by phone and fax. Better a good agent outside the city than a mediocre one based in New York.

What are the common causes of an agent/writer relationship souring?

Publishing relationships between agents and writers suffer many of the same problems that romantic relationships do. Unrealistic expectations may exist for what an agent can or should do for you. Don't ignore each other, communicate whenever possible, be considerate and respectful, say thank you occasionally, but be aware that everyone has other demands put on them. Respect each other's need for privacy, but also expect that your agent will respond quickly if there is a problem that needs to be fixed. Learn to trust each other.

How do I attract the attention of a good agent?

A lot of writers chase agents who are too busy to respond most of the time. They have their hands full just with their regular clientele. The agents *are*, however, on the lookout for successful writers who are unrepresented. These writers are published in magazines and anthologies, have written book reviews for local or national newspapers, have gotten their name in print somewhere and often more than once, and somewhere in the article their byline says something like, "Ethel Ethelridge is currently working on a nonfiction book about water management," or, "a novel about the Alamo from the Mexican perspective."

Go to writers conferences and network. I hate the idea of writing as a blood sport, but, if you can deal with it, enter competitions and win prizes. Get your writing noticed by people whose opinion counts for something and who can talk to friends or colleagues in the business about you and your work.

Find out who is starting up on their own or has just joined an established agency. These days, with editors losing editorial jobs in the changes that are wracking the publishing industry at the moment, many of these former editors are setting themselves up as agents and are on the lookout for new clients.

One of the best ways to find a good agent is by word of mouth. Try querying members of an organization such as AAR, though not all good agents are members.

Other good sources are R.R. Bowker's *Literary Market Place* (also called the LMP), which also has rules about who can be listed as an agent in its pages.

Lists of agents can also be found in Writer's Digest *Guide to Literary Agents* and Jeff Herman's *Writer's Guide to Book Editors, Publishers, and Literary Agents.*

If I write in two different genres using different pen names, can I legally use two different agents?

Of course you can. The question becomes "Should you?" If you have a good relationship with your agent, you should be able to discuss problems and career moves openly. Certainly, after discussing this situation with your agent, if you both decide it's OK, it can be a good move. Most agents these days are interested in getting the best deal for their clients because they stand to gain as well. Some writers, however, want to pursue smaller or less career-advancing projects for a variety of reasons, aesthetic and otherwise.

Unless they are in contact or somehow work together, two agents for one client can be a problem, however, when the contracts they procure for the author start to clash in terms of delivery dates of projects, option clauses (that means a particular publisher has an exclusive first choice in making an offer on the author's next work) and general expectations.

If possible it's always best to work with one agent who can represent the totality of your work.

My agent wants me to make editorial changes to my manuscript. Should I do it, and how many changes should I make?

Revision is an interesting topic these days. Many editors are not as skilled at line editing as they once were, and they also don't have the time to work on manuscripts the way they once could. Consequently, they're looking for manuscripts that are in near-perfect condition. Of course that's rarely the case, but agents know that in order to stand any chance of getting a book published, it needs to be in good shape editorially. Many agents have editorial backgrounds (many were editors at one time in their career); and, in general, the onus of editorial work on a manuscript has fallen more on the agent's shoulders than ever before.

There's no point making editorial changes to a manuscript, however, if they don't make sense to you. You'll never please anyone if you don't please yourself first. This is not saying that you shouldn't develop as objective a view as possible of your work, particularly when it comes to genre and structure.

What's the average commission percentage that an agent asks for?

Book agents commonly charge 15 percent for domestic sales and 20 percent for foreign sales, which are often shared with a foreign subagent.

Ask an agent at the beginning of your relationship what he charges.

Does this commission include not only the original sale but subsequent sales as well?

An agent's commission is payable on anything the book earns as long as he is the agent of record on that project.

How do I get a really powerful agent for my fiction?

Make sure you are a client that a powerful agent will find attractive. That means you have to have more going for you than just your opinion that you've written a "hot" novel.

The simple answer after that is to keep an eye out in newspapers, magazines or online sources such as publisherslunch.com for reports of deals agents have made. Bear in mind though, that some established agents, like myself for instance, don't always bother to report deals to the media. In many cases we get new clients through recommendations and word of mouth and less from the slush pile.

Should you go to an agent with a completed piece, a partial or just an idea?

If you've written a novel, finish the manuscript if you haven't been published before.

Nonfiction, on the other hand, is usually sold as a proposal and sample chapters. This should be put together in a particular way, however. (In chapter five you'll find advice on how to put together an effective nonfiction proposal.)

OK, enough about agents. What does an editor's office look like?

An editor's office looks a lot like an agent's—a jumble of books, manuscripts and loose sheets of paper. Each editor's office is likely to have floor to ceiling shelving, often taking up at least three out of four walls, groaning with published books and manuscripts to be read and edited, and copies of edited books transmitted and in "the system."

On the editor's desk and his assistant's desk sit piles of paper in an assortment of trays and out of them, while often on any free chair (and if they're senior enough, on a couch, too) sit more manuscripts and papers. In a corner somewhere there may be filing cabinets, while outside, where the assistant sits, are more filing cabinets.

What happens to my manuscript when it arrives at a publishing house?

Your manuscript arrives as part of a huge daily delivery of letters and parcels that are doled out by staff in the mail room. If you're lucky, the editors get their mail the same day it arrives, but sometimes the mail room decides to move at its own pace. (The guy in charge, having survived several mergers and downsizings in the last couple of years, is unfazed by the concept of urgency in mail delivery to editors who may not even be employed by the company anymore. When challenged, he indicates the bags of unsorted mail by the door as the mail person hefts in yet another sackload.) So it may be a couple of days before an editor gets to read all his mail.

Usually the mail is opened and logged in by his editorial assistant. Senior editors get their own assistant, while other editors sometimes have to share.

What's important about editorial assistants?

Editorial assistants often sit in open planned cubicles, with their computer screens and telephones the most obvious equipment on their desks next to piles of paper under neon strip lighting, in a long line facing the offices of the editors, who get to have windows. They can be some of the most important people you get to know in publishing. Why? If the submission the assistant logs in is a manuscript or proposal the editor is eagerly awaiting, the editor will take it home that night and respond as quickly as he can. More frequently, the submission will languish in a pile on a shelf waiting to be read, having been sorted by an agreed-upon priority system. Solicited agented mail tends to get a higher priority than unsolicited, which will be read before "over the transom" un-agented mail.

Very often, especially when it comes to fiction, the assistant will give the manuscript a first read. The assistant's experience grows by doing this type of work, and she will eventually get promoted to assistant editor and then full editor. (She may have to move to other houses, though, to get those promotions. That's one reason editors change jobs a lot.)

Is it a good idea to make friends with an editorial assistant? Shouldn't I be trying to attract the attention of her boss?

If you are working with an editor who is preparing your book for publication, it's more than likely you will spend more time dealing with the editor's assistant than with the editor. Editorial assistants are the people who get things done: They follow up on in-house problems for the editor, they transmit manuscripts and coordinate a lot of the editor's work. You don't have to buy them flowers or chocolates (although occasionally a card is nice), but make a point of saying please and thank you to them. They work hard, and it's nice to have your efforts noticed and applauded on occasion.

If you're submitting to the editor for the first time, it's likely that the assistant is the person who will look at your material first.

The assistant gives each submission serious consideration because she's looking for promising material. Finding a solid seller is like panning for gold, but that's how she will make her name in the company and in the industry in general, so she has an incentive to find good projects. Her editor is relying on her help.

Because she's worked for the editor for a while now and has typed all his letters and helped him with the day-to-day details of acquiring and rejecting material, as well as followed up on the transmittal details of books in the system, she has a good sense of what the editor likes and is looking for and, more importantly, what the editor does not like or want.

Why has publishing become so hard-nosed these days?

Many writers have quaint notions about publishing that have about as much to do with the modern realities of being an editor as Revolutionary War soldiering has to do with serving in the Gulf.

A mythical, romantic idea became known that editors (nearly all male) used to sit around wearing cardigans and smoking pipes, engaging in Dorothy Parker-like witty repartee. Of course it was never like that. The truth is that publishing (and those who buy books, by all accounts) is overwhelmingly female, and most of an editor's time is taken up with producing and moving "merchandise," not "books."

What do editors do?

Apart from editors like, say, Judith Regan at HarperCollins, the glamour in publishing is minimal. There are occasional publication parties, industry conferences, business lunches and glimpses of TV greenrooms once a year if you're lucky.

The reality of an editor's life is a daily grind of meetings, building positive consensus for books whose merits seem obvious to them, feeling guilty that they haven't read all that has been sent to them quickly enough, not paying enough attention to their private life and not finding enough time to read published books that they really want to read, which is why they went into publishing in the first place.

Ah, the endless meetings: editorial meetings to acquire the book, scheduling meetings to figure out if the publication of a book is on track and when to publish it, cover conferences to discuss the jacket design. Then there's catalog copy and book flap copy that must be written for the books on the editor's upcoming list, presentations for sales reps at sales conferences that must be prepared, problems and emergencies that need swift handling, phone calls to authors and agents returned, new proposals to be read from agents who gently—and sometimes not so gently—nag you for being too slow.

Editing is somehow done at home by stealing a day here and there, and reading is often done in bed at 10 P.M., while back in the office the word is out: "Find best-sellers. Get another Grisham or Steel or Patricia Cornwell if you want to keep your job."

Understanding and appreciating something of what an editor's life is like will help make your submission more professional and more geared to an editor's work schedule, and this in turn will make an editor's job easier if she likes your project and increase the likelihood that the editor will help you turn your project into a published book if it isn't quite in sync with what the house is looking for.

How do editorial departments work?

An editorial department is headed by the editorial director, who answers to the publisher. A good publisher not only has the responsibility of balancing the financial books and watching the bottom line, but often has a good editorial eye as well, at least in terms of recognizing potential moneymakers when their staff bring them up at editorial meetings.

The next in charge after the editorial director is the executive editor, and below her are a number of senior editors, editors, associate editors and editorial assistants.

The acquisition of a new book usually requires the agreement of the editorial director as well as the whole editorial board, which includes the sales director and sometimes the publisher, who may act as the de facto head of the editorial board.

Senior editors, particularly if they have their own imprint, can at times buy books they love up to a certain price, but they rarely exercise that option without getting some other editors on their side first.

Editors are becoming concerned that as publishing corporate types emphasize the bottom line more and more, an editor's future job security will be tied to the sales records of the books they buy. Buy enough flops and you'll likely be out on your ear after your annual review. Such pressures affect one's judgment.

As well as acquiring and editing books, the editorial department is often responsible for the overall coordination of other activities in the publishing house. This is usually the responsibility of the managing editor, who oversees the progress of a manuscript as it passes through the various stages needed to turn it into a published book.

Do publishers believe there is always room for another book?

Of course, that's what they're in business for. That's what editors live for, but finding a good book project is surprisingly difficult. So many new authors haven't mastered their craft, their idea is familiar, they lack the expertise to carry off their nonfiction idea or a myriad of other things.

That's why, if you learn your craft and develop your imagination in a way that takes advantage of the marketplace, the chances of being published are quite high.

If you're asking how open editors are to new writers, the answer is generally a positive one. Obviously, they are always on the lookout for experienced, money-earning writers who know how the game is played and can exploit it to everyone's advantage.

But truthfully, some great books and authors have come from the slush pile. Editors know this and are partly haunted by the fact that they could turn away the next Terry McMillan or Tom Clancy, so they continue to find a way to go through the unsolicited submissions with an eye toward finding a winner.

Can you tell me something about the sales and marketing department?

After editorial, the department that has the most impact on how and what books are acquired by a house is *sales and marketing*.

Publishing, whether newspaper, magazine or book, has always been an uneasy alliance between art and commerce. Since the advent of huge royalty advances to authors, the input of the marketing department has become even more crucial to book acquisition.

In editorial meetings, emphasizing the bottom line is what makes everyone smile and gets the editor what she wants. These days publishing is all about numbers—getting stock out and making sure it doesn't get returned. That's the job of sales and marketing.

The marketing department explores different and innovative ways to sell books, coordinating publicity and promotional campaigns and figuring out ways of getting the reading public to pay attention to a new book and new author.

In some cases, book buyers for major bookstore chains have suggested to publishing company sales reps the kinds of books they want to sell. The reps have reported back to the head of sales and marketing, and she in turn has informed editorial of the kind of books they ought to be buying. Before you know it, the tail is trying to wag the dog.

This is not to suggest that everyone in that chain doesn't have a valid role and valid opinions. Editors *should* spend time listening and talking with book buyers and sellers.

However, a finely honed balance of power seems to be tipping more in favor of sales and marketing, *i.e.*, commerce and conservatism, and away from editorial, *i.e.*, art, creativity and innovation.

Lacking the will and the courage to potentially fall on their face in an effort to publish new and inventive things, companies lose the ability to find and exploit new talent and reap the considerable rewards that can accrue as a result. They tend to throw money at more proven projects and authors rather than spend the time and roll of the dice developing their own.

Sales and marketing's most crucial decision is made when a manuscript is first acquired. Very often the proposal that sold that book will be used as the basis for the sales and marketing campaigns, which are put into gear way before the final manuscript is turned in. If the proposal is woolly or unfocused, then the subsequent marketing campaign may well reflect that lack of focus and the book will not do well.

Heaven help the publishing company whose editorial and marketing departments are either weak or at odds with each other.

What does the art department do?

The art department creates dust jackets and book covers, and the work is largely produced by freelance artists from guidelines given to them by the art director and the acquiring editor. It is unlikely that the artist has read the book. At cover design meetings everyone must sign off on the art before it is put into the system.

Rarely will a publishing company pay attention to an author's ideas about what should be on the cover. Authors are usually wrong and lack any real understanding of the task a book cover has to do. Publishing companies are exceedingly jealous of their control over how a book will look in its finished version. The best they'll sometimes do is give "cover consultation," which means they'll listen to what you have to say and then most likely ignore it.

Submitting sample jacket sketches is a sure sign of amateurism on a writer's part.

What can you tell me about the production and design department?

The production and design department designs the look of the book: the type-face, the page margins, the design of each chapter page, facing pages and so forth. They coordinate with the printer and are responsible for turning the inside of a book into something you recognize in a bookstore.

What do I need to know about the promotion and publicity department?

The promotion and publicity departments create adverts, which usually boast of a book's success or announce the latest book by a best-selling author with an eager and impatient audience waiting for its publication. They also create point-of-sale display materials for bookstores and book fairs and the like.

Publicity gets copies of the book to reviewers and others, arranges media coverage, schedules book tours and tries to shout loudly about a book to anyone who will listen.

The sad truth is that these departments have limited resources and limited personnel; they pick and choose which books they will expend effort on and which books will sit on the vine, like grapes, and wither from inattention.

The odds are that your book will sit on the vine, so you must be in the vanguard of promoting and publicizing your book. Keep in regular touch with the sales and marketing and publicity departments, who will probably assign someone to work with your book, but don't expect them to do much for your book. They're just too overworked.

However, where you lead, they will follow. Many a successful book became that way because of an author's efforts to initially get a book noticed.

What does the subsidiary rights department do?

If you've given the publishing company any rights to your book—for example, paperback rights or book club rights, which are commonly held by publishing companies—the subsidiary rights department is responsible for selling them on your behalf. The proceeds are usually split 50/50 between you and the publishing company. Other rights are split in ways that the publishing house and an author agree upon during the contract negotiations.

If the company also has foreign or translation rights, once again, the subsidiary rights people are the ones who will sell them. Very often, with high royalty advances paid for books, the money from such "subrights" sales goes toward a company recouping some of their initial outlay to an author.

What should I know about the distribution department?

The distribution department receives finished books from the printer and, in coordination with leads from sales and marketing, distributes copies of the book to various places around the country and sometimes outside.

What happens in an editorial meeting?

Once an editor finds something that "speaks" to him, he has to start a campaign to get others in the company to see the commercial merit in the project that he sees.

The editor will photocopy the proposal, or perhaps have his assistant make a copy of a manuscript, which will then be circulated to other editors and the sales and marketing director, perhaps with a note from the editor explaining what he finds appealing and publishable about the project.

A publishing company has two conflicting needs that continually have to be resolved. "Should this book be published?" and "How many copies can I get into the bookstores? Is this book promotable?"

If sales and marketing are not keen on a book, they can veto the acquisitions process or severely cripple it by making sure there's a very low print order.

One of the problems of conglomerate publishing is that while editorial departments remain independent of each other, the sales forces of merged companies are collapsed into one unit. The sales force is reduced, and suddenly at editorial meetings a sales director is saying, "But Imprint X is already doing a book something like this. Do we really want to publish two books on the same topic?" The project is then nixed, unless, of course, Imprint X's book does so well that everyone in sales and marketing wants more books just like it.

A major paradox of contemporary publishing is that everyone wants to publish a trend-setting book, but no one wants to be so far ahead of a trend that the book-buying public is running to catch up.

I've heard a lot about large companies buying a number of small publishers. How does this affect publishing and the people I'm working with?

Publishing has headed more and more in this direction as bigger companies gobble up smaller ones. It has always been a business that has a large financial risk attached to it for the publishing companies. In many instances, a handful of commercially successful books carry the financial burden of the rest of the publishing house's list, allowing the company to publish smaller selling but more prestigious "quality" literature, be it fiction or nonfiction, and maintain its credibility as a house that supports serious books on cultural, artistic and scientific topics of importance to us as a society. These financial "also rans" sometimes break even and sometimes never recoup the money spent on them.

One of the consequences of the changing economics of book publishing is the coalescing of smaller companies into bigger ones. Giant, diversified groups, so the theory goes, do not suffer so acutely from a shortage of cash and can even up the balance of power when dealing with large bookstore chains such as Barnes & Noble or Crown in terms of the discounts the chains demand for stocking and selling the publishing company's books.

Some conglomerates believe in the power of cross-fertilization, that is, that the various businesses within the group will benefit from a particular book's acquisition. Another type of conglomerate has arisen as a result of a sort of corporate cooperative, where several companies have banded together but remained editorially independent, as though different rooms in a house owned by an overarching financial authority.

As they greedily gobble up one of their rivals, conglomerate heads always declare that the various editorial departments will function independently and become stronger and increase the diversification of book titles available to the reading public. This resolve lasts about six to nine months. What then usually happens is that various imprints within the new combined entity are collapsed into one another and the streets of Manhattan run red with the blood of sacked editors yet again. On one occasion, the firing of the editorial staff took place in alphabetical order, and no one unconnected with the company was allowed into the building while the carnage took place.

Quite commonly the first people to go are the sales staff as sales forces are combined into a selling behemoth. What this means is that the various independent editorial departments find themselves presenting their new acquisition projects at editorial boards that include the same sales force representatives as the rival imprints within the same publishing group two floors up. The sales force rep says, "We already have a book like this from imprint X, why should we compete with ourselves?" and the editor is forced to reject the book. The public is then gypped of the chance of hearing perhaps a better writer's view on a serious topic that deserves various opinions published to create a debate. If, of course, book A is successful, conglomerate salespeople usually can't get enough of them, and that's all they want the editors to buy.

How can I make sure that someone will read my query? If it's rejected, what are the odds that it'll end up somewhere else under another writer's name?

To put together a professional query, make sure your query letter is no more than a page long and looks clean and well written, with no grammatical or typographical errors.

Make sure it's well researched, and mention early on why you are the best person to write the book and why the book should be published despite the other books that may already be published in that field. If you are asked to send fifty pages, or the first three chapters, don't send ten pages, or the whole manuscript—send what you are asked to send.

Amateur writers worry endlessly about their work being stolen; but the fact is, if it's good enough to steal, it's good enough to publish. Editors and agents aren't just looking for a good project to sell; they're looking for a writer who will produce many successful projects and who will grow into a moneymaking concern.

Just suppose a project is stolen. And suppose further that it is a big success—a writer's nightmare come true. But it's a nightmare for the editor or the agent who stole it because the public clamors for more, and there is no more to give.

The truth is that publishing is made up of reputable people who long to find publishable material and the writers who can produce it. But an idea is not copyrightable; in fact, ideas are ten-a-penny. What's important is what you do with the idea, how you realize it. If you can prove that someone plagiarized your work, you can always sue them and win compensation.

How do I approach editors or publishers?

Do some research. Books such as the Writer's Digest guides or Jeff Herman's *Writer's Guide to Book Editors, Publishers, and Literary Agents* can help. Plus a multitude of frequently asked questions on a number of writers forums can be found on the Internet.

After you've found the best publisher and the name of the editor who handles the kind of material you want to write about, write a one-page query letter with perhaps a synopsis of your story or an overview of your nonfiction project explaining why you're the best person to write this book.

If I publish on the Internet, can I still publish with a print publisher?

Theoretically, yes. However, anything that has been previously published, whether it is self-published in print or electronically, becomes a kind of "damaged goods" in the eyes of many publishers until the book starts to get good sales figures. Then the situation changes—an audience has been proven for the material—and print publishers will be far more receptive to the project. Remember that a best-seller electronically is usually fewer than one thousand copies.

What does copyright protect?

(The following copyright information is used courtesy of the Library of Congress. For more information, see the Web site: www.loc.gov/.)

Copyright protects original works of authorship including literary, dramatic, musical and artistic works such as poetry, novels, movies, songs, computer software and architecture. Copyright does not protect facts, ideas, systems or methods of operation, although it may protect the way these things are expressed.

When is my work protected?

Your work is under copyright protection the moment it is created and fixed in a tangible form so that it is perceptible either directly or with the aid of a machine or device. In other words, as soon as you put words on paper or on a computer screen your material is copyrighted.

Do I have to register with the Library of Congress (LOC) to be protected?

No. Copyright exists from the moment the work is created. You will have to register, however, if you wish to bring a lawsuit for infringement of a U.S. work.

How do I get in contact with the Library of Congress?

The LOC has a FAQs page with extensive, up-to-date information about copyright. The Internet address of the LOC is www.loc.gov/. The Public Information Office telephone number is (202) 707-3000.

Why should I register my work if copyright protection is automatic?

Many choose to register their works because they wish to have the facts of their copyright on the public record and have a certificate of registration. Registered works may be eligible for statutory damages and attorney's fees in successful litigation. If registration occurs within five years of publication, it is considered prima facie evidence in a court of law.

Is the LOC the only place I can go to register a copyright?

Although copyright application forms may be available in public libraries and some reference books, the U.S. Copyright Office is the only office that can accept applications and issue registrations.

How do I register my copyright?

To register a work, you need to submit a completed application form, a nonrefundable filing fee of $30, and a nonreturnable copy or copies of the work to be registered.

How long does the registration process take?

The time the Copyright Office requires to process an application varies, depending on the amount of material the Office is receiving. You may generally expect a certificate of registration within approximately eight months of submission.

Do I have to renew my copyright?

No. Works created on or after January 1, 1978, are not subject to renewal registration. For works published or registered prior to January 1, 1978, renewal registration is optional after twenty-eight years but does provide certain legal advantages.

Can foreigners register their works in the U.S.?

Any work that is protected by U.S. copyright law can be registered. This includes many works of foreign origin. All works that are unpublished, regardless of the nationality of the author, are protected in the United States. Works that are first published in the United States or in a country with which we have a copyright treaty or that are created by a citizen of a country with which we have a copyright treaty are also protected and may therefore be registered with the U.S. Copyright Office.

What do fair use and public domain mean?

Fair use generally applies to a limited use of a small part of a copyrighted work for specific uses, such as commentary, criticism or scholarship. Fair use is a narrow and highly technical legal doctrine, and you can really only know whether or not it was applied legitimately *after* a lawsuit for copyright infringement has concluded and the court has decided! Always get written permission to use another's material in some way in your own work.

Once a copyright on a work expires it passes into the public domain. It can then be freely used without the permission of the former copyright holders. If you're not sure about its legal status, contact the Library of Congress and ask them to do a copyright search. Once a book passes into the public domain it can't be recopyrighted again. However, if a *new* work is created, based on the work in the public domain (*Les Misérables*, the musical, for example, was based on Victor Hugo's nineteenth century novel) the author of the new work may well be entitled to a separate copyright for the new work.

What is a work made for hire?

Although the general rule is that the person who creates the work is its author, there is an exception to that principle: the exception is a work made for hire, which is a work prepared by an employee within the scope of his or her employment; or a work specially ordered or commissioned in certain specified circumstances. When a work qualifies as a work made for hire, the employer or commissioning party is considered to be the author.

How do I copyright a name, title, slogan or logo?

Copyright does not protect names, titles, slogans or short phrases. In some cases, however, these things may be protected as trademarks.

How do I protect my idea?

Copyright does not protect ideas, concepts, systems or methods of doing something. You may express your ideas in writing or drawings and claim copyright in your description, but be aware that copyright will not protect the idea itself as revealed in your written or artistic work.

How long does copyright last?

The Sonny Bono Copyright Term Extension Act, signed into law on October 27, 1998, amends the provisions concerning duration of copyright protection. The terms of copyright are generally extended for an additional twenty years. Specific provisions are as follows:

• For works created after January 1, 1978, copyright protection will endure for the life of the author plus an additional seventy years.

• For works created but not published or registered before January 1, 1978, the term endures for the life of the author plus seventy years, but in no case will expire earlier than December 31, 2002. If the work is published before December 31, 2002, the term will not expire before December 31, 2047.

• For pre-1978 works still in their original or renewal term of copyright, the total term is extended to ninety-five years from the date that copyright was originally secured.

How much of someone else's work can I use without getting permission?

Under the fair use doctrine of the U.S. copyright statute, it is permissible to use limited portions of a work including quotes, for purposes such as commentary, criticism, news reporting and scholarly reports. There are no legal rules permitting the use of a specific number of words, a certain number of musical notes or percentages of a work. Whether a particular use qualifies as fair use depends on all the circumstances.

How much do I have to change in order to claim copyright of someone else's work?

Only the owner of copyright in a work has the right to prepare or to authorize someone else to create a new version of that work. You cannot claim copyright to another's work, no matter how much you change it, unless you have the owner's consent.

What is a copyright notice? How do I put a copyright notice on my work?

A copyright notice is an identifier placed on copies of the work to inform the world of copyright ownership. While use of a copyright notice was once required as a condition of copyright protection, it is now optional. Use of the notice is the responsibility of the copyright owner and does not require advance permission from, or registration with, the U.S. Copyright Office.

Somebody infringed my copyright. What can I do?

You can file a civil lawsuit in Federal district court. If you believe that your copyright has been infringed, consult an attorney. In cases of willful infringement for profit, the U.S. Attorney may initiate a criminal investigation.

Is my copyright good in other countries?

The United States has copyright relations with more than one hundred countries throughout the world, and as a result of these agreements, we honor each other's citizens' copyrights. However, the United States does not have such copyright relationships with every country.

How do I get permission to use somebody else's work?

Ask for it. If you know who the copyright owner is, contact the owner directly. If you are not certain about the ownership or have other related questions, ask the U.S. Copyright Office to conduct a search of its records for a fee of $65 per hour.

Could I be sued for using somebody else's work? How about quotes or samples?

If you use a copyrighted work without authorization, the owner may be entitled to bring an infringement action against you. There are circumstances under the fair use doctrine where a quote or a sample may be used without permission. However, in cases of doubt, get the owner's permission.

chapter four

Marketing Your Work: From Idea to Bookstore

I've got this great idea. What do I do now?

The first question you need to ask yourself is: "Is this idea really a book? Would it work better as a magazine article or (if it's a piece of fiction) a short story or even a play?"

If you're confident you can write at least 250 double-spaced pages without padding, then your idea could well be a book.

Having decided that, start the process of introducing that irritating piece of sand (your idea) into an oyster (your outline or proposal), which promises in turn to become a beautiful pearl (your book).

It's a mistake to think that writing is about putting down words on paper. That's *technique*. *Writing* is about *thinking*.

Publishing industry professionals primarily stay in the industry because we love what we do. Our love affair is not just with books—our passions are about ideas. It's a heady thought to realize that the publishing industry is really a marketplace for ideas, especially those with strong emotional impact.

What do you mean by "Make your story emotionally gripping"?

Apart from the obvious need to make us care about the characters in your story, books that sell well invariably touch some sort of communal nerve. Of course, divining what that communal nerve will be is guesswork based on honed intuition, objective observations of the world around us and experience studying your topic and the kinds of books audiences are attracted to.

Successful books on a subject not only tackle the problem in a simple, inventive way, they also speak to the reader in a reassuring and positive way that makes the reader feel empowered.

Nonfiction can work in the same way in the sense that, if possible, it should always have an appeal to the reader on a benefits base. What I mean by this is that the book will have a tangible benefit to the reader that can be demonstrated.

(Look at the proposals advice in chapter five for more discussion about this.)

What do you mean by "Define your audience"?

When you start to develop your idea, the most important questions are: "Who will buy this book?" and "What category does it fall into?" From the beginning, define your audience.

Catching the reader's attention isn't just a function of how well you write your proposal or your book. It's about how well you structure and think through your idea and how you tie that idea into a reader's expectations.

What do I mean by that? We've already seen that genre is a guide to a reader's expectations. Another element to ponder is that with all the thousands of books published every year that remain unread, why will enough people be interested in what you have to say that they'll spend their hard-earned cash on your book? Make sure your idea is told in such an emotionally gripping way that it will appeal to as wide an audience as possible.

Should I approach writing my book from the point of view of my audience?

Approaching your book this way forces you to become more objective, and that in turn helps you reexamine, reshape and if necessary restructure your idea.

In general, it's worth remembering that certain constants apply, particularly in the nonfiction field. People who like romances, for example, don't just buy one. They tend to collect them. Similarly, people who buy self-help or health books usually do so because they have a problem they're trying to solve. Regardless of the fact that they may have bought six other books on the topic before buying yours, the other six didn't work for them and they're hoping that yours will provide the key to the problem they're grappling with, be it a way to quit smoking or an inability to lose weight.

Objectively compare your idea with what has already been published in this area. What does your book add to the field? If it's only your thoughts and philosophies, unless you're an expert whose opinion is sought after by colleagues in the field, your book might be a tough sell. If, however, you know your subject well enough that you realize there's a "hole" (*i.e.*, something that hasn't been written about much yet), you're probably onto a good thing.

How can I figure out how many readers I'll get for my book idea?

Answer this question for yourself: "Do I honestly believe that fifteen thousand people will buy a trade paperback version of my book?" If the answer is "no," then this is either a small press book or a magazine article.

Does the subject matter you're interested in writing about have a fan base? Is there a magazine devoted to it? Are columns written about it in national or regional magazines?

Read magazines and newspapers that cover your area of interest. If you see a lot of articles about new trends in the subject, perhaps there might be a corresponding interest in a new book on the topic. You must let your passion for a topic drive you, but you must also be objective about its sales potential.

How do I go about sizing up the competition?

First see if there are other books on your topic and, if there are, how successful they've been. Go online to Amazon.com or Barnes&Noble.com and check the category or subject you intend to write about. After you've done that, visit your local bookstores and browse the shelves. Has anyone written something like your book and published it recently? What are the names of the publishers who publish books like the one you propose? Who are the big-selling authors in this genre and what are the titles of their latest and/or most successful books?

Go to the library and check out *Books in Print*. In particular, look up books that have been published on your topic in the last five or so years. The results can be daunting and need to be interpreted, but the most important thing about *Books in Print* is that it's an exhaustive catalog. Concentrate not on the academic and barely-in-print titles, but on those by mainstream and small press publishers that you can find relatively easily in any neighborhood bookstore of some quality. The point is to size up your audience and see if your idea has already been done.

With your *Books in Print* list in hand, start browsing the shelves of your local bookstores. See if any editor or agent names are mentioned in the acknowledgments of the books you've got stacked beside you. Make a note of them.

Pay particular attention to competing and complementing books. You'll need all this information when you construct your proposal.

Once I've targeted my audience, what do I do next?

Do the books already published on the subject fit a pattern? Can you fit into or manipulate that pattern to your own advantage? For example, are all the books expensive hardcovers? Could there be room for a cheap paperback that would appeal to a large mass of people? Publishers always determine the price and style of the book, but in your proposal you can always suggest the broad aim of the book and temper its language and appeal to fit more easily into a type of book.

My idea is very time sensitive. How do I get an editor or agent to look at it quickly?

If it's that time sensitive, your best outlet is a magazine. It can take as long as two years from the time a book proposal is contracted by a publishing company to the time it reaches a bookstore's shelves. A book copyrighted 2002 may well contain, at best, 2001 information. In other words, it *could* be out of date.

Has anything really changed in the field in the intervening period that might make publishing a more up-to-date book worthwhile? One of the big problems with publishing books in the computer and Internet field, ironically, is that things change *so fast* it's almost impossible for a book to keep up. As a result, publishers tend to try and find topics that will have a long and more stable backlist life.

Ideally, you want to write a book that will maintain a strong selling life after the initial enthusiasm has died away and it's left pretty much to its own devices.

How do I find out what's hot and take advantage of the trend?

The big problem with trends is that by the time you've responded to them, it's too late. Here's a rough timetable to give you some idea of how things work:

    From idea to research to book proposal: two months

    From book proposal to literary agent: six months

    From agent to editor and book contract: six months (if you're lucky)

    From contract to delivery of manuscript to editor: nine months

    From transmission to editor to finished book on the shelves: nine months

    Total time: two and a half years

You might think from this that you could go straight to the editor and gain some time; but the truth is, an agent knows exactly who in a publishing house is looking for material and what his or her tastes are, so the agent will probably shorten the time it takes to get an editor to accept the book. They can also send the book to more than one editor at a time. It's tougher for an author to do that. Your proposal could languish in an editorial slush pile for months before it gets rejected and you have to start the process all over again.

If you are an experienced writer with a track record of some kind, it's possible you can work directly with an editor to put out an "instant" book. You must prove that you can work quickly and accurately, that you're the best person to write the book and that there is a compelling (usually financial) reason to do the book in six to eight weeks or so.

These kinds of books are usually done through an agent and rarely directly with an editor who does not know you because the pressures to get it right the first time and the time constraints are too great. Feel free to approach them, but don't be disappointed if nothing happens.

Unless it's an instant book on, say, the death of Princess Di, or Elian Gonzalez, or a Three Mile Island– type meltdown, the book probably doesn't have to be crashed. "Crashing" a book is time intensive to the detriment of everything else an editor may be responsible for and very hard on a publishing house. The chances are high that an editor who must do an "instant" book will approach either a writer he knows or an agent he has worked with before whose clients he knows and trusts can do the job quickly and well because there is little time for "second takes."

I live in a remote part of the country. How am I going to find all this information?

Actually living in a rural or suburban area can be an advantage. You can become a local or regional celebrity and build on that.

Bookstore owners and managers, for example, generally love to talk to authors if they have the time. Find out from them what sells well in your region. What backlists "well" (sell) locally and what kinds of new books cause excitement? Try out your book idea on the bookstore owner and see what sort of reaction you get.

If there are a lot of new books on a topic, maybe it's not such a good idea for you to write this book *unless* you really do have something new to say. All those books would indicate publishers think the topic is a hot seller, so they might be interested in something worthwhile on the topic. Bear in mind that subjects get overbought and that hot now is often cold later.

What else should I do to track markets and audiences?

Call publishing houses and ask for their latest catalogs. You can find the numbers in *Literary Market Place* (LMP), at your local library, in the Writer's Digest *Writer's Market* or in Jeff Herman's *Writer's Guide to Book Editors, Publishers, and Literary Agents*. Publishers are usually happy to send prospective authors free catalogs. It's a lot easier to help educate a writer than to cope with inappropriate and unprofessional submissions that take up valuable time to examine and reject.

Once you get the catalogs, study them carefully. They'll tell you what the publishers intend to publish in the upcoming season. Is there a book on your subject? Study the entry carefully. Are they making a big deal of it? Does it get a full page? Are there marketing and advertising plans? Pay attention to the author's qualifications. How do yours stack up?

How do I keep my material cutting edge?

Nonfiction is sold on a proposal and sample chapter. A novel has to be completed (unless you already have an existing relationship with an editor who's in a position to buy your next book).

At present, genre fiction is much more likely to sell than any other, and the genres that are a little easier to break into tend to be:

Mystery and crime

Romance

Sci-fi and fantasy

Middle grade and YA fiction

Everyone wants to write fiction. Every publisher that publishes fiction wants to find another John Grisham, Mary Higgins Clark, Anne Rice, Stephen King or Tom Clancy, but there are only so many of these kinds of authors to go around and only a handful of publishers who can afford them.

Remember, editors are looking for outstanding books with a strong voice and strong characters an audience can get involved with.

"Cutting edge" means more than just "relevant" to a contemporary audience.

It has to appeal to a broad audience while at the same time presenting a unique new voice and take on a familiar subject. Obviously, this gives talented young writers and those from cultures other than the mainstream a slight edge when it comes to writing about or viewing the mainstream.

As we become culturally more diverse, things in our society change and become more familiar. (Consider what is understood or taken for granted in the world of a thirteen-year-old today as opposed to a thirteen-year-old in 1925, 1945 or 1960, for example.) We reinvent ourselves as a society, and in the act of reinvention, talented and imaginative writers show us how we can view anew things that are familiar to us. This is not limited to age or ethnicity, but to flexibility of thinking. (For example, Sid Caesar is as funny now as he was in the 1950s because his humor was based on reality.)

I've heard the expression "niche" publishing. What does it mean?

Niche publishing means identifying a specific area of the marketplace and publishing books that will appeal to that audience.

New Age and New Age health is such an area, as are computer and technology books. In the commercial trade arena, Jack London-esque, man-against-nature narrative nonfiction is also doing well. As the baby boomer generation ages, it has more time to read; and since it came of age in the 1960s, it has always been a generation fascinated with itself and its problems.

So a niche in this case can have quite a large audience. The danger is to think that all baby boomers or all African Americans or all Hispanics are monolithic groups interested in a particular topic that should appeal to them, when the likelihood is that it will be splinter groups within these broad classifications whom you should be targeting.

An editor I know asked me, "How many copies can YOU help sell?" Was he serious?

Let potential editors know if you have a regular newspaper or magazine column or a constituency of some kind that could be a potential market for your book.

This is especially true if you teach a course or regularly hold a seminar on the topic you're writing about. Publishers are interested in the bottom line, and anything that helps book sales and promises to pay for itself is looked upon with more enthusiasm.

But I'm not an expert; I just write well. What do I do now?

If you're not an expert in an area, find an expert to work with. Chances are, if you *can* write, she can't or doesn't want to. Use your intelligence; keep up with current events and trends.

If you're not hooked up in some way with an expert in the field you're writing about, or you're the expert, try to find a well-known (and ideally well-respected) colleague or expert to endorse your idea or who will look at your book with an eye to endorsing it when it's finally published. Even if you're an eminent physicist, if Stephen Hawking or Lawrence Krauss say they'll write you a blurb or better yet an introduction to your book, your chances of getting published increase exponentially.

Are there any national organizations, museums, clubs, etc., that you have access to whose name might increase a book's visibility and marketability?

What are the five most important things I should know about pitching an idea to an editor?

• Make sure your idea is a fresh idea. If you've seen it or read it, don't try and rewrite it in order to get published. You need to look at the world and see it with fresh eyes. Difficult? Who said that writing publishable material was easy?

• Make sure what you send in is well written. That means don't use "fiction novels" and other equally redundant phrases. Learn to use words gracefully and well. They are your tools, so become comfortable with them and know how to use them effectively.

• Be professional. If you don't know what this means, read this book and others like it about what editors like and expect from authors they deal with.

• Be able and willing to communicate clearly and effectively with the editor you're submitting to.

• Be willing and able to promote your work.

Should I copyright my manuscript or proposal before I submit it?

No. Because you've written it, it is automatically copyrighted. If you're worried that someone might steal your idea, remember that an idea can't be copyrighted, only the way it is executed. If you see your idea in print somewhere, consider that ideas seem to float in the ether and when they are "ready," several people seem to get them at the same time. However, if there is a clearly provable case of plagiarism, you can always sue.

One of the simplest ways to informally copyright material (i.e., prove authorship), particularly with plays and screenplays, is to go to the post office, register a copy of the manuscript and then mail it to yourself. When it arrives, put it, still sealed, on a shelf and keep it like that until you need to prove you wrote something at a particular date. (For information on formally copyrighting material, see chapter three.)

How do you gauge how crowded with submissions a given market could be?

First, go to a big bookstore, maybe a good, independent bookstore, browse the shelves and talk to the bookstore staff. These people really know books.

Check out what's in print using Amazon.com and Barnes&Noble.com. Go to the library and use *Books in Print* and also read back copies of *Publishers*

Weekly, *Library Journal* and other publishing industry newsletters and magazines. Study the sections that cover your topic.

If it's a crowded field, make sure that your book is covering a topic or aspect that has not been dealt with or which places the subject in a new light. You'll also need to be an expert or well known in the field.

My publisher is a small house. How do I get my books into the bookstores?

Bookstore buyers first learn about your book from the new catalog your publishing house puts out. If your book is given a whole page rather than a half-page or two pages rather than one, the store's book buyer gets an immediate sense of how important, in commercial terms, the publisher considers the book.

Several times a year sales reps for the company touch base with bookstore accounts. Some reps have large geographic areas, such as New England or the Pacific Northwest, and others have large volume clients such as Crown or Barnes & Noble. The larger publishing companies have full-time sales forces, while the smaller houses use commissioned reps.

The problem with commissioned reps is that they often represent more than one publisher at a time and only earn money on the books they place. The inherent problems of the system are obvious. If the rep selling your first novel is, at the same time, promoting Stephen King's new novel, guess who's going to get the short end of the stick?

The best way to combat this is to develop the "ripple in a pond" strategy. Drop a pebble in water and watch the ripples move out ever wider from a central point. The central point of your marketing and sales strategy should be local stores and local media outlets. If you can get local bookstores to stock your book with the help of your publisher and if you can imaginatively get the book to the attention of a local audience, through, say, the local newspaper, local radio and TV (the story would be both what the book is about and the fact that you are a local personality), then its success will cause statewide interest, then regional interest and eventually national interest.

If you've written a stamp collecting mystery, make sure that stamp collecting groups nationwide know about it and that the book is advertised in and reviewed by any stamp collection newsletters there are. Get as many endorsements from famous relevant names as you can. In other words, catch the store book buyers' eyes without being an irritation.

Does having a large publisher make a difference in terms of getting better exposure for my book?

It's something of a trade-off. A big publisher may ignore your book until it starts to catch on and then they can get it out to bookstores through their distribution networks very effectively.

A smaller publisher may put more time and effort into promoting you because you are a "star" to them. However, they may be hampered by a poor or weak distribution network.

Which one you choose and why is sometimes a moot point if you only have one offer, for example, Conari Press wants to make you an offer for your book, and Random House turns you down, and those are your last two viable options besides self-publishing.

What do a book company rep and bookstore buyer talk about?

The meetings between a buyer and a rep can be somewhat distracted affairs. The rep has about two minutes or so to present each of the season's new titles, and will often go through the catalog page by page for the buyer, discussing each book. He learned about these books from the editor firsthand at a sales conference not long ago.

The rep basically discusses three things. (They're a variation on the same things you should put in your book proposal.) They are:

- A description of the book
- The publisher's plans to promote and sell the book
- The author's credentials and past track record, including sales

The question now becomes, how many copies of your book will the buyer take?

What do editors mean when they talk about "legs" and "the numbers game"?

Legs means an author's successive books are getting more and more sales, or "legs." Bookstores track sales of inventory, that is, books, on their computers. A few years ago, a bookstore would buy, say, a month's worth of inventory; now, they take about two weeks. If they need to restock, they'll get more copies from a book wholesaler. With less money tied up in inventory, the theory is that the process becomes cheaper for the bookstore.

During the meeting between the rep and the book buyer, they may check the computer to look at sales for a particular author or for a particular genre of book. The number of copies the store takes will be affected by a perceived current popularity of that type of book or that author.

Does the number of copies of a book taken by a store depend on how many copies the author's last book sold?

Yes. Often, a new book by an author with a proven track record will be more appealing to bookstore buyers. If his books have sold well in the past, odds are his new ones will sell, too, thus earning everyone more money.

New authors and authors whose previous books haven't sold well may not get as many advance orders from bookstores. However an author who's a good self-promoter is always of interest to book buyers. Media appearances, self-marketing, hot topics and good writing can all alter an order.

What happens after the reps get all their advance orders?

Once all the advance orders are in, the publisher will have the warehouse ship the books to the stores. These days, publishers try to keep print runs low (a print run is the number of books a publisher prints in total when the book is published). Print runs are perhaps three to five thousand copies on average. They restock by going back to press as demand merits. Returns (that is, unsold books shipped back to the publisher by the bookstore) will also end up in the warehouse, so publishers may wait critical marketing periods if they think a book will return and then redistribute, rather than print more copies immediately.

So what will my publisher do once my book is published?

The short answer is, "Not much," once the book is in the stores. However, they will usually follow where you lead.

What about the publicity person who's been assigned to work with me and my book?

The publicity department will get out copies of your book to reviewers and others who can help in the promotion of the book. They'll also help you get local signings, maybe make follow-up calls and, if appropriate, arrange interviews.

Bear in mind the publicity department is often small and overworked, they have limited and finite resources, and those resources are generally earmarked for the books that a committee has determined will benefit the company's bottom line most.

How can you tell if your book is one of the favored siblings? How much space, compared to other titles, did your book get in the sales catalog? There's your answer.

How can I get a publisher to help market my book if it's not going to be a lead title for them?

Ask what the company's publicity and marketing plans for your book will be. Ask specifically if they intend to tour you. It's not likely, but you should be prepared in case they say yes. Find out who's going to pay for it, at least in terms of hotel and traveling expenses, and make sure it's them. If you do go on tour, make a space in your schedule to accommodate your publisher's plans. If you have any problems, get your agent involved.

If it's possible—and certainly after you've had a couple of books published that give you a decent track record (say, sales of twenty thousand copies or more)—choose a publisher who is known for selling and marketing books like yours well. Check bookstores, the Internet, writers conferences, etc. Develop your own marketing plan (obviously, it needs to be down to earth and practical) suggesting how best to market your book.

These things have a common root but will vary from book to book, fiction to nonfiction. Can the book be marketed directly to your audience? What contacts can you exploit?

In the case of fiction, marketing a book is difficult because the book tends to rise or fall in a promotional context based on who the author is. At the least, start a Web site and refer as many people as possible to it.

My publisher refuses to advertise my book. Surely that's costing me lots of book sales.

Not really. In general, advertising an unknown book by an unknown author is expensive and achieves little. Adverts for books work in two ways: They boast of a book's success in prizes and sales, essentially telling its audience, "Don't miss out on this hot property everyone else has read!" and they tell the eager fans of famous authors (or those interested in the specific things the book is about) that the author's next book is imminent. Clancy fans or King fans eagerly await the next novel, and the adverts tell them it's on the way.

The publicity department will promote your book for about three months before they move on to another author. If you ask nicely, they may give you a copy of their marketing plan and a copy of the press kit they used for the book. If you have a problem getting hold of these, ask your editor or your agent to get them for you. No marketing plan? There's your answer.

My publisher won't promote my book. This really stinks, doesn't it?

Believe it or not, there is a positive side to that. In general, where an author leads, a publisher will follow. So you hold your own fate in your hands, and you can show the so-called experts exactly how it should be done. If you're right, they'll applaud you and put the weight of the company behind you again. If you're wrong, well, that's a lesson learned, isn't it?

How do I go about promoting my book?

Initially, the Internet is one of the best ways. There are plenty of sites that offer advice (use www.askjeeves.com or www.google.com as a starting place), and a search for a target audience for your book helps you inform them that your book exists.

The simple answer to selling books is publicity—as much as you can get for yourself and your book. Start with local publicity, then expand to regional and finally national.

How many people live in your town, your county, your state? What organizations are interested in your book's subject matter? How many members do they have?

If you can sell ten thousand copies regionally, you're already beating the odds big time and getting the system to work for you. Remember, even though all ten thousand were sold in the Barnes & Nobles in and around your town in the north, a Barnes & Noble in Florida or Texas consults the computer and sees total figures nationwide. If a book looks like it's moving, they may well want to get on the bandwagon and provide a hot property for their customers, with some encouragement.

How do I go about encouraging bookstores to take my book, short of using a sawed-off shotgun and making them an offer "they can't refuse"?

It's almost never too soon to start working on publicity for your book but with this provison: If you get people excited about the book before it's available, you will lose momentum and will have to work twice as hard to get it back later on. Timing in publicity is critical.

Once your manuscript is completed and handed in, draw up two lists. The first is of half a dozen people whom you can approach to ask for a quote or "blurb" once they've read the book. They should be both well known and relevant to your endeavors. The second list should be a wish list of famous people (obviously, they must all still be alive and approachable) whom your agent and/or editor might be able to help you reach, with the same objective— to get a quote. These should be writers or experts in the field you've chosen to write about and whose work you genuinely admire. With the backing of a publishing contract in particular, many people will ask you to send them something when it's ready.

It's your job to ask and their job to say "yes" or "no." But it's business, so don't take rejection personally. Many authors have their own deadlines to meet, and many are simply burnt out from the process of being asked for quotes based on their celebrity.

How do I write a letter to a "famous" person asking for an endorsement?

A writer friend of mine use to call these "worm" letters. The best answer is, approach writers whose work you admire and write from the heart. You're a writer; you'll find the words. Such a letter—short, succinct and to the point— can be hard to resist from someone who can write and who is clearly a fan. Include a brief synopsis of your book and a short bio.

What if I ask a "famous" person for an endorsement and I get no answer?

There's a saying in publishing that "no news is no news." However, if you haven't heard after seven or eight weeks, check the address and send another letter.

If you get a "yes," promptly send out the manuscript or galleys with a cover letter that says thank you. If you haven't heard anything after a month, politely get in touch by phone if you have the number (presumably it will be on the person's letterhead when they responded to you), and ask whether the person received your manuscript. Check in once a month, no more. Be persistent and polite until you either get your response or you realize they're too busy to look at your book after all. Then drop it and move on to someone else.

If you're successful early enough in the publishing process, it's possible for your editor to get the art department to put the quote on the front cover of the book. Anything that will make you and your book stand out, that you're comfortable doing, is worth trying.

Keep in touch with your publisher's publicity department. When they ease back, start to pick up the slack, continuing the book's marketing momentum.

What do I do if my editor and imprint are swallowed up in a merger or a reorganization of the parent publishing company?

One of the nightmare scenarios of contemporary publishing is the "orphan syndrome." This is where an author loses an editor (who moves on to another company or gets fired) or, in a worst-case scenario, the whole company goes on the auction block and everything is put on hold until after the sale is completed and the new regime has decided what kinds of books they want to do.

Agents spend a lot of time dealing with exactly these kinds of situations. Sometimes the answer is to wait and see, and sometimes it is to get back the rights to the book and resell them. If it is a situation where an imprint has been folded into a larger house, then the best thing you can do is try to ride on your editor's back through the rough water. In the end, the same marketing and publicity department will probably be working on the book.

If you have a new editor, you and your agent should try to bond with that editor if possible so that the editor thinks of the book as "hers" and not some "cuckoo child" she's been stuck with.

This is a tough situation and not easily resolved, except by time and positive actions.

What does "having a platform" for my book mean?

One of the first elements you should emphasize when writing your proposal is your ability to sell copies yourself. From the moment the editor reads your proposal, the question everyone asks is: "Does this author have a platform?"

A great deal of importance was placed on your claims to be able to promote your book. Now it's time to put your money where your mouth was.

• Don't promote your book ad hoc. Get a plan.

• Be persistent, but don't badger people. You want them on your side, not annoyed at you.

• Start publicity efforts early, but not too early. Timing is critical. Make sure you can follow through if you strike gold.

Bear in mind that promoting a novel and promoting nonfiction are different. In general, promoting a novel is much tougher because you are focused much more specifically on who *you* are than what the novel is about, unless it won an award or a prize. Few of the people you'll deal with will have the time to read it, and conversations will be about what you went through to write the book, what inspired the story and so forth.

With nonfiction you have an easier time of promoting both yourself and your book's subject. Sad, but true, the book's success is far less tied to how well it's written.

Should my marketing goal be to sell as many copies of my book as possible?

Actually, no, strange as it may seem. That goal is too vague. Aim for something more concrete, for example: Get as much positive publicity for you and your book as you can.

There are specific steps you can take to achieve this. List the resources you can approach. Here are some basic ideas that can be applied to both fiction and nonfiction projects, although not every one will work well with each genre. You'll have to decide what's best for you and your project on a case-by-case basis.

• Create a Web page and use the Internet to advertise and sell your book.

• Talk to anyone in the PR or promotional fields who can give you advice or contacts.

• Approach newspapers, newsletters and magazines who might be interested in knowing about your book's publication and for whom you can perhaps write articles.

• Buy adverts in the newsletters of appropriate groups to let the membership know about your book.

• Think of places that might review your book.

• Come up with talks you can give in public or seminars you can be invited to as a guest speaker, where you can promote yourself and your book.

• Create a variety of press releases, fliers and postcards that can be sent to newspapers, magazines and specific groups interested in your book's topic or in knowing you have a new book out.

• Arrange author signings in bookstores, either organized or impromptu (that is, wander into a bookstore, quietly make sure they're carrying your book, then introduce yourself to the manager and offer to sign copies if she would like you to).

• Give media interviews, especially radio and TV—as many as you can. People who listen to the radio often read books. Radio interviews can be done over the phone from home, so they're a relatively cheap way of reaching a wide audience.

• Join an organization such as Sisters in Crime or Romance Writers of America and become a part of the joint adverts they put out at industry events such as Book Expo (formerly known as the ABA), Bouchercon for crime writers or World Fantasy.

• Study how others have promoted their books.

Are there organizations or places I can contact to help me publicize my work?

There's much to be found on the Web. Also, Sisters in Crime (SinC, which actually also includes Brothers in Crime) puts out an excellent pamphlet about self-promotion. They can be contacted at:

Beth Wasson
Executive Secretary
Sisters in Crime
P.O. Box 442124
Lawrence, KS 66044-8933
www.sinc-ic.org

If you're interested in radio and TV, check out *Radio-TV Interview Report* magazine, which goes out to about four thousand radio and television producers. *Radio-TV Interview Report* is published by Bradley Communications, 135 E. Plumstead Ave., Lansdowne, PA 19050-8206; (800) 989-1400 or (610) 259-1070 (ext. 408). Ask for a free issue. It's worth looking at to see what other talk show guests are doing.

Should I hire a publicist?

Before you take this step, make sure you can take advantage of anything she puts your way. A good publicist is expensive, and a bad or mediocre one probably can't do much more than you can do for yourself. Far better to learn the lesson of the *Blair Witch Project* filmmakers and use the power of the Internet to target your ideal audience.

A great deal of publicity and promotion is knocking on doors and getting them politely slammed in your face. What you get with a good publicist is her Rolodex of sources, whom she knows personally and whom she can call up and often talk into giving you an interview. That means she will be picky about the books and authors she takes on because her credibility is riding on your ability to come across with "the goods" for her contact.

To do interviews, learn how to get your point across quickly, succinctly and, well, sexily. I'm not referring to overt sexuality, but making sure that you know what it is about your book that's going to whet people's appetites to hear more and get them to pick up a copy next time they're in their local bookstore.

How can I learn to become media savvy?

Take an evening class in media communications. Media trainers are available but expensive, although they are worth considering if you can find a good one. Try to develop an ability to think fast on your feet.

Before you start doing interviews, jot down on a "cheat sheet" (a 3″×4″ index card, ideally) what you want to get across. Come up with at least four major points of conversation. Always, if you're able, turn a question into something that will allow you to promote your book.

Acquire a small library of witty stories and practice using them. Even if your topic is deadly serious, be a fun, energized guest.

If you can accomplish this, you'll help a potential publicist by giving them someone that TV and radio talk show hosts and their producers will want to have on their shows, regardless of the book you've written.

Before you cringe at the thought, consider this: What's more important, remembering the title of one book or the name of an author who may have written several books that are available?

This is not about art—this is about selling. You need to learn to get strangers to pay attention to you and your book, despite the noise and chaos of their lives, and then fork out money to read it. We watch interviews with authors not to hear them talk about their latest book, but because they are interesting *thinkers* and witty raconteurs.

How can I get myself on TV?

If you want to get on TV or radio, start locally, and convince producers you've got something interesting to say and that you'll be an entertaining guest.

Study and research what works on camera and what doesn't. Learn how to sit and how to make the camera like you, because it can be a pretty cruel instrument. Think about the image you want to project. Make sure it doesn't detract from your ability to talk seriously about the topic you've been asked to discuss.

In much the same way that you got yourself an agent and a book deal, you need to sell yourself to TV producers when you contact them. Send them a photo to demonstrate how photogenic you are, plus a list of topics that they could base shows on and a suggested list of thought-provoking and "sexy" questions they might want to talk with you about. Is there something in the news, some current event, that you can tie into? Can you take questions from the audience or your interviewer that test your knowledge of your subject in an entertaining way?

Don't expect anyone other than maybe a research assistant to actually read your book.

Use every opportunity to promote and sell your book, from an on-air display, if that's possible, to setting up local bookstores for signings ahead of time for when you fly into a new town to give your interview. Make sure they know you're going to be a "celebrity" on local, regional or national TV. Milk it; sell books.

What Web sites can I go to for help with marketing and publicity?

Check out these links to marketing and news sites about the publishing industry.

www.publisherslunch.com

Created and run by Michael Cader, this is one of the most enjoyable, informative *free* Web sites about publishing out there.

www.amazon.com

Amazon.com Books, the oldest and biggest online bookstore. If you want to see if a book is currently in print, this is a good place to start. Plus, you can always buy a book you're looking for if you find it.

www.barnes&noble.com or www.bn.com

Barnes & Noble—your neighborhood bookseller now in competition with Amazon.com. You can use it similarly to check if a book is in print.

www.ingrambookgroup.com

Ingrams is one of two major book distributors in the United States and Canada. (The other is Baker & Taylor.) Once you're at their site, go to the "Book Kahoona," which will give you free, top fifty lists on a wide variety of subjects.

www.nyt.com

The New York Times on the Web. You can access their book review section and also look at their top thirty best-seller lists.

www.bookwire.com

R.R. Bowker's Bookwire site. A lot of it is subscription, but you can get some basic information for free, and it has gateways to the AAR Agents site, *Publishers Weekly* and many others.

http://publishersweekly.reviewsnews.com

Publishers Weekly home page. PW is the industry's weekly "bible" and everyone reads it in publishing. It's worth checking out as often as possible to keep up with the latest news and views in publishing.

www.sinc-ic.org

Sisters in Crime (and brothers). A support organization for writers of crime and mystery novels, they also have material that can be used by those who write books other than crime fiction.

Developing Ideas and Creating Book Proposals

What should I write about?

The sarcastic answer to this is, "How long is a piece of string?" The real answer is, "If you really don't know, don't bother writing." However, what most writers mean when they ask this question is: "I have so many ideas, I don't know how to choose the best one."

I was a journalist for about ten years before I finally finished my first novel. While having lunch with a friend, I said I was going to write a novel, and she challenged me to put my money where my mouth was. Five years later, it was done—and unpublishable. However, the lessons I learned along the way were invaluable.

The problem now was what to write next.

We all think that once our first book is published, it will be all plain sailing. But, of course, it isn't.

Believe it or not, developing book ideas is not the problem. The problem is distinguishing a good idea that will sell from a weak or mediocre one that won't.

Ask yourself: Who is my audience? Is it men? Is it women? Is it people who are enthused with bird-watching? Someone who reads a certain type of science fiction?

When considering nonfiction, ask yourself: Am I affected by this topic? And if not, is someone I know—a friend or relative perhaps—affected by it? With fiction, in the absence of a compelling idea that won't let go, start thinking *what if* or *suppose*.

How do I figure out what makes a bad idea?

Most bad ideas come into existence because the writer was drawn to them for the wrong reasons. My friend Gary Provost used to say that there are three things that can tip you off to a bad idea, and they are all based on the *writer's needs*, not the *reader's needs*.

A bad idea appeals to a writer because it makes the writer's life easier. It is often an example of weak and shallow thinking and clichéd writing, and it avoids dealing with the inventiveness and grace it takes to write strong, clear and involving prose.

Gary believed that the warning signs of a bad idea involved one or more of the following:

1. Familiarity. Books, narrative nonfiction or fiction, however subtly, are about the *meaning* of the event and how it affects the characters emotionally, not just a straight reporting of what happened. You can read a newspaper for that. In fiction, in particular, the event or scene should be a metaphor for the internal life of the character, if you write well enough.

Because you know about something isn't enough to make it an idea worth writing about in a book. It's what you make of the event and how it affects you and others that's significant.

2. Importance. Because something affected you profoundly, it doesn't mean that it will automatically make a worthwhile subject for a book.

Being a victim of the Oklahoma bombing, having a loved one die of cancer, losing a limb and becoming a sports champion anyway, striving against overt racism, recovering from a debilitating addiction, surviving a devastatingly difficult childhood—all these things can be the pivots of making you a better and stronger person and are shared by others. Consider *Angela's Ashes*, for example.

What makes it a success is the universality and emotional power that Frank McCourt put into his book. It wasn't the importance of the subject that made that book memorable; it was the lucid and emotionally powerful writing. And "emotionally powerful" does not mean lots of adjectives and adverbs. In fact, it's quite the reverse.

3. Truth. God save me from the inexperienced writer who responds to criticism with a plaintive, "But it's *true!*" Just because something really happened doesn't automatically mean it is a good idea for a book, particularly when it comes to ideas for fiction. Sometimes something that's true isn't even necessarily believable. Credibility is an important element of writing, whether it's fiction or nonfiction.

How do I recognize a good idea?

First, start thinking about the reader's needs. If you're going to write fiction, study your genre so well that you're familiar with what's been done and *what hasn't*. What's fresh and new and yet familiar enough that it can still fit into the main body of books published in this area?

Next, look for holes. What's a hole? Something that hasn't been done quite that way before. Find a hole, and you will usually find a good idea in there somewhere.

What do you mean by "a reader's needs"?

Ask yourself this: Why do people buy books? People read fiction and narrative nonfiction to spice up their lives and enjoy an emotional or intellectual rollercoaster.

Strong stories, whether fiction or nonfiction, take us to new worlds and introduce us to new and interesting people and ideas. Readers want stories about characters resolving ethical and moral dilemmas.

Good stories are about people who *take action*. Without an active character, there is no emotional power to your narrative. In other words, it's *boring*.

It's not *what happens* to a character that makes her interesting, *it's what she does about it*. Do your characters have *clear and definable goals*? What does your character want? What will victory cost her? If you're asking people to sit down and read a three hundred or four hundred page book, there better be something important at stake. If there isn't, your readers will be aggravated.

In many ways, stories are about watershed events in a central character's life. The story begins when the trauma or watershed event begins, and it ends when the trauma is resolved.

There are books that manage to become successes that defy these guidelines. Some nonfiction books, for example, don't have emotionally grabbing characters. What they have instead is a focus on how to make the reader's life better. They offer a tangible benefit. Arguably *The Celestine Prophecy* would fall into this category, or *Chicken Soup for the Soul*, an anthology of wisdom in story form.

Are there any exercises I can do to develop ideas?

There are lots of ways to get your "idea muscles" working. Here are just a few to start you off. Check out Anne Bernays's and Pamela Painter's *What If?: Writing Exercises for Fiction Writers* if you want more help.

- Scour newspapers, magazines and other sources of current events.
- Invent lives for strangers you observe as you go about your daily business.
- What if something that happened to you or someone you know had gone differently?
- Rewrite fairy tales and legends as modern stories.

What's a book proposal?

A book proposal is primarily a sales tool. It describes the structure of your proposed book and includes a sample chapter to demonstrate the voice or tone of the piece.

The first thing to think about when writing a book proposal is that editors have hundreds to review at any one time. So your proposal had better stand out, and it better be well prepared and professionally presented. Trust me, if it isn't, the next guy's will be.

With all that mail, you'd think such promising material would be easy to find, but it isn't. That's why if you do a terrific job on your proposal, you start way ahead of the pack.

A nonfiction book is essentially about the appeal and marketability of an idea, and it's less concerned with a writer's ability to put down words on paper.

However, what will catch people's attention first and foremost is a strong voice in the work. If an editor or agent gets caught up in the world of the writer from the first sentence, you are way ahead of the game as a writer.

Buying an unfinished (or in some cases, barely started) book by an unpublished and unagented writer is a huge act of faith on an editor's part. And that's before dealing with the complications and trauma of having an editor leave a publishing house halfway through a project. The book can suddenly become the unwanted stepchild of a new editor who has a completely different view of how it should be written and published.

What are the basics of writing a good book proposal?

The basic philosophy behind writing a book proposal is to describe to the editor the book you want to write and provide the editor with sufficient ammunition in the form of facts and figures for her to convince colleagues in both editorial and sales and marketing at an editorial board meeting that the proposed book is not only a quality piece of work, it will *make money for the publishing company*.

A good book proposal is, in essence, a justification for why your book should be published. Martial all your facts and figures, competing books, marketing material, the book's uniqueness, etc., then present them in the most effective and positive light.

Demonstrate that you know your subject, but beware of getting so caught up in the demonstration that you lose sight of the forest for the trees. Once you start getting too technical or too involved in minutiae, it can seem that you're trying too hard. Including a sample chapter, a good proposal should be about twenty-five to thirty pages long. You can push it to forty pages, but any longer than that and you're in danger of overwriting.

If you can, mention how long the book will be and how long it will take you to write it (if it's not finished yet, as in the case of most nonfiction books). For example, "I estimate my 75,000-word book on this topic will take approximately a year to complete."

As with all sales tools, a book proposal can be broken down into two broad categories: features and benefits.

For example, editors are interested in not only seeing the equivalent of, "This is a high-quality blue, four-wheel, eight-seater, all-terrain sport pickup truck," which is a descriptive set of *features* included in the proposal, but also the *benefits* of this truck, e.g., "This truck will allow you to not only look good when you take your family to church on Sundays, but will let you travel offroad into unpaved wild country for relaxing weekends of hunting and fishing."

Explain what's meant by "benefits" and "features" sections of a book proposal.

The following are what we refer to as the "benefits." I'll go into these in more detail later on in this chapter. In brief they are:
- Title page
- A clear, clean format
- The one-paragraph hook overview
- The larger overview
- Marketing analysis
- Competing books

The following are what we would say are the "features" of a book proposal. Again, I'll explain these in more detail elsewhere in this chapter. In brief they are:

- Table of contents
- Chapter-by-chapter descriptions
- Sample chapters
- Author biography
- Cover letter

If I'm writing, say, a history proposal for an editor who specializes in history, can I assume he'll know what I'm talking about?

One of the golden rules of writing a book proposal is: Don't assume anything. The editor may not remember, until you point it out, that there's a strong link between your book and a current best-seller. Your book, however, is unique because _____ (fill in the blank).

If you have good writing credits, particularly if they are relevant to the book proposal subject, make sure we know about them early on in the proposal.

If your mother and your boss have promised to buy five thousand copies each and you know others who can get multitudes to buy your book, mention it; if you're best friends with Tom Clancy or Kay Hooper and they'll give you a blurb, say so; if you've won the Nobel Peace Prize, the Pulitzer or just first or second place in a writing competition, let us know. If your book has a huge and clearly identifiable audience, point it out; and make sure you do all of this fairly close to the beginning of your proposal.

How do I create a nonfiction proposal?

All nonfiction books have one thing in common: They pose a question and then answer it. This question proposes a simply stated thesis that the book will focus on proving.

A nonfiction proposal should be about an idea that has universal appeal and could sell at least ten thousand or more copies. Anything narrower in appeal and we're in the realm of small press and niche publishing books.

It's worth remembering that on average it can take two years or more from a nonfiction book contract being signed to the book appearing on the shelves, so your book idea must be appealing enough that in two or three years, people will still be excited about it.

Another book recently published on your subject may not necessarily be a fatal blow to your book idea, because you may find once you've read the published book that the author treats the subject differently from the way you intend to treat it.

It's important that you let editors and agents know that this other book is in the marketplace and why it won't be a problem for your book idea. If an editor puts forward your idea in an editorial meeting and someone around the table says, "But so-and-so just published a book exactly like this," that editor will have been made to look stupid. Guess whose book they're *not* going to buy?

Work on the table of contents (TOC) early. As you develop the proposal you'll need to continually revise this, but it'll provide an excellent overall map to the project while you're working, as well as a guide to its final form when completed.

Present the strongest arguments against your thesis, and then defeat them to establish your thesis's *bona fides*. One-sided arguments rarely hold a reader's interest or imagination as effectively as a well-turned debate.

How do I create a fiction proposal?

In fiction, we need to reassure an editor that an idea for a novel can be expanded successfully to book length, usually three hundred to four hundred manuscript pages, double-spaced. *Editors usually want to see the completed manuscript rather than buy a novel on what is called a "partial."*

If you have not published fiction before, unless you are writing fiction based on your widely recognized field of expertise (e.g., you're a NASA astronaut writing a sci-fi thriller based on your experiences), editors are not likely to take a chance on an unfinished manuscript. They don't really need to, because there are so many accomplished writers with finished manuscripts eager to be published.

Most successful fiction proposals come from experienced writers an editor knows can provide a well-written finished manuscript. The editor is concerned not with "Can he write a good novel?" but with "Is this a good idea for a novel that we can successfully sell to the public?"

The fiction proposal will once again provide the hook and a brief overview. It will also include a synopsis of the story that details, in broad narrative strokes, the beginning, middle and end of your story over the shoulder of the main character(s). It should also include a bio of the author, emphasizing writing experience and publications, etc., and the *first* ninety to one hundred pages of the book. If the first few chapters aren't the best in the book and don't hook the reader, it doesn't matter how brilliantly written the rest of the chapters are because the reader will never get to them. If a fiction writer sends chapters other than the first chapters to an editor, the suggestion is that the first chapters need work and that the book is not ready for submission.

If the book is part of a series, include a half-page or one-page description of a few more titles in the series, as well as a brief series overview.

Don't inundate an editor or agent with a shopping list of ideas at one time on the basis of, "If you don't like this, then try that." It's unprofessional and shows a lack of commitment and passion to the project.

Is there a recognized structure I should follow when creating a proposal?

Obviously you need to take these suggestions and fit them to the particulars of your project, but they generally can be adapted to work on both a fiction and nonfiction project.

A good book proposal should ideally be in a 12-point clean Times Roman, pica or elite typeface, double-spaced with inch margins all the way around. Better to have more pages and fewer words on the page, which is easier on the eyes, than cram a load of small-sized words on one page in an effort to make the proposal look shorter than it is.

Each of these should be thought of as a separate element that comprises the whole—the completed proposal.

1. The Cover Letter. This should be brief, warm and probably contain the hook. It should include your address and phone numbers, relevant information such as you're a prize-winning writer, a member of this or that group, an expert in the topic you propose, that you were referred by a writer or agent, whatever. Mention the book's title and what kind of book it is, then let the proposal do the rest of the work. Try to keep it to a page if you can.

2. Title Page. Center your title and the subtitle of the book proposal. Under that add your name, address and telephone number, voice and fax if you have it (perhaps even an e-mail address). Make yourself easy to reach. Does your answering machine work? Is there a professional message on the machine when an editor or agent does get through? All these things count.

3. Make sure that every page of the proposal is bylined in some fashion and easily recognizable with continuous numbering (except for the first page). If an editorial assistant drops the pages by accident, he should be able to easily reconstruct the proposal. Try to avoid pictures and graphics, etc., unless they are extremely well done and relate directly to the proposal's subject.

4. The Hook Overview. The first overview is the hook—an in-a-nutshell description of the book that helps the editor sell the book to colleagues in thirty seconds or less. (This works particularly well with high-concept fiction.)

5. The Larger Overview. The second overview is a development of the first. If colleagues say, "Tell us more," you now provide the editor with broad facts and figures (if applicable) and a general overview of the project:
- Why is there a need for this book?
- What's the problem? What's the hole that needs to be filled? What suffering can you help alleviate in your readers' lives? What information do they lack? What predicament exists in society, or what vacuum needs to be filled?
- In what new ways can your readers be entertained?

- State your case as dramatically as you can without being overly sensational; startle us from the outset and make us consider your topic with fresh eyes.
- How will your book meet this need, fill this hole, etc. Don't answer these questions with hype or rhetoric. Nobody's interested in your opinion of how great this book idea is. Convince us with solid content summed up in a paragraph or two.
- How is your book different from others in the field?
- Why are you the best person to write this book?
- How long will the manuscript be, and how long will it take you to write it?
- Close your overview with something that sums up the benefits or merits of the book, reminding the reader of the book's importance.
- Try to do all of this in no more than four double-spaced pages, and ideally two.

6. Marketing Analysis. In this section explain who's going to buy your book. Use facts and figures you have researched. How many people belong to organizations or subscribe to magazines that deal with this topic? What other books out there have proven there is a successful and eager audience for your proposed book? Why will these people still be interested in reading about your topic in two or more years' time? If you have experience or knowledge in selling, marketing or promotion, mention that here. Do you have a seminar that you take around from place to place, or do you lecture to groups of people regularly? What can you do to translate your experiences into book sales? A strong marketing plan accompanying a book proposal will go a long way to selling the proposal. Are you a member of organizations who will help publicize your book and, ideally, buy lots of copies? Could you help sell bulk quantities of your book to organizations that might want to give them away as gifts to members? Do you have a connection to well-known people who might endorse your book and help increase book sales that way?

(Fiction sells on the strength of writing; however, some awareness of a book's marketability is always a plus as long as you don't make too big a point about it.)

7. Competing Books. What we mean here is a list of a half dozen or so of the most successful and most recent books published in the field you propose to write about. Nothing breeds success like success, particularly if you have a new take on a successful idea. In your comments about the books, mention title, author, year of publication, publisher, a one- or two-sentence description and a line pointing out the difference between your book and the published book. Every competing book gives you an opportunity to make a new point about your book idea, so take advantage of the opportunity.

8. Author Biography. Nowadays you have to be an expert or a professional writer who is working in collaboration with one or more experts to get a nonfiction book successfully published. You have to be an expert because you will be competing with others who are experts who have published books in this field, even if their books aren't very good. So establish your credibility both as a writer and as an expert in the topic you are proposing. That may mean publishing articles on the subject you propose in your book in magazines before you start querying editors and agents with your book idea. Write this bio in the third person, rather than first person, unless you have a life experience that makes your view particularly valid.

9. Table of Contents. Explain how the book will be structured and what it will say. The simple table of contents will list the number of chapters you intend to have in your book and what the title of each chapter will be (e.g., Chapter 1: I am born; Chapter 2: I get my diaper changed; Chapter 3: I get hit on the head by a baseball, etc.). The TOC provides an at-a-glance guide to the book's content and organization and perhaps a glimpse of the wit or seriousness you intend to bring to the project. At least 75 percent of a book proposal's success lies in its organization. (This is not needed for a fiction proposal.)

10. Chapter-by-Chapter Descriptions. Follow the TOC with a half-page to one-page description of what you plan to cover in each chapter. The key here, as throughout the proposal, is your ability to write succinctly, yet dynamically about your subject. In general, state your premise, then explain how you will develop it. Make sure that your passion and interest for your subject come through. (This is not needed for a fiction proposal.)

11. Include Sample Chapters. A nonfiction book needs a mixture of narrative, emotion and logic, so it doesn't matter what chapters you include, but you should aim at about fifteen to twenty pages. No more than two chapters need to be included. If you use partial chapters, make sure everyone knows this is not the complete version of the chapter. If you're working on a fiction proposal, include the first ninety to one hundred or so pages and a synopsis.

12. Estimated length of the finished book and how long it will take you to write it.

13. Include a stamped, self-addressed envelope (SASE) if you want your work returned.

14. Include any enclosures, such as press clippings, testimonial letters, proofs of book sales if the book is self-published, brochures or PR material that's relevant to either you as a writer or your proposal subject.

Other points to bear in mind:

• Never, ever send original material. Always make sure you keep the originals at home and that you submit clean, crisp copies. Accidents happen, so be forewarned and prepared.

• Don't bind or staple your proposal. If you want to keep it together, use a clip and/or slip it into a folder, or take a piece of cardboard as a backing and slip a large rubber band around everything.

What are the guidelines for submitting a proposal for a collection of short stories?

Collections of short stories are extremely difficult to sell unless you have had some material published in major magazines like *The New Yorker*. You also need to have a pretty good literary pedigree, having studied with some major figures at the Iowa Workshop or some other prestigious program. Finally, the stories really need to stand out.

That said, you would submit pretty much as explained here. Query an editor; and if invited to submit, find out what their submission guidelines are, then submit your stories as you have been invited to do.

How do I sell articles I have had published?

This is rather like the question about short stories. A collection of essays of feature articles by an unknown writer is a particularly difficult sale. What holds the pieces together? Why would anyone want to read these essays? Better to focus on a book project, get a reputation, then see if that will help you sell your material.

Are there any dos and don'ts about writing and submitting a book proposal?

DO find out a person's correct name and title before you send in your proposal and query letter to them.

DON'T misspell names and technical words in particular. Do some research.

DO make sure you put the correct postage and address labels on both the letter you send out *and* the SASE you include.

DON'T use antiquated equipment if the printed copies it produces are hard to read.

DO make sure the proposal is easy to look at and read, with double spacing and inch margins all around.

DON'T handwrite anything, except your signature.

DO come to the point quickly in your query letter, and keep it short.

DON'T bother to make statements like, "I've registered the proposal with X, so no one can steal it," or "I'll only take a minimum of $250,000 for this book." If it's good enough to steal, it's good enough to represent. If not, who cares? And as far as price is concerned, you'll get what you're offered. Accept it or not as you please.

DO behave professionally, and try to help the agent or editor to help you.

DON'T inundate an editor or agent with a shopping list of ideas at one time on the basis of, "If you don't like this, then try that."

DO try and remember you're not the only writer the agent or editor has to deal with. The volume of mail and telephone calls they have to go through is *enormous*.

DON'T worry about rushing your book proposal into print. By the time the book's ready, if the subject is that timely, it'll be too late. No one will remember or care what your book was about. You're better off writing a magazine or newspaper article.

DON'T submit e-mail proposals unless you're asked to.

DON'T send full manuscripts unless invited.

DON'T call every day asking if we've either received the manuscript or read it yet.

If an editor at a publishing house has rejected my manuscript, can I send it to another editor at the same house?

Maybe. Agents know how to finesse these kinds of things; authors often don't. If editor A rejects a proposal and editor B brings it up to the editorial board a few months later, editor A will say, "I already saw this and rejected it because of x, y and z." Editor B will now feel rather stupid because he didn't know someone else in the house had rejected the manuscript, which makes it twice as hard to generate support for the project. He'll have been made to look foolish, and he probably won't go to bat for the project or that author.

An agent, on the other hand, knowing the taste of certain editors at certain houses, knowing that editor A was the wrong editor to have sent the proposal to in the first place and that editor B was the best chance for this book, will first of all get the client to work on the project. The agent will then resubmit the manuscript to editor B, telling him that editor A rejected *an earlier version* of this project, but the author has reworked it. Editor B now goes to the editorial board meeting armed with the knowledge that editor A rejected a *different manuscript* from the one he is hoping to get support for. Now when editor A says, "I already rejected this," editor B can reply, "No, you didn't reject *this version*." Maybe he'll get lucky. At least he's not made to look foolish.

How long should I wait before I contact the editor or agent to see whether they have read my material?

It's a good idea when originally submitting to ask how long the editor or agent will take. However, six to eight weeks is not an unusual amount of time to wait. It's probably not a good idea to start nagging until four weeks at the earliest have gone by.

I hear a lot about "high-concept" ideas. What does this mean?

A high-concept idea is an idea that can be stated in a short paragraph. It's often outrageous and compelling, but it doesn't have to be.

For example: *Imagine (if you can) a Muppet version of* The Seventh Seal. (The scene where Death plays chess with Kermit the Frog on the beach, while Big Bird and Miss Piggy slowly die of the Black Death is even funnier than *Bill and Ted's Excellent Adventure*!)

Or, *What if a young man plays hooky from his life for a weekend in order to find himself.* (*Catcher in the Rye*, J.D. Salinger)

Or this one: *Suppose a young lawyer, straight out of law school, gets his dream job only to find he's signed a Faustian pact with the devil he has to try to break.* (*The Firm*, John Grisham)

There's nothing new about high concept: *A bookish young prince discovers that his mother and his uncle conspired to murder his father and steal his throne.* (*Hamlet*, William Shakespeare)

Not every story has to be high concept, but the idea of marketing your work with one tight sentence is becoming more and more important.

High concepts are almost entirely marketing tools usually created by the writer, or, in some instances after a book has been bought, by the sales and marketing staff. From a writer's point of view it can help to focus attention on the book's heart. If you have trouble reducing your story to this essence, it can suggest that it is not focused enough.

What is meant by a "narrative hook"?

A narrative hook is really another way of talking about high-concept ideas. The hook is what catches your attention and makes you want to enter the author's world. It is usually used in marketing your book to a reader—ideally an editor or agent. If the hook is strong enough, it will eventually make its way down the line of events until it is used by a book sales rep to entice a bookstore owner to stock the book.

Hooks are used all the time in Hollywood—take a look at the opening crane shot of *The Player* as it swoops and soars, eavesdropping on a variety of pitches. ("Think: *High Noon* in space!" is typical of what Hollywood types throw at each other. The resulting movie was *Outland*.)

The hook is about the marketability of your story. A good one-sentence hook in a query letter describing a novel will catch an agent's eye, who, after reading the manuscript, decides to take on the book. In his submission letter to an editor, the agent will use that one-line hook because it had such an effect on his decision to represent the book and the writer. The editor will read the book with enthusiastic anticipation because of that one-line hook. She will go to an editorial board and use that one-line hook to convince her colleagues in editorial, sales and marketing that this is a book they should buy because not only is it good, but it will also make the company money.

When your book comes out, the publisher's sales representative goes to a bookstore and tries to sell your book, along with ten or twenty others, to the bookstore owner. He's going to have maybe a minute to convince the bookstore owner to stock your book. What's the bookstore owner going to say to the customer to excite her about your book? More than likely, they'll use the hook you came up with in your query letter—the letter that got you an agent in the first place.

Are there any writing organizations I can join or that can help me become more professional?

There are so many it's almost frightening. Below is a list of just a couple of the more well known ones.

American Society of Journalists and Authors
1501 Broadway, Suite 302
New York, NY 10036
Voice: 212-997-0947
Fax: 212-768-7414
Internet: 75227.1650@compuserve.com
(JFORUM on CompuServe is ASJA's official online service)
Alexandra Cantor Owens, Executive Director
New address of the ASJA Web page: www.asja.org/
> Founded in 1948, the American Society of Journalists and Authors is the nation's leading organization of independent nonfiction writers. The membership consists of more than one thousand freelance writers of magazine articles, trade books and other forms of nonfiction writing, each of whom has met ASJA's exacting standards of professional achievement.

Author's Guild

31 E 28th Street

10th Floor

New York NY 10016

Voice: 212-563-5904

Fax: 212-564-5363

www.authorsguild.com

> The Author's Guild is the nation's largest society of published authors. It is a leading advocate for fair compensation, free speech and copyright protection.

National Writer's Union

National Office East

113 University Pl. 6th Floor

New York, NY 10003

Voice: 212-254-0279

Fax: 212-254-0673

E-mail: nwu@nwu.org

National Office West

337 17th St. #101

Oakland, CA 94612

Voice: 510-839-0110

Fax: 510-839-6097

E-mail: nwu@nwu.org

www.nwu.org

> The National Writer's Union (NWU) is the trade union for freelance writers of all genres who work for American publishers or employers. It is committed to improving the economic and working conditions of freelance writers through the collective strength of our 6500 members in seventeen local chapters throughout the country.

Local Writer's Workshop

www.elanworks.com/lww/members.html

The LWW is a forum where writers can post works-in-progress. They meet once a week in a chat room to discuss each other's work.

The Police Writers Club

℅ Knight Management Corp.

P.O. Box 416

Hayes, VA 23072

www.policewriter.com

The Police Writers Club provides those who write about or for the police with the knowledge, resources and networking capabilities they need to share their expertise with others. Both fiction and nonfiction writing and publishing are covered, and they welcome both published and unpublished writers. Current members include writers of magazine articles, technical books, true crime articles and novels. Many members are active or retired police officers, but that is not a membership requirement.

Rocky Mountain Fiction Writers

P.O. Box 260244

Denver, CO 80226-0244.

www.rmfw.org

Rocky Mountain Fiction Writers (RMFW) dedicates the efforts of its volunteers to supporting published and unpublished writers of novel-length fiction. RMFW limits its membership to residents of Colorado, Montana, New Mexico, Utah and Wyoming. Membership, however, is not required for participation in the annual Colorado Gold Writing Contest and Colorado Gold Conference.

Romance for Writers

www.rwanational.com/

Romance for Writers is a group for romance writers to have writing critiqued and discuss problems/issues of being a romance writer and/or romance writing. This is a worldwide group, though mainly English language writers participate. All correspondence should be sent to ashton@osn.de with RFW in the subject line. You will be sent information about the group and how the information chain is set up.

Mystery Writers of America

www.mysterywriters.net/

A group much like Romance Writers of America, except this one is geared toward those who write mystery and crime fiction.

Are there any useful sites about writing on the Internet?

There are so many it's impossible to list them all. Again, besides the ones listed above, here are a few others to start you off.

www.prlit.com

The Web page for the Peter Rubie Literary Agency. You'll find a couple of pages dedicated to publishing sites and sites dedicated to writers and writing.

www.authorlink.com

Authorlink! About writers. Authors can post manuscripts and get information about publishing insiders.

www.writersdigest.com

Writer's Digest— The Insider's Guide to the Writing Life. The publishers of this book. Enough said.

www.writerexchange.about

An interesting forum for writers, particularly if you have questions.

Book Buyers and Sellers

www.amazon.com

Amazon. The world's largest online bookstore, they claim. Useful for buying books and seeing what's in print.

www.abebooks.com

The Advanced Book Exchange home page. A network of used book-stores that can find almost any published book you might look for if you can wait long enough.

www.barnes&noble.com

Barnes & Noble. The World's Largest Bookseller Online, they claim. Useful for buying books and seeing what's in print.

www.Bookfinder.com

Bookfinder.com lets you search for out-of-print and used books.

Publishing

www.publishersweekly.com/aar/

The official Web site of the Association of Authors' Representatives.

www.ingrambookgroup.com

Ingram is one of the major distributors of books. This is their Web site, which can be helpful when putting together marketing information about competing books. Check out the "Book Kahoona"— the Web surfer's source for book industry information.

www.bookradio.com

BookRadio provides audio interviews with authors.

www.literaryleaps.com

Literary Leaps. Information about thousands of publishing, publisher, author and book links from BookZone.

www.literarymarketplace.com

Literary Market Place home page. The industry bible for names and addresses. To get the full information you have to subscribe.

www.publishersweekly.com

Publishers Weekly home page. The official magazine of the publishing industry. A good place to go for weekly news and reports.

www.publaw.com

Publishing law and articles on publishing. Legal information about publishing.

www.publink.net

PubLink is a community of book industry participants working together to provide an open platform that all authors and publishers are welcome to join. Its goals are to make it easier for authors to reach their fans, for readers to find what they are looking for and for publishers and booksellers to be able to provide it.

Sites About Writing

www.gmu.edu/departments/awp

Associated writing programs. College programs to help you learn writing. A national database.

www.inkspot/craft/courses.html

Courses and workshops for writers.

www.noveladvice/index.html

NovelAdvice. Devoted totally to the craft of writing.

www.writers.net/index.html

Writers.Net. An Internet resource for writers, editors, publishers and agents.

Writing Tools

www.refdesk.com

My Virtual Reference Desk. A one-stop site for dictionaries and other reference material. Reportedly Colin Powell's favorite site.

www.bartleby/index.html

Bartleby Library. Great books online.

www.bartleby/141/index.html

The Elements of Style online. If you don't know what this is, you haven't been reading this book properly!

www.eb.com

Encyclopaedia Britannica online.

www.wordorigins.org/home.htm

Dave Wilton's etymology page. It's all about words.

www.gutenberg.net/list.html

Project Gutenberg. E-text Listings. Free classic books online.

www.loc.gov

The Library of Congress's home page.

www.pantheon.org/mythica
  The Encyclopedia Mythica. A dictionary of mythology.

http://tech-two.mit.edu/Shakespeare/works.html
  Shakespeare's works online.

www.theslot.com
  The Slot. A Web site devoted to copyediting and copy editors.

Search and Research

http://goon.stg.brown.edu/bible_browser/pbform.shtml
  Browse the Bible and search for passages.

www.infoplease.com
  Information Please. Another all-in-one online dictionary, Internet encyclopedia and almanac reference.

www.lights/publisher/us.html
  A list of publishers in the United States.

www.monash/spidap.html
  The Spider's Apprentice. Tips on searching the Web.

Questions Databases

The following search engines will answer questions written in normal English.

www.allexperts.com
www.AskMe.com
www.askjeeves.com
www.askanexpert.com
www.worldfree.net/

Web Search Engines

Look for it on the Web with these.

http://ixquick.com
www.google.com
www.searcher.com
http://qbsearch.com
http://altavista.com
http://mamma.com
www.metacrawler.com
www.dogpile.com

chapter six

The System: How Your Manuscript Becomes a Book

Why do I keep getting rejected?

There are many reasons a book or book proposal is rejected, but by far the most common is that the writer (a) was ill-prepared, either in technical ability or technical information in the proposal, or (b) presented a weak idea poorly.

On average, something like 90 to 95 percent of material sent to editors and agents is rejected.

That's a tough market to crack, you might think. But looked at another way it means that if you've got a polished and well-written book idea, you're in competition not with all the others who submit, but only with the 5 to 10 percent whose material cries out to be taken seriously by editors and agents. Now *that's* a much more workable situation.

Rejection may feel personal, but it isn't. It could be simply that other books on that topic have been recently published by the company or are in the system. Perhaps the publisher had a bad experience with a book such as you suggest and lost money.

If you write to an editor to ask for a reason for rejecting your book, they'll likely ignore your letter. Most editors don't have the time to critique or analyze your work if it's not for them. Rejections are not personal; they're about the suitability of that project with that particular agent or publishing house. There is also no point writing a rude letter in response to a rejection letter no matter how exasperated you feel. My advice: Success is the best revenge. Get your book published elsewhere. If it's as good as you think, someone will pick it up and publish it.

If you get a rejection with a handwritten note from an editor or a comment of any kind, pay attention to it. Editors and agents don't do these things unless they see promise, as you probably realize by now they don't have the time.

Take heart, pay attention to what's suggested, then go back to the fight with renewed vigor. Obviously if you've gone from getting standard rejections to personalized ones, you're heading in the right direction.

I'm an American living abroad, but it seems that no one is interested in my work. Not the publishers in Europe where I live, or Britain where they speak my language (sort of), or the United States because I'm told I live too far away. What do I do?

The simple answer is to write a compelling book. If your material is good enough and compelling enough, it will overcome all obstacles.

The problem is that distance does play a role, because there is no author available to promote a book once it's published. And in fairness to other countries, they have local markets that they are interested in serving. It's great when they have a book that will appeal to the U.S. market as well as their own, but such books are few and far between.

Just keep writing until you write that compelling book no one can put down.

I'm writing a nonfiction book. Should I write the complete manuscript before I submit it?

Nonfiction is usually sold on a proposal and sample chapters, so while you'll need to have the book planned out, the entire manuscript doesn't need to be completed. The stronger and more focused the proposal, the more chances you have of not only selling your book, but having it published well. (See page 140 for a definition of this.)

I'm a really prolific writer. Ideas just keep tumbling out of me. Is it OK to include several queries in one mailing to an agent or editor?

This is not a good idea. Agents and editors are looking for quality, not quantity. There are, after all, only so many books by one author you can sell at a time without running the risk of (a) boring your audience, who generally wants variety, and (b) marking yourself to be a "hack" writer with little substance who dashes off material.

If you can really pull off writing quality books quickly, the answer is to do them under a pen name.

Why is it called the slush pile, and do editors ever really read it?

No one really knows how the term came about, and some of us would rather call it the unsolicited pile. Perhaps it's called slush because on some days it seems as though you're ploughing through that horrible, dirty, slushy snow when you're reading it. Manuscript after manuscript, proposal after proposal of, at best, competent, but usually very amateur writing and poorly thought out ideas. But then you come across that gem! It stands out like a jewel in the rough and is usually easily spotted, rewarding you for all that slogging effort.

The slush is not always read by editors. Acting under the guidelines of an editor who knows exactly what she wants and likes, it is often the task of an editorial assistant to keep the office from being overrun by unsolicited mail.

The assistant wants to make a good impression with the editor and wants to find good material, so she will tackle that pile of manuscripts with much greater optimism and enthusiasm than an editor. Unless you've met the editor or agent or have a networking connection to him or her, let the system do its work. If you can write, you are that gem everyone is searching for. Trying to subvert or bypass the system may well work against you and reveal you as an amateur when what we're all looking for are professionals.

Are book titles really important?

Pay attention to book titles and subtitles: Is your title too longwinded? Is your publisher's title too trite? Listen to what others have to say, but if your instincts insist that your title is the way to go, don't compromise if you can help it. Know exactly who your core audience is, then choose a title that will resonate with them.

If you're working on nonfiction, come up with something that has "How," "What" or "When" in it.

A good title should be both informative and provocative. You should know at once what the book is about and at the same time, ideally, strike just the right chord with the reader.

Here are a few of examples of strong titles:

The Physics of Star Trek
The Seven Habits of Highly Effective People
Chicken Soup for the Soul
What to Expect When You're Expecting
When Bad Things Happen to Good People
Toxic Parents

A book title is usually a collaborative effort between author and publisher. However, in a few cases, publishers make a decision—usually based on a marketing perception that a certain title will help the book sell well—about what a book will be titled, and the author will not have much to say that will affect the decision.

What happens once I get an agent?

Most people in publishing work primarily on a gut level first. Does the book move me? Despite any reservations I may have, do I want to spend more time with this piece? Then the analysis creeps in. Can the book be improved? Does it have a potential to make money?

Once these decisions over a new manuscript are made, an agent will call or at least contact an author and say that she wants to take on you and your book, but she'd like you to make some changes to the book.

You make the changes the agent suggested, and several weeks later, you and the agent come to an agreement on representation. Perhaps you'll sign an agency agreement with that agent, agreeing to her exclusive representation of your work for a year.

The agent then asks you to supply her with four more copies of your manuscript, which she uses to submit your book to select editors.

Weeks go by and still you don't get that million-dollar offer your spouse said was almost certainly in the bag. After a month or so you call your agent "just to say 'hi.'" The agent is understanding enough to say the book's been rejected by a couple of houses already, but there's lots of interest in it whenever she calls editors and pitches the project to them.

A good agent knows when to throw in the towel and get you to move onto another project and when to stick to her guns and continue submitting to smaller, more specialized houses in an attempt to get someone to publish your book.

What happens after an editor makes my agent an offer on my book?

If your book is "hot," it may sell in as little as a few days, usually for a reasonable amount of money. What does that mean? Perhaps $150,000 or more depending on the topic and the publishers interested. If more than one editor wants the book, then your agent will find himself in an auction situation, with several houses bidding for the book. Some editors may want to avoid the auction scenario by making a preemptive bid, offering enough money to convince you and your agent to take the book off the market prior to an auction.

More usually, maybe six months after your agent starts submitting the book, your phone will ring and you will hear your agent say, "I've got an offer from an editor. Is this a good time to talk?"

It's $15,000 for world rights payable in thirds: on signing a contract, on delivery and acceptance of the final manuscript, and on publication. It's certainly not the million plus you expected, but somehow none of that matters: Someone—a professional—thinks something you've written is *publishable.* What's more, they're prepared to pay you money for it!

Now you have your vindication! And you didn't tell your boss to go shove his job, so you still have a day job, thankfully. You realize in calmer moments it may be a while before you'll be able to write full time and earn a living from it. The agent asks if you will accept the deal, and you tell her to go ahead. If she can improve the offer, so much the better.

Your agent goes back to the editor and manages through force of will and personality, plus good arguments about treating right authors whom the company wants to groom for stardom without costing them too much money, to get the editor to give up translation, foreign and some other subrights so you can sell your book abroad and get some more money from it. So now the $15,000 world rights deal is worth a lot more because the publishing company is only taking North American rights. Things are looking up.

You chat with your editor, and she loves your book. She has some ideas for improving it, and once again, even though you thought it was perfect, she helps you see all sorts of things that can be done to make it better. So you set about rewriting your book.

How can I get help getting my children's book published?

Start by looking at the latest Writer's Digest *Children's Writer's and Illustrator's Market.* Go on the Web and find the Society of Children's Books Writers and Illustrators (www.scbwi.org). SCBWI has local and national conferences across the country. If you can get to one, it will prove a great source of information and networking contacts. The process for submitting is the same as with houses that publish adult fiction and nonfiction.

How do you submit poetry?

The cute answer is: very carefully. More seriously, you submit poetry as you would an article or a book proposal. Request guidelines from the place you want to send your material to and then follow them. You can get more detailed information in the Writer's Digest *Poet's Market*.

What is normal when getting a book published? How will I know if I'm being taken advantage of?

The truth is that amateur writers—and they are usually unpublished as well—worry far more about being taken for a ride than professionals who are published. Publishers don't take advantage of writers in the way that most unpublished writers fear. What publishers do try to do is slant book deals as much in their favor as possible, and that includes royalty rates, advances, as many subrights as they can get their hands on, etc. (See chapter eight for a full discussion about subrights.)

What is normal? For a midlist novel or genre paperback novel, it could be $5,000 world rights for a 5,000 copy print run, and 4 percent paperback royalty. Is this good? Of course not. But you also need to consider as objectively as you can that few books hit the best-seller lists, and if your book happens to be one of them, regardless of the kind of rotten deal you think you signed, you'll earn money on the "back end" (i.e., after the book is published in earned royalties). The total amount earned and the cumulative sales will stand you in very good stead for the next book you write.

Plus, you'll establish a solid track record of sales that both publishers and bookstores will want.

What kind of money can I expect to make on my first book sale?

This is another of those "how long is a piece of string" questions. The general formula for an advance is shaped by a guesstimate on how much the publisher thinks a book will earn. However, this is modified by the number of editors who are excited about a project and may want to buy it in an auction or for a preemptive bid, and elements the author can provide that can establish a strong audience for the book such as seminars, fan clubs, etc.

The average first novel sells anywhere from $3,000 to $30,000.

Is an author paid a commission on sales?

In a sense. They're called royalties. For each book sold, the author gets a percentage of the net price (usually), the amount of which is laid out in the contract.

Does the author have to meet with the publisher? Or can all business arrangements be handled via telephone, fax and mail?

If a publisher wants to meet an author or send an author on a book tour of bookstores, etc., the publisher will pay the reasonable expenses of travel and lodging. Usually, it is not necessary for an author to meet with a publisher face to face. The same is true of meeting one's agent. Often, when editors and agents are at nearby writers conferences, the author and editor and/or agent will take advantage of the proximity and make a point of getting together. Otherwise telephone, e-mail, letter and fax are the preferred means of communication.

Is a book deadline a flexible thing?

Yes and no. Contractual deadlines are not suggestions. That's why, during the negotiations stage, both your agent and your editor asked you how long you thought it would take you to write (or rewrite) your book. That was one of the factors involved in setting down a manuscript delivery date in your book contract.

It is the wise writer who always hands in his manuscript on time, or perhaps a little early if possible. If there's going to be a problem or a delay in hitting your deadline, *talk to both your agent and your editor about it ahead of time.* Don't wait to the last minute; it makes everyone's job twice as hard. The editor is answerable to others, as you've seen, from the art department, to marketing, production and so forth, all of whom need to be kept informed about a book's progress so they can adjust their schedules if necessary. If you leave your editor dangling by missing your deadline and not letting him know that you were going to do that or why, you make him look unprofessional and incompetent in front of his colleagues. This is not a good way to go about nurturing a long-lasting business relationship. Usually, and within reason, he'll give you the extra time you need if you ask for it.

What do editors mean when they talk about being "well published"?

Most publishing houses understand the kinds of people their books appeal to. St. Martin's Press, for example, does not do the same kind of high-toned books that Farrar, Straus & Giroux publish, and Warner Books does not publish the same kinds of books that Basic Books publishes.

The sales and marketing departments and their staffs know who to approach to maximize the sales possibilities of a book they are bringing out. If they decide suddenly to bring out a book they are not usually associated with, they must alert their bookstore accounts, plus find different outlets that are interested and reach the target audience.

A book that is published well not only understands who its core audience is, it is intelligently marketed to reach that audience. This is not as common as you would think and is partly the responsibility of a good editor who can get the enthusiasm and the expertise of his company in harness behind a book.

What happens if the offer for a book is much less than I know others have received?

Obviously, you want as much money up front as you can get. However, to get a reputation as a successful writer, that money has to be earned back in copies sold, royalties earned and subrights sales. If you want to make a career as a writer, sometimes starting with a modest royalty advance is a better bet, because a book that makes money and has good sales figures puts an author into a much stronger position for her next book.

If a book ends up being as successful as everyone feels it should be, you'll make money in royalties from copies sold.

An author who got a huge royalty advance for her first book but didn't sell enough copies to earn back the royalty advance will have a much harder job getting the same kind of advance for her next book. Better to get more than less for your next book.

Why does it take so long for a publisher to get me my contract and acceptance check once they've decided to buy my book?

A number of people, including your editor, the editorial director, the publisher, the contracts manager and the chief financial officer, all have to sign off on the acquisition of your book.

Your contract could be on someone's desk for ages while they're on vacation, out of town, ill or just plain busy. Even in large conglomerate publishers, contracts departments are often small. They do the contracts for all the editors in a house and are usually logjammed. Checks are usually cut once a week toward the end of the week. If the okayed contract arrives on your editor's desk the day after checks have been cut for that week, you'll have to wait another week before you see your money.

Should I hire a lawyer to look at my contract once my agent sends it to me?

There shouldn't be any need to hire a lawyer if you have a reputable agent. You'll be paying two people to do the same job twice. Agents may not be lawyers, though sometimes they have lawyers on staff or on retainer to help them with contracts. Most agents learn how to go through publishing contracts as part of their training and publishing experience. Unless a lawyer is familiar with publishing law and publishing contracts, they may well do you a disservice by not knowing what clauses are known to be flexible and what clauses the publisher simply won't budge on. Agents also develop boilerplate contracts with individual houses that they modify according to the client and the book being acquired but that may have already established certain "bottom line" things in the author's favor.

Nevertheless, study your contract, call your agent and ask her to explain the clauses you don't understand. (A very good guide to publishing contracts is *Kirsch's Guide to the Book Contract.*)

When you're ready, you'll sign all the copies of the contract that were sent to you (adding your social security number), initial any paragraphs where changes to the contract have been made, then return the contracts to your agent. Don't make changes to a contract because you don't like a clause; it could well negate a contract and at the least will extend an already painfully slow process. All changes to a contract have to be agreed on by all parties concerned. If you've got a problem, call your agent and have them negotiate with the editor any change you want to make.

Pay attention to the length of the book the company wants, that is, the number of words stated as acceptable in the contract, and also the delivery date.

Hopefully, about a month to six weeks after you've sent back the signed contracts, you'll get your copy of the countersigned contract from your agent—with the signing check, usually about one-half to one-third the total advance, minus your agent's commission.

What happens after I hand in the book?

There are accepted formats that editors and production departments like; before you change them, it's wise to know what they are. It's important to look and act like a professional at all times, and that includes handing in a professionally finished document that looks good and reads well. Don't handwrite anything or use single spacing except in cover letters, and carefully check all the grammar and spelling before you decide it's ready.

Quite often the publishing house will give you a style sheet when you sign the contract, explaining how they want the manuscript to look. In general, they will ask for:

- a hard copy, which is to say, a version printed out on paper; and,
- an electronic version, which is a version saved to disk.

If you can, use a modern, widely used word-processing program like Microsoft Word or Wordperfect.

Save your files on a disk in either MSDOS/Windows, or Mac formats, clearly labeling on the disk the operating system (i.e., Mac, Windows) as well as the word-processing program used. It's better to save the files as individual chapters rather than in one long file, and *always, always, always back up* your material. *Never, ever send an original of anything*. Guaranteed, it will get lost by somebody.

How do editors expect the finished manuscript to be formatted?

Unless you've been asked to do something different by your editor, print your manuscript this way:

- Use a deskjet or laser printer, not an old-fashioned dot matrix if you can help it. But whatever you use, make sure there is a new ribbon or new cartridge or plenty of toner so the words on the page are clean, clear and easy to read.
- Use a readable font (not too small), e.g., a 12-point Times Roman, Courier or Elite typewriter face.
- Print on clean, white 8½″ × 11″ paper.
- Along the top of each page, print a running head and page count something like the following:

  Your Name/Book   CatchWord   Page (#)

  where (#) will be a continuous running page number.
- Use a one-inch margin around the page.
- Use double spacing.
- Indent each paragraph. Don't space paragraphs, unless you are introducing a break in the action, when a one-line space is common.

- Make text unjustified, that is, ragged right text.
- Send the manuscript loose leafed and in a box, not bound.

How should I handle illustrations with my submission?

Unless you're a professional illustrator, don't submit illustrations. It's much harder to get a manuscript/illustration package accepted than if you simply sent along a manuscript.

However, if you *must* accompany your work with illustrations, make two or three photocopies of your "final" illustrations for the book and send them along with your manuscript. You could also create a "dummy" or mock-up of the book showing the art and text. The artwork in the dummy can be rough, as long as it's accompanied by more polished samples.

What's the format for a children's picture book in verse?

It should be the same format as any other submitted manuscript, which is covered elsewhere in this book.

You don't need to put a different verse on each page, but if you want to gently indicate where you think it might work, that's OK. Page breaks and illustrations are usually decided by the publisher.

What does it really cost to make a book?

A publisher's total investments, including overhead, sales and marketing, etc., is around $60,000, assuming the author's advance is under $10,000. For a big-name author who gets a big advance, the cost is much higher, of course.

How long should it take for an editor to read my manuscript and get back to me?

It could take a month or more. Remember, editors don't have just your book to work on, they have to oversee sometimes more than ten books at any one time in various stages of the publishing process.

In your cover letter when you deliver your manuscript, politely ask that when the editor makes a change, he adds a brief note about why he made the change.

When he's ready, you'll get either an editorial letter from your editor or you'll have a long telephone conversation with him, detailing suggestions and changes that in his view will improve and tighten the book. Writing a book is a collaborative effort, although it's clearly your talent and hard work that will carry things through. Your editor is objective, though, and provides a great sounding board. If you feel he "gets" your book, you'd do well to listen to him.

How much revision will an editor typically ask me to do on my book?

This is another of those "how long is a piece of string" questions. So much depends on the original quality of the manuscript. Presumably, it was in good enough shape to capture an editor's attention and encourage him to go through the somewhat arduous process of convincing his colleagues to let him acquire the manuscript.

That said, there have been instances when editorial letters are one page long and others where they are twenty pages long. In nonfiction, the revision process is more dynamic because this may be the first time the editor has had a chance to read the full manuscript.

In fiction that's not so much the case, as most fiction (certainly first fiction) is acquired on a full manuscript, not a partial.

An editor will often see things that are not obvious to an author, particularly when it comes to improving the emotional pull of a book and its structure. The point is not to change a dog into a cat in your manuscript, but to understand why there is a dog there at all. It is this developing of trust between author and editor and the editor's ability to articulate to the author that he "gets" the author's work that will make the revision process go smoothly. The best authors are those who not only follow an editor's notes, but look for other places in a manuscript where they can tighten, clarify and otherwise incorporate changes that pull everything closer together.

What do I do if the editor wants me to make a change I hate to the book?

Most editors welcome discussion about the book, and it's worth remembering that they are objectively dealing not with what you intended to say, but with what you actually wrote. Let's assume you've tried to discuss things nicely with your editor, but the two of you seem to be heading toward an impasse at breakneck speed.

If your editor asks for changes that you have real problems with, *don't* argue with him. Be noncommittal; say something like, "That's interesting. I hadn't thought of it like that. Let me think about that a while." Then call your agent and say how you really feel and what your concerns are.

Your agent is experienced in dealing with these kinds of situations. She'll have read the book herself and will be able to discuss the situation with you and the editor, taking any heat or unprofessional behavior out of the situation. She almost certainly has a good personal relationship with the editor and will try to cash in on that.

This kind of situation is occurring with increased frequency as editors indulge in the "musical chairs" of leaving one house to take up a more senior position somewhere else. The new editor may not share your vision of the book, and it's highly unlikely you will be able to move the book to another house with the former editor.

What does it mean when your book becomes an "orphan"?

In publishing terms, an orphan is a book that has lost its acquiring editor. It can become particularly troubling when the original acquiring editor is no longer at the publishing house for one reason or another. The book is still going to be published, and a new editor who has a very different view of what the book should be will step forward to look after the "orphan."

What should I do when I get phone calls from people in the publishing company besides my editor?

You'll quite often get phone calls from people in the various departments involved with creating your book. Be kind and helpful to them, even if you've already answered the question for someone else. Don't answer a question with an exasperated, "I've already told my editor this." Gracefully tell the caller what she wants to know. If they want something faxed to them, don't say, "My editor already has this." Fax it again. Cultivate a reputation for being a sweetheart to deal with. If necessary, develop a good cop–bad cop act with your agent. If there's a problem that needs a tough stance, get your agent to take care of it.

My book needs charts and illustrations, etc. Whose responsibility is it to provide all that?

If you examine your contract carefully, you'll see that nine times out of ten you are responsible for this material. Getting permission for pictures and copyrighted material in general to use in your book is your responsibility, not your editor's and not your agent's. Illustrations for children's picture books and cover art should not be confused with interior illustrations or graphics that are used to illustrate the text.

Creating and developing the cover art is completely the decision of the publisher. If you're lucky, your agent may get you "cover consultation," but that means only that the publisher will patiently listen to your opinions before going ahead and doing what they wanted to do in the first place more often than not. Cover consultation is about catching mistakes in a cover that purports to illustrate something from the book.

Similarly, children's book illustrations are usually provided by the publisher, though if you present the publisher with the work of a professional illustrator, they may take a serious look.

Why am I talking to my editor's assistant more than to my editor? Doesn't she like me anymore?

Far from it. Your editor's assistant will be overseeing a lot of the day-to-day business of turning your manuscript into a book for the editor. It's likely that you will get to know each other quite well in the months your book is in process.

Assistants help editors organize "stuff" and are often more accessible than your editor. You would be well advised to cultivate the friendship or at least a positive acquaintanceship of your editor's assistant, and thank her occasionally for what she and your editor are doing for you. Not enough writers do this, and it's nice to know that your efforts are appreciated every once in a while.

What happens after I send back the revised and corrected manuscript?

About six weeks after you return your corrected manuscript, you'll get it back from the copy editor. The book has moved from your editor's world to the world of the production editor or managing editor, though you will maintain contact with the process mostly through the good offices of the editorial assistant. (The managing production editor is responsible for overseeing the rest of the stages of the manuscript's transformation into a book.)

The copy editor's main job is somewhat pedantic. She makes sure things are spelled correctly, grammar is correct, facts and figures are accurate, details are consistent within the book and so forth.

Seeing the copyedited manuscript will come as a shock. The manuscript pages will be covered in indecipherable red pencil marks and bristle like a porcupine with yellow notes asking some extremely pedantic questions, particularly about names, dates, places, attributions and correct spellings. If you're interested in learning more about this process and its signs and symbols, read *Words Into Type*, which is many a production editor's bible if the publishing house hasn't developed its own style manual.

Answer all the questions on the copyedited manuscript as best you can, and make any changes you feel have to be made. This is your last chance to make major alterations to your book.

Sometimes, copy editors can be overzealous, so be warned. However, unlike when your editor line-edited your manuscript, if the changes the copy editor made are more stylistic than technical, consider stetting material if you don't like what she did. ("Stet" is the term used to reinstate material marked as a deletion.) It might be an idea to discuss things with your editor or the managing editor first.

Basically, editors edit for three reasons: to improve clarity of meaning, promote brevity of language and make the clumsy graceful. They also remove redundancies and smooth over inconsistencies in the text. They'll work on perfecting your book's structure, trimming excessive length or helping you find ways to expand material that needs more development.

If some poor decisions have been made in the editing of your book, it may well be because you have not explained yourself as clearly or explicitly as you could have. So rather than stetting, perhaps you can clarify your words in a way that overcomes the problem an editor thought was caused by clumsy or unfocused thought and language.

What happens after I send back the copyedited manuscript?

Once you've reviewed and returned the copyedited manuscript, you'll wait a few months before you receive the page proofs, or galleys. At one time these were different things, but today the terms are becoming synonymous. Once you get the copyedited manuscript, you can make substantive changes to the text of your book. At page proofs, however, you're looking for typos and minor typesetting errors.

What are "galleys" and "page proofs"?

Various publishing houses approach this stage of the process differently from each other. In nearly all cases you will see some printed version of your manuscript to correct before the book is printed and bound into a final version.

In general, page proofs or galleys are quite literally a first draft—or pass—print run (hence the term "first pass") of what the final pages of your book will look like. They are reviewed by, among others, your editor, the managing editor and the art director. There's usually at least one more pass, sometimes two. You'll be sent copies of the book in this form to read for typos, particularly of names and particular things you would know are misspelled. Apart from correcting typos, you may make a particular number of changes for free. This number will be spelled out in your contract. The cost of the author's alterations (or AA's) in excess of 10 percent of the cost of composition is charged to the author.

Why can't I make big changes in the galleys for free?

The simple answer is because it's expensive. Book pages are printed up in "signatures," that is, multiples of eight, sixteen or thirty-two. If you make a change on the last page, there should not be too much of a problem. However, if you make a change on page 2, it may alter the number of words and lines on all the pages thereafter, and the whole signature will have to be reprinted and possibly the next signature, if the last page is pushed over. This delays things terribly and ratchets up the cost of publishing the book.

Second-pass galleys input all the changes and corrections that everyone noted on the first-pass pages. The final pass is checked by the proofreader just before the book is shipped to the printer.

The printer prepares your book, and this version is called the "bluelines," which most people shorten to "blues." It's unlikely you'll see these.

What can I do to help the publisher promote and publish my book?

This is a big question. First, fill out any publicity forms you're asked to complete. The author questionnaire will ask about your background, influences, likes and dislikes, credentials, where you live, your publishing history—anything that might help them promote you and your book and sell copies locally and nationally when the time comes.

There are a number of things that you may do over the next few months to make the job of your various editors and the promotion of your book a little easier.

A fundamental philosophy that pervades publishing is that the professionals in the industry know more about how to print and market a book than unpublished or barely published writers. In general, this is an informed philosophy, though it has its weaknesses. Both writer and publisher should be prepared to listen to what the other has to say because both, presumably, are experts when it comes to knowing the best way to exploit the commercial prospects of a particular book.

If you want to have a positive effect on how your book is published, acquire and apply tact and diplomacy. Try to see things from your publisher's point of view. The name of the game is selling books. The point is to make sure the essence of your vision is uncompromised and that your publisher and editor don't feel their considerable experience and expertise is being belittled or ignored. They, too, have a bond with this book, and this affinity can and should be gently exploited by you.

If you know, without any doubt, that what you want to achieve is right, then enlist your agent's help in the battle. She'll almost certainly see things much the same way you do.

When it's time for your editor to write catalog and flap copy for your book, have him fax you a copy. Editors and marketing people are quite skilled at boiling a book down to a pithy, exciting nub—a sizzling one sentence that just "nails" the book. But you can still make a few suggestions for improvement if you're tactful. This is especially true if you've developed pamphlets, seminars or brochures that have already done this job of selling you or your work to the public.

My editor keeps ignoring my ideas about the cover of my book. Can I do anything about it?

Publishing houses will *try* to accommodate your ideas, but they have the last word, even though it's your book. Nine times out of ten, with hindsight, they are usually right about how they've decided to market and present your book. But not always.

If you're not sure about your book cover, go to your local bookstores—you have made friends with the staff there already, haven't you?—and get their reaction to the cover art. It will certainly be more objective, and its point-of-sale perspective may be very informative for you.

Again, if the problem persists, call your agent before you call anyone else and see if she can sort things out for you with the editor and the art department.

Go to a bookstore and really study covers, taking note of the ones you thought most effective. Then send your editor a memo early on in the process, detailing your thoughts on a cover design and mentioning the names of these books, especially if they're successful and involve bold, simple designs, colors and motifs. Is there a particular illustration that you think is "just right" for your book's cover? Mention it, but be prepared to be ignored, politely.

At the very least, you should be able to clearly read both the book name and the author name on the front cover. In many cases, disputes about the cover really involve disputes about how the book is going to be marketed. Again, that's an area the publisher feels they know better than anyone. In most cases they're right, but if you really know your core audience and what appeals to them, use all the guns at your disposal to make sure that the cover doesn't offend or put off people in this core group.

The book designer designs the look of the pages and the general inside of your book. Ask your editor's assistant to send you a couple of pages of page design when they're ready. If you really don't like it, call your agent and see if the two of you can get the editor to alter or remove the elements that are bothering you.

Why does it take so long for some books to be published, especially those by new writers?

A book's publication date depends on a publisher's schedule. Most publishers publish books in "lists"—usually fall and spring—and they are working at least a year, sometimes two years in advance. Consequently, the first available "slot" for a book may be in a list at least a year to eighteen months away. In fact, most publishers in their contracts now ask for a twenty-four-month period within which to publish a book once a contract is signed before they are considered in breach of contract for not publishing the book (excluding acts of God).

In general it takes about nine months to a year from handing in a manuscript for a book to appear in the stores. However, big-name authors, who earn the publisher lots of money, take precedence over new authors in terms of who will get what available publishing slot. So it could take as long as two years for your book to appear in the stores, though this is not likely.

There is also a tactical aspect to publishing. A romance book could do well on Valentine's Day, a horror novel could be launched on Halloween, etc. This could mean waiting to get the book the best marketing boost.

What's a sales conference?

About twice a year, sometimes three, your publisher holds a large get-together for the sales and editorial staffs. This is known as a sales conference. It's designed to let the sales reps know through face-to-face contact with the book's editor what that editor's coming book list looks like and which books are expected to perform well or exceptionally.

Sometimes your editor may ask for a photo or even videotaped material by or about you that she can use to sell you and your book to the sales reps. If ever there was a time that your editor could be thought of as your in-house agent, it's now.

What is a publication date?

The honest answer to that question is that it varies depending upon the publisher. For some it is the date the book is shipped to the warehouse, for others it is the date the book appears in the stores, for yet others it is an artificial date created to make sure the book has sufficient lead time to be reviewed in newspapers and magazines, some of whom need to see galleys as much as six months ahead of time.

When will I finally get to see the finished book?

Several months after you've turned in your manuscript, answered all the phone calls, gotten to know the promotions person detailed to help push your book, read the galleys and returned them, a padded manila folder will arrive in the mail.

You rip it open, and lo and behold, there's a pristine copy of your book, compliments of your editor. Set it prominently on a mantelpiece, and break out the champagne to celebrate. Your book—*this* book on your mantelpiece—will soon be for sale in the stores.

Reading the Contract

This chapter is only a map to what's in a contract. It's designed to help you understand some of the more important things that are in a contract and why they should or should not be there. You follow my advice at your own risk.

I make no pretense at being a lawyer or well versed in the law. I do, however, have a working grasp of reading a publishing contract. Be warned: Each publisher has a variation on this contract, and I am not too proud to ask for help from those more knowledgeable than I am if I don't understand a clause. You should do the same.

If you're a published writer, consider joining the Author's Guild, which provides a free contract information service to its members who pay an annual fee. The Writer's Union, which you can join without publishing anything, provides something similar.

Author's Guild
212-563-5904
Fax: 212-564-5363
http://authorsguild.org

National Writer's Union
212-254-0279

Fax: 212-254-0673

E-mail: nwu@nwu.org

Are there any good books about contracts you can recommend?

Several books have been written on the subject by lawyers and more experienced agents versed in publishing law. One of the best is *Kirsch's Guide to the Book Contract* by Jonathan Kirsch. It goes into the clauses and their meanings in publishing contracts in more readable detail than almost any other book I know of and is probably more comprehensive in 260 pages than books twice its size.

Other books to look at are: *How to Be Your Own Literary Agent: The Business of Getting a Book Published* by Richard Curtis and *Negotiating a Book Contract* by Mark L. Levine.

What is a book contract?

Contracts are about many things, but principally they're about what each party wants and needs out of the contract. They include contingency plans for awkward or difficult situations down the road that could put either party in breach of contract, who owns what and for how long and what each party in the contract is responsible for doing. In effect, a contract is about what you and someone else have mutually agreed over something and what to do if something goes wrong.

I can't be bothered to read all the fine print. Surely it's not important for me to read the contract all the way through, is it?

Publishing contracts are heavily weighted in favor of the publishing house. The boilerplate contract usually tries to take a share of every earning possibility the publisher can get their hands on. What's more, publishers want writers to work at the publisher's convenience, not the writer's convenience. If you're not careful, a contract can mean it could be two years or more before your next book is legally able to be published.

I found the publisher myself, and I then contacted an agent to negotiate the deal. Do I still have to pay the agent 15 percent?

Agents earn their commission just on the contract negotiations. There are broad similarities in all publishing contracts, but each publisher's contract is different. Every decent agent has their own boilerplate changes that they've negotiated with the various publishing houses they do business with, establishing precedents with that house.

Editors hate to have to become Jekyll-and-Hyde personalities who have to deal with an author on business and editorial matters. However good a deal an author gets for himself, ninety-nine times out of a hundred an agent could have gotten a better deal.

Is it OK for a publisher to just send me a contract and say we have a deal?

Until the contract is signed and countersigned, there is no deal. In general, it's not acceptable for a publisher to just send you a check and then claim that certain rights have been automatically transferred to the publisher by your acceptance of that payment.

Contracts may be transmitted by fax or e-mail. These days if both parties are in agreement, a faxed signature can be considered legally binding. E-mail is trickier, although the new law (2001) making e-mail signatures legal and binding may well come into play if there is software to allow it to happen. Usually, an e-mailed contract lacks the editor's signature, and you'll have to print it out to sign it.

What should I beware of in a contract?

Keep an eye out for loopholes and clauses that claim additional rights without additional payment.

All contracts should contain at least this much information:

• The title of your work.

• The specific rights being purchased (e.g., print, electronic, reprint rights, translation, etc.).

• The exact fee offered for your work, how it will be paid, and when you can expect to receive it.

• Your obligations and liabilities. Some companies specify issues of accuracy, originality and libel. Make sure you can reasonably meet their demands.

When making a deal, also consider the following:

• If a publisher offers no contract (or confirms a sale simply by sending a check), protect yourself by creating your own letter of agreement. Keep it simple, don't get clever, just outline what's been verbally agreed and leave it at that, if you can get the publisher to sign it. At least make sure there is a written record of the agreement that's been sent to the publisher, ideally by registered mail. This way you can substantiate that there are terms the publisher has implicitly agreed to (by not disagreeing) if they publish your material.

• A verbal agreement is usually binding but can be hard and expensive to enforce in court.

• Always confirm oral agreements with a memo or letter covering the terms.

• If you want to change a contract, get the agreement of everyone concerned in writing. This is usually just a signature or an initial on the change. However, it isn't enough to simply delete or rewrite clauses you don't like.

• If an editor is unwilling to negotiate, ask yourself, "Do the positives of this deal outweigh the negatives?" Think hard before you commit yourself. Almost certainly you'll start to have second thoughts; but if everything's signed, you're committed. Just move on and learn from the experience.

Would you give an example of a simple contractual letter of agreement?

An example of such a letter from an author to a publisher might be as follows:

Dear _____

Thank you for accepting _____. I have received your check for

$ _____ in payment for _____ and I look forward to receiving

my author copies on publication on _____.

Sincerely,

What do you recommend trying to negotiate or change in a contract?

• **Advance.** How much and when you will receive your royalty advance on your book. Publishers try for a publication payment (pub payment) these days. Avoid them if you can. Go for half on contract signing and half on manuscript delivery and acceptance.

• **The option clause.** Try to limit the option as much as possible, either by confining it to the next book exactly like the one you've written (e.g., a mystery featuring Joe Smith, professional golfer and amateur detective) or something like it (e.g., the author's next mystery). You should also not have to submit more than a proposal and sample chapters if it's nonfiction and a synopsis and the first fifty pages if it's a novel.

Ideally, the publisher should have no more than sixty days to consider the material exclusively, which begins thirty days after the current manuscript has been accepted for publication.

There should not be any "topping" or "matching" privileges. These clauses basically give up the author's ability to decide who he next wants to do business with. These privileges mean that the publisher can reject your next project but insist that if someone else wants to buy it, they have the right to change their mind and either match the offer (matching) or improve it (top it) by a set percentage (often 10 percent), depending upon the wording of the contract.

In other words, if House B offers $10,000 for your novel that House A (your current publisher) has rejected, you are obligated to give it to House A if they offer (match) $10,000. If A has to top the offer by 10 percent, then A has to come up with $11,000 to keep the book.

• **Reversion rights.** Most books have a life of about three years before going out of print. If the author's career eventually takes off, these books can be worth good money; therefore, make sure you have had the rights to your books reverted back to you from the original publisher.

Make sure you get the publisher to specify what they mean by out of print. If the book is still in print, you won't get your rights back. Make sure you get the publisher to define what they mean by this term; otherwise, publishers can hold onto your rights for a long time if you're not careful.

A good starting point for determining what defines out of print is if a book earns $250 or less in two royalty periods (basically, a year). Publishers often like to talk about numbers of copies sold over a set period (e.g., four hundred copies sold in a year). Either way, it's important to define these terms.

• **Electronic rights.** A vague and controversial area. Try to limit them as much as possible. Most publishers are demanding them as deal breakers. However, it is possible to insist that if nothing happens with them within, say, eighteen months, the rights revert to the author on written request. Also, distinguish between electronic version and electronic rights. (These are defined in chapter nine.)

• **Royalties.** Each publisher has their own version of what they think a royalty statement should include. About the only thing they have in common is that they all manage to report inadequately what the author needs to know. Ideally, your statement should include:

Number of copies printed cumulatively and also this royalty period.

Number of copies shipped or distributed cumulatively and this royalty period.

Number of copies sold cumulatively and this royalty period.

Type of royalty (whether regular, special discount, foreign export, etc.). [These are too complicated to go into here, but the books mentioned on page 156 will explain these terms in detail if you're interested.]

Number of copies returned.

Details of the reserve against returns (explained in chapter eight).

Details of subsidiary sales, contracts and income.

Be advised that publishers usually won't change their contracts for a lowly writer whose earning power is not in the seven figures range. It is good to know about these things, however, and see what you can get.

• **First proceeds clause.** If the book is cancelled for some reason and the author is obligated to repay all or part of the advance, make sure that you have the option to resell the book and pay the original publisher the money they claim you owe from the proceeds of the new sale. This is called the *first proceeds* clause because it deals with a payment from the first proceeds of a resale.

• **Publication of the manuscript.** This used to be within eighteen months of signing the contract, but is now more likely to be within twenty-four months of signing. If they fail to publish within the agreed time (excluding acts of God), then the rights revert to you without your having to repay any advance that has been made to you.

- **Subsidiary rights.** Hold onto as many of these rights as you can because they can be worth money to you; however, not all agents are good at foreign sales. If the publisher's offer is decent but includes foreign rights, it's worth considering that 75 or 80 percent of the foreign is better than no sale at all.

Unless the offer is close to or over seven figures, do not give away dramatic rights, and even then make sure it is at most 75/25 in your favor. The same is true with audio rights.

- **Flow-through.** This means that all subsidiary income should be passed along by the publisher (i.e., it flows through) within thirty days of the publisher receiving the money. (This assumes your royalty advance has earned itself out.)

- **Bankruptcy.** If a publishing company goes out of business, make sure you don't have to buy back the rights to your book. They should revert to you automatically.

- **Grant of rights.** If it's not there, try to add the phrase "Any rights not expressly granted herein remain exclusively the Author's."

Are there any clauses I shouldn't bother with in the contract?

Don't get upset about a basic options clause. It only means the publisher has the right to view your next work. It doesn't mean you have to sell it to them.

Don't get concerned about the indemnity clause and the competing works clause. Publishers are unlikely to budge, and these clauses aren't that important except in rare cases.

Don't try to negotiate cover approval, an advertising budget or to get your picture on the front cover unless you can muster some substantial negotiating leverage. The odds of a publisher granting these things is very small.

Don't try to negotiate the kind of paper or the design of the book or typeface. Again, it's not worth the time and phone calls.

A sample contract with comments

This is a fictional contract for *GigantaMegaCorp* Publishing House. It's important to remember that different houses have different boilerplate contracts that include and exclude a number of things. One house may or may not change certain aspects of the contract that another house will give you without difficulty.

This particular contract is heavily weighted in favor of the publishing house. Bear in mind that legalese is not there just for effect. In the law, certain words have specific meaning and that meaning may not necessarily coincide with the common everyday usage we associate with it. For example, in immigration law the term "refugee" does not mean legally what we mean when we use the word in everyday conversation. So be cautious and don't assume anything. If you don't understand, ask or look it up.

The following contract is for a book called *All You Need to Know to Make a Zillion Dollars in Publishing* by Bean Gornan Dunnit. Comment appears before a clause in boldface type.

The following clauses define the parties in the contract and what it is about.

AGREEMENT made this 31st day of February, 2099, between Bean Gornan Dunnit (the "Author"), and *GigantaMegaCorp* Publishing House Trade Publishing, a division of Worldwide GigantaMegaCorp Publishing Group, Inc., of 2003 1st Street, New York, New York 10000 ("*GigantaMegaCorp* Publishing House");

The parties to this Agreement wish to publish and have published a certain Work (the "Work") provisionally entitled:

All You Need to Know to Make a Zillion Dollars in Publishing in consideration of the mutual promises in this Agreement, the parties agree as follows:

The Work. The Author shall deliver to *GigantaMegaCorp* Publishing House a new and original manuscript comprising a Work containing approximately 80,000 (words) 350 (book-length pages) [and 12 photographs or illustrations which are integral to the Work].

#2. This describes the work that is being contracted.

2. Description of the Work. The Work shall be a book about making a fortune as a writer of books, by selling a book about making a fortune as a writer to other writers.

#3. There next follows the Grant of Rights. This clause details what specific rights and territories you have allowed the publisher to sell their version of your book into.

Broadly the terms are "U.S. and Canada," also called "North American rights," and American dependencies such as Guam, Puerto Rico, U.S. Virgin Islands, etc.; "World English," which is any English-speaking country such as North America, Great Britain, Australia, South Africa, etc. The percentage splits between author and publisher for these sales, usually handled by the publisher, are detailed in Paragraph 12. The last of the three is World Rights, which grants the publishing company a negotiated percentage of all the foreign and translation rights to your book.

Nonexclusive distribution means the Open Market. Any American publisher can export a certain number of their version of a book into a foreign country on a nonexclusive basis. This means you may be able to find the American version of your book in a bookstore in Holland, even though a Dutch publisher is also selling a Dutch language translation.

3. Grant of Rights; Territories. The Author grants to *GigantaMegaCorp* Publishing House, during the full term of copyright available to the Work in each country covered by this Agreement, the exclusive right to print, publish, distribute, sell and license any and all editions and or formats of the Work, in whole or in part, throughout the World (the "Territories").

Because of a law passed in the early 1990s in Australia and New Zealand, the following means that Australia has retained for itself the right to produce their own version of the book within a set period after the initial publication in the U.S.

If the Grant of Rights herein does not include the right to sell the Work in Australia/ New Zealand, *GigantaMegaCorp* Publishing House may nevertheless arrange for non-exclusive distribution of the Work in Australia/New Zealand if the Author has not entered into a publishing agreement with an Australian or British Commonwealth publisher for publication of the Work in Australia/New Zealand within thirty (30) days of *GigantaMegaCorp* House's first publication.

#4. This outlines how much you'll get as an advance against royalties and how the company will pay out that advance. Traditionally it has been half on signing the contract and half on delivery by the author and acceptance by the editor of a completed manuscript. Publishers are trying to change this, particularly on higher advances, to include an on-publication payment.

4. Advance Against Royalties. @*GigantaMegaCorp* House shall pay to the Author, as an advance against and on account of all moneys accruing to the Author under this Agreement, the sum of eighty thousand dollars ($80,000), payable as follows:

$20,000 on signing this agreement

$10,000 on delivery and acceptance of the first half of the manuscript

$30,000 on delivery and acceptance of the remainder of the manuscript

$20,000 on publication of the manuscript

#5. Outlines when the manuscript is due to the publisher.

(a) (1) This says if the Author doesn't deliver the manuscript by the due date (stated in 5 (a)(1)), that is, the date agreed upon in the contract, he must repay any money he's collected from them and then wait three years to resubmit this manuscript or one a lot like it to another publisher.

5. Delivery and Acceptance of Manuscript. (a) One (1) original of the complete Work in print form and one copy on computer disk, as described in Paragraphs 1 and 2 and in the following Subparagraphs of this Paragraph 5, shall be, delivered to *GigantaMegaCorp* House no later than December 31, 2099. Prior to the delivery of the complete Work, the Author shall deliver Progress Materials as follows:

The first 40,000 words by July 30, 2099.

The final 40,000 words by December 31, 2099.

(i) If the Author fails to deliver the complete Work by the due date, after a thirty (30) day grace period, *GigantaMegaCorp* House may demand, in writing, that the Author return all sums in full paid to the Author by *GigantaMegaCorp* House in connection with the Work. Upon receipt of these sums, this Agreement shall terminate. The Author may not, for a period of three (3) years after termination, submit any partial or complete manuscript or proposal for the Work or for a similar work to any publisher before offering it to *GigantaMegaCorp* House under the same terms contained in this Agreement.

(ii) It is common to expect an author to pay for photos or illustrations unless he has negotiated some sort of "Photo or Illustration Budget" ahead of time. If you have illustrations in your book, the cost of getting the license to use the pictures should be known ahead of time and built into the royalty advance if possible. Very often the money for this is like a line of credit, available for expenses incurred, but otherwise not forthcoming. The money often comes as part of an advance against projected royalties.

(ii) If *GigantaMegaCorp* House determines that the published Work requires materials such as photographs, illustrations, an appendix, a bibliography, or other supplementary matter ("Related Materials"), the Author shall furnish these to *GigantaMegaCorp* Publishing House in reproducible form at a time mutually agreed; if the Author does not do so, *GigantaMegaCorp* House may supply them at the Author's expense.

(iii) Again, permissions are an accepted Author responsibility.

(iii) If permission from others is required for publication of any material contained in the Work, including any visual material, or for the exercise of any other right conferred by this Agreement (including the right to promote the Work), the Author shall be responsible for obtaining such permissions at Author's own expense and shall submit them, in form satisfactory to *GigantaMegaCorp* House, with the complete Work, but *GigantaMegaCorp* House may, if *GigantaMegaCorp* House deems it necessary, assist the Author in obtaining the necessary permissions. Such permissions shall permit the exercise by *GigantaMegaCorp* House and its sublicensees of all the rights licensed to *GigantaMegaCorp* House in the Territories.

(iv) & (v) Indexing is difficult to do properly. Most authors think they can index their own books until they try, then learn that it's a real art. The cost will come out of your royalties, however, so you won't feel the pain too much. I always find this to be something of a hidden tax on an author's earnings.

(iv) *GigantaMegaCorp* House shall have the right to commission the preparation of an index, reasonable to the size and scope of the Work, at the expense of the Author, unless the Author provides an index at the time of delivery of the complete Work or within a mutually agreeable time period following the submission of the completed Work.

(v) Any sums that *GigantaMegaCorp* House has paid on the Author's behalf by reason of Subparagraphs 5(a)(ii-iv) may be deducted from any portion of the advance payable to the Author pursuant to Paragraph 4; if the total advance has already been paid, however, any such sums will be billed to the Author directly, or, at *GigantaMegaCorp* House's discretion, charged to the Author's royalty account.

(b) This part details how long the editor is allowed to take before getting back to the author with revisions, if any are needed. If the editor takes longer than the ninety days specified, the author can reasonably assume the book has been accepted and he should be paid his delivery and acceptance payment.

(b) *GigantaMegaCorp* House will inform the Author in writing whether the Work or Progress Materials which are delivered pursuant to Paragraph 5(a) are acceptable within ninety (90) days of receipt of the complete Work or the Progress Materials. Acceptance of the Progress Materials shall not be deemed acceptance of the complete Work.

(b) (i) Read a certain way, this next clause says that an Author doesn't automatically get the opportunity to fix a delivered manuscript the publishing house judges unacceptable (note the phrase: "in its sole judgment" and all the "or" clauses). *GigantaMegaCorp* House can reject an unacceptable manuscript (or Progress Materials, *i.e.*, parts of a manuscript) the first time it's submitted. Again, this is a contingency situation that should be addressed in the author's favor.

(i) If *GigantaMegaCorp* House concludes that the Work or the Progress Materials delivered are unacceptable but could be revised to *GigantaMegaCorp* House's satisfaction in a timely fashion, *GigantaMegaCorp* House and the Author shall agree on an appropriate period of time for the revision process and *GigantaMegaCorp* House will provide written editorial comments to the Author with respect to the revisions required. Should

GigantaMegaCorp House, in its sole judgment, conclude that the Work or the Progress Materials as first submitted cannot be revised to its satisfaction within a timely period, or after the agreed revision period, should *GigantaMegaCorp* House find that the revised Work or the revised Progress Materials are still unacceptable for any reason, *GigantaMegaCorp* House may reject the Work by written notice to the Author.

(b) (ii) This next section is called "The First Proceeds Clause." This version says that if the Work is rejected, an Author may keep 50 percent of any money already received from *GigantaMegaCorp* Publishing House and repay the Publishing House the other 50 percent within twelve months from the proceeds of a sale to another publisher, if the author can get one. The Publishing House sees this as a major concession to the Author. If an author is lucky— and he absolutely shouldn't count on it— unless large sums of money are involved, the publisher probably won't ask for the money to be returned. However, strictly speaking, if the book has not been sold within the specified time period, the author is still liable to repay the money if he is asked to do so.

(ii) If the Work is rejected, the Author may retain fifty percent (50%) of any amounts advanced to the Author pursuant to Paragraph 4 and shall repay *GigantaMegaCorp* House fifty percent (50%) of the amount advanced within twelve (12) months. The Author will be authorized to negotiate the sale or license of rights in the Work to any third party on the condition that the Author will be obligated to repay to *GigantaMegaCorp* House the amounts retained from the advance pursuant to this Subparagraph 5 (b) (ii) from all proceeds from any sale or license by the Author of rights of any nature in the Work to a third party (the "First Proceeds"). The Author agrees to use best efforts to license or sell the rights in the Work on terms most likely to result in the repayment in full to *Giganta-MegaCorp* House. The Author agrees to notify *GigantaMegaCorp* House of the financial terms of any agreement with any third party involving rights in the Work and the Author will ensure that any agreement with any third party provides that *GigantaMegaCorp*

House will be paid directly first proceeds under that agreement until amounts in the Work and the Author will ensure that any agreement with any third party provides that *GigantaMegaCorp* House will be paid directly first proceeds under that agreement until amounts retained by the Author under this Agreement have been fully recouped.

(c) Unlike the clause above, which deals with a work being rejected for being "unpublishable," this next clause discusses specific circumstances of a manuscript being unpublishable because it puts the publisher at legal risk in some fashion. It gives the publisher the right to have their lawyers decide whether or not there is anything libelous or that could otherwise put the publisher at legal risk. If Author and Publisher cannot make the manuscript legally acceptable, the Author must fully repay the Publisher (not partially as in 5b.ii.) Notice that it is *GigantaMegaCorp* House's lawyers who decide what's acceptable.

(c) If *GigantaMegaCorp* House requires that the Work receive a legal vetting, the completed, revised manuscript will be submitted to *GigantaMegaCorp* House's attorneys. The Author will cooperate with the attorneys in the legal vetting process. If *GigantaMegaCorp* House's attorneys conclude that publication of the Work may lead to legal liability, *GigantaMegaCorp* House and the Author will cooperate for a period of sixty (60) days to make it legally acceptable to *GigantaMegaCorp* House's attorneys. If they are unable to do so, the Author shall return to *GigantaMegaCorp* House any amounts advanced and, when *GigantaMegaCorp* House has received this repayment, this Agreement shall terminate. If *GigantaMegaCorp* House finds the Work is legally acceptable for publication in the United States but changes are advisable for publication in other territories, and/or if *GigantaMegaCorp* House's attorneys deem changes advisable after the first publication, the Author shall agree to make the changes. The Work may be deemed acceptable only when it is legally acceptable. In no event shall *GigantaMegaCorp* House be obligated to publish or continue to publish a work which, in the judgment of its attorneys, may lead to legal liability. No changes or revisions made pursuant to this Paragraph shall be deemed to alter or affect the warranties and indemnities contained in Paragraph 15 of this Agreement.

#6. In the clause below, notice the last sentence uses the phrase "from time to time" following first publication. What does this mean? In contracts, words and their meaning are very important. Don't assume you understand what something means. Legal definitions can be different from the same word's common usage outside a contract.

The revision clause should be amended to include some intent by the publisher to pay the author for extensive revisions to his work at a later date on terms to be mutually agreed upon. I mean, if they are prepared to pay someone else to do the work, why shouldn't they pay the author to do the same thing? Some publishers get this argument, while others do not.

6. **Proofreading and Author's Corrections.** Following *GigantaMegaCorp* House's acceptance of the Work, the Author shall cooperate in making any required corrections, approving the copyedited Work, and reading, correcting, and returning promptly all galley proofs and dummies. The cost of the Author's alterations, in type or plates, other than those that are due to printer's errors, in excess of ten percent (10%) of the cost of composition, shall be paid by the Author. The Author shall be entitled to see the typesetter's bill for such charges. Following acceptance of the Work, no changes other than copyediting shall be made by *GigantaMegaCorp* House without the consent of the Author. Upon *GigantaMegaCorp* House's reasonable request, in order to keep the Work topical, the Author shall revise/update the Work from time to time following first publication.

#7. This clause basically says the Author must wait a minimum of two years and then can keep partial payment from the publisher if publication doesn't occur. Publishers keep their options open about how they will publish a book. The buzz on a book, numbers of the print run or the quality of the final manuscript can make a difference between plans to go into hardcover or paper.

The eighteen-month publishing window is common. Some publishers push it to two years because they are already that far ahead in the publishing calendar. If *GigantaMegaCorp* House does not publish, an author can either go with another publishing house and pay back *GigantaMegaCorp* House or give *GigantaMegaCorp* House six more months to publish. If they still don't publish the book, the Author can keep the money *GigantaMegaCorp* House already paid as a "cancellation fee."

7. Publication. GigantaMegaCorp House may publish and distribute the Work in any format, style, and manner, and under any of its imprints, and with a jacket, cover or package and at a cover price as it shall determine. The final title shall be mutually agreed between *GigantaMegaCorp* House and the Author. *GigantaMegaCorp* House shall publish the Work within eighteen (18) months of its acceptance of the complete Work and Related Materials, as described in Paragraphs 1, 2 and 5. If *GigantaMegaCorp* House has not commenced production within such time, other than for reasons beyond its control, such as strikes, wars, government restrictions, or Acts of God, or because of a business decision made in consultation with the Author, then the Author shall have, as a sole remedy, either of the following options: (i) Upon written notice to *GigantaMegaCorp* House, the Author may grant the rights to the Work to another publisher provided that the Author repay *GigantaMegaCorp* House all sums advanced for the Work under this Agreement out of First Proceeds received from the grant of rights to another publisher; or (ii) the Author shall grant *GigantaMegaCorp* House an extension of six (6) months from the date of *GigantaMegaCorp* House's receipt of written notice in which to publish the Work, with the understanding that if *GigantaMegaCorp* House should fail to publish within this additional six (6) month period, this Agreement will terminate, all rights in the Work will revert to the Author, and the Author shall have the right to retain all sums already received by the Author pursuant to Paragraph 4 as liquidated damages for *GigantaMegaCorp* House's failure to publish the Work.

#8. The publisher wants to make sure that it can use all means at its disposal (that is, personal appearances by the author, radio and TV interviews, etc.) in

order to promote the book. Although not mentioned specifically here, it is commonly accepted that tours and traveling and room and board will be at the publisher's expense not the author's if the impetus comes from the publisher.

"Selections from the work" are excerpts, usually of no more than 5,000 or 10,000 words. It's not the same as first serial and second serial subrights mentioned in paragraph 12. This clause talks about advertising and promoting the book by using an excerpt. For example the first chapter might be printed as an insert in a magazine, though no payment will be forthcoming to the author.

8. Promotional Materials/Promotion by Author.

(a) The Author shall cooperate with *GigantaMegaCorp* House in obtaining, at Author's expense, a photograph of the Author of quality acceptable to *GigantaMegaCorp* House to be used in connection with the publication of the Work.

(b) *GigantaMegaCorp* House may use, or permit others to use, the Author's name and the likeness of the Author obtained pursuant to Paragraph 8(a), the title of the Work, and selections from the Work in advertising, promotion and publicity related to the publication and/or licensing of the Work, including broadcast, without charge, by radio, television or cable, or distribution via any form of electronic transmission, including online or satellite, and/or licensing of the Work, including broadcast, without charge, by radio, television or cable, or distribution via any form of electronic transmission, including online or satellite based data transmission.

(c) All details of the advertising and promotion of the Work shall be determined by *GigantaMegaCorp* House. If *GigantaMegaCorp* House requests the Author's cooperation in promoting the Work, the Author shall be available for such promotional activities.

#9. In this next clause we discuss the number of free copies of your book you will get. This is a negotiable number within reason, and many editors will send you a few more gratis copies after you've used up your contracted quota. Your agent will probably want to insert "and 10 to the Agent" after the hardcover and paperback numbers. These will be used for subrights submissions by the agent. The copies mentioned here are personal copies for the author and should not impinge upon copies that the author wants *Giganta-MegaCorp* House's publicity and promotional department to send to reviewers and people who will or have provided blurbs for the book.

9. **Author Copies.** Upon *GigantaMegaCorp* House's publication, it shall give twenty (20) hardcover and twenty-four (24) paperback copies of its edition of the Work to the Author. The Author may purchase additional copies for personal use and not for resale at one-half (½) the cover price. The Author will be billed for these copies and payment shall be made prior to shipping unless the Author's royalty account has sufficient excess royalties accrued over and above the advance paid to the Author so that these charges can be recouped from the Author's royalty account.

#10. In #10, notice that publishers usually agree to register copyright with the copyright office. Copyright is valid and enforceable without registration, but in a global marketplace where intellectual property is becoming more and more valuable, it makes a lot of sense to have work definitively registered *before* there's an infringement. Registering at the copyright office carries important added benefits. However, if the publisher won't do it, the author/agent should if they realize it becomes their responsibility to do so.

10. **Copyright.** Notice of copyright in the Work shall appear in each copy of the Work printed by *GigantaMegaCorp* House and be in the following name:
Bean Gornan Dunnit.

#11. This next paragraph contains an important set of clauses to examine. They define what the royalty rates will be for the book under various circumstances. It's very hard to get publishers to alter these rates in any significant way, though in some circumstances there is a little flexibility. Note the phrase "on the sales less actual returns and less a reasonable reserve for returnable copies." This means, in essence, that the publisher can hang on to money that you have earned until they deem that it is time to pay you everything you've earned. The fear is that they'll print too many copies, ship them out to booksellers who buy them on consignment, and then six months later decide they can't move them off their shelves and ship the copies back to the publisher, who is forced to issue a credit.

Publishers sometimes add "performance bonuses" or "best-seller bonuses." These are bonus royalties paid if the book performs unexpectedly well to an agreed-upon level. Best-seller bonuses are tied to a particular list, for example, *The New York Times* list, and pay varying amounts for a fixed period, say ten weeks, according to the position on the list the book hits. So much for each week a book is in positions one through three, a little less for positions four through seven, etc.

11. **Royalties.** Royalties on *GigantaMegaCorp* House's editions of the Work shall be based upon sales less actual returns and less a reasonable reserve for returnable copies, at the following rates:

(a) *Hardcover.* (i) On copies of a hardcover edition sold in the U.S., except as described in subparagraphs (k) through (p) below: 10% of the U.S. cover price of the first 5,000 copies, 12 ½ % of the next 5,000 copies, and 15% on all copies thereafter.

(ii) On copies of a hardcover edition sold in the British Home Market (defined as the United Kingdom, Republic of Ireland, and the Channel Islands), except as described in (k) through (p) below: 5% of the U.K. cover price.

(b) *Trade Paperback.* (i) On copies of a trade paperback edition sold in the U.S., except as described in (k) through (p) below: 7½ % of the U.S. cover price.

(ii) On copies of a trade paperback edition sold in the British Home Market, except as described in (k) through (p) below: 5% of the U.K. cover price.

SMALL PRINTINGS: After two years, if a book sells less than five hundred copies annually, then on printings of 2,500 copies or fewer, the author will get half the regular royalty rate. It's an attempt to keep a book in print rather than revert the rights to an author.

SMALL PRINTINGS. For the purposes of keeping the Work available as long as possible, the Author agrees that if, at any time after a period of two (2) years from the date of initial publication of the Work, the semi-annual sales in the hardcover or trade paperback edition shall be less than Five Hundred (500) copies, then *GigantaMegaCorp* House shall pay the Author one-half (½) of the royalty rate set forth in Paragraph 11 (a) or 11 (b), provided these copies are sold from a printing of Two Thousand Five Hundred (2,500) copies or fewer (such printing not to occur more than once per calendar year), this reduction being made by reason of the increased cost of manufacture per copy.

(c) *Mass-Market Paperback*. (i) On copies of a mass-market paperback edition sold in the U.S., except as described in (k) through (p) below: 8% of the U.S. cover price.

(ii) On copies of a mass-market paperback edition sold in the British Home Market, except as described in (k) through (p) below: 5% of the U.K. cover price.

(d) *Calendar*. On all copies of a calendar based on the Work: 10% of the amount received by *GigantaMegaCorp* House.

(e) *Special Library/GigantaMegaCorp House Special Book Club Editions*. On all copies of any edition sold in these Editions (regular or giant), 5% of the cover price except as provided in (k) through (p) below.

(f) *Large Print*. On all copies of a large-type edition of the Work sold in the U.S.: 5% of the cover price on the first 5,000 copies sold, and 7½% of the cover price on all copies sold thereafter with respect to a hardcover edition of the Work and 5% with respect to a paperback edition of the Work; and on copies of a large-type edition sold in foreign countries, by direct response, or in bulk quantities: one-half (½) of the rate specified above.

(g) *Omnibus*. On all copies sold of any omnibus volume containing the Work and other works by the Author: 8% of the amount received by *GigantaMegaCorp* House for the omnibus as a whole except as provided in (k) through (p) below.

(h) *Canadian*. On all copies of any edition published by *GigantaMegaCorp* House and sold in Canada by any affiliate of *GigantaMegaCorp* House, except as described in (k) through (p) below, two-thirds of the prevailing U.S. rate for that edition based on cover price.

(i) *Australia*. On all copies of any edition sold in Australia and New Zealand, except as described in (k) through (p) below: two-thirds of the prevailing U.S. rate for that edition based on cover price.

These next clauses define other types of royalty possibilities. (j) for instance, defines a royalty for what is called Open Market sales, that is, sales of the U.S. edition in a foreign country; (k) is a form of Special Sale and deals with situations where, for example, Costco or QVC may take several thousand copies at a time; (o) through (p) are also kinds of Special Sales, for example, a special edition for a college or a book club.

(j) *Other Export Sales.* On all copies of any edition sold in foreign countries outside the United States of America, its territories and possessions, military bases and other than those specified above, except as described in (k) through (p) below: 10% of the amount received by *GigantaMegaCorp* House for the original hardcover edition of the Work; and 5% of the amount received for any lower priced edition.

(k) *High Discount Sales.* On all copies of any paperback edition sold at a discount of 60% or more and on all copies of the hardcover edition or calendar sold at a discount of 55% or more: 10% of the amount received by *GigantaMegaCorp* House.

l) *Premiums.* On all copies of any edition sold for premium use: 5% of the amount received by *GigantaMegaCorp* House.

(m) *Mail Order Sales.* On all copies of any edition sold to direct marketers as part of a direct marketing program for sale directly to consumers: 5% of the amount received from the consumer.

(n) *Educational— Book Clubs and Book Fairs* On all copies of any edition sold to book clubs or book fairs supplying the educational market: 6% of the amount received by *GigantaMegaCorp* House.

(o) *College Sales.* (i) On all copies of any special hardcover edition sold with a lower cover price as college textbooks: 10% of the cover price; and (ii) on all copies of any paperback edition sold with a lower cover price as a college textbook: 5% of the cover price.

(p) *Adult Book Clubs.* On all copies of any edition sold to an adult book club on a royalty inclusive basis: 10% of the amount received by *GigantaMegaCorp* House.

Audio. There are two types of audio rights: abridged and unabridged (the complete text of the book). There are also dramatic readings and dramatized readings. Note that if *GigantaMegaCorp* House owns the recording, they want the author to record the tape for free for them ("participate without cost"). A professional actor would be paid to do the work if he or she was employed. The author ought to get some compensation as well. It is a negotiable clause, and the author would do well to retain these rights if she can.

(q) *Audio.* (i) On all copies sold of any audio recording developed from the Work and sold through regular trade channels: 10% of the amount received by *GigantaMegaCorp* House.

(ii) on copies of the audio recording sold through special markets such as mail order and premium (including copies sold by *GigantaMegaCorp* House in bulk at a royalty-inclusive unit price for resale to third parties) or coupon advertising or radio or television advertising; one-half (½) of the regular audio recording rate; and,

(iii) on all sublicensing of audio recording rights in the Work to book and record clubs, continuity programs, mail order marketers, foreign publishers and other third parties such as electronic publishers, or for broadcast; 50% of the advance and/or royalties received by *GigantaMegaCorp* House.

If more than one work of the Author is recorded on the audio recording, the royalty paid to the Author shall be in proportion to the amounts from each work used on the audio recording.

If *GigantaMegaCorp* House has or acquires audio recording rights, the Author, upon *GigantaMegaCorp* House's request, agrees to participate without cost in the recording of the audio edition of the Work in order for the audio work to be published simultaneously with the first publication of the Work.

11(r) *Electronic Rights*: Note the distinction between Electronic Book and Electronic Version. An electronic book is usually a verbatim reproduction of the book on some sort of computer screen. Electronic versions are adaptations that enhance the book with elements not in the originally printed version. Publishers should pay for the right to take that book and present it in an altered or clearly different form from the original, just as movie studios must pay for the right to turn a book into a film.

Royalties received by the author on e-books are defined as 15 percent of amount *GigantaMegaCorp* House receives. However, it gets more interesting: In clause #12 electronic book rights are listed among the various subrights and are split 50/50 between Author and Publisher. So, if *GigantaMegaCorp* Publishing House licenses e-rights out, then the author will get 50 percent of the sale, but if the e-book is treated as a Publisher's "edition," they'll only give the author 15 percent. This is also a very low figure for this right. Commonly, publishers are giving between 25 to 50 percent royalties on these rights.

The penultimate paragraph is also worth noting. If the Author retains an electronic subright and gets an outside offer for it, the Author must first offer the right to *GigantaMegaCorp* House.

(r) *Electronic.* On all copies of the Work sold as an "Electronic Book" or "Electronic Version" as defined herein: 15% of the amount received by *GigantaMegaCorp* House. As used in this Agreement, Electronic Book means the text of the Work in complete, condensed, adapted or abridged versions by any means of distribution or transmission, whether now or hereafter known or developed, intended to make the text and any illustrations or photographs contained in the Work available in Visual form for reading.

Electronic Versions mean the text of the Work in complete, condensed, adapted or abridged versions whether sequentially or non-sequentially together with added sounds, images, or graphics which are more than incidental to the text and distributed in electronic formats.

(s) *No Royalty Copies.* No royalties shall be paid on copies sold to any party (including, in the case of "remainders," affiliates of *GigantaMegaCorp* House) below or at cost (including direct expenses incurred) or given away for review, advertising, sample, sales promotions, or like purposes, or on portions of the Work appearing as previews in other books published by *GigantaMegaCorp* House or on portions of the Work used or sublicensed for advertising or publicity without compensation.

#12. This next clause discusses in more detail the breakdown of the subsidiary rights the author has granted the publisher. If the author and the publisher share subsidiary rights (as in this case because in Paragraph 3 we agreed to give the publisher World Rights), it is useful to ask for a "pass through" for monies earned through a sale of subsidiary rights within a fixed period, say, thirty days.

This means any money owed the author as the result of a subright sale will be passed through to the author within thirty days of the publisher receiving that money. They can make you wait for ages if you don't do this. You only get royalty statements every six months. Remember, every subrights sale that *GigantaMegaCorp* House makes on your behalf, if you've agreed to share the income, means that your share of the money will go toward paying off the royalty advance you initially received when the company gave you money up front on signing and delivery.

12. Subsidiary Rights. The Author grants to *GigantaMegaCorp* House the exclusive right to sublicense other rights in the Work as specified in this Agreement in the Territories upon terms as *GigantaMegaCorp* House deems advisable. The net proceeds of these sublicenses shall be divided as set forth below and paid (less the amount of any advances then unearned) at the time of the next accounting. Upon Author's written request, *GigantaMegaCorp* House will provide the Author with copies of executed licenses in which the Author's share of the proceeds is Five Hundred Dollars ($500) or more.

	GigantaMegaCorp House's Share	Author's Share
First Serial (use of serializations, condensations, excerpts, digests, etc., in newspapers, magazines or other periodicals before publication of the Work in book form)	10%	90%

Second Serial (use of serializations, condensations, excerpts, digests, etc., in newspapers, magazines, other periodicals or books after publication of the Work in book form)	50%	50%
Book Club	50%	50%
Permissions (including the right to grant transcription or publication rights in the Work in Braille or in other nonbook formats specifically for the physically handicapped without charge)	50%	50%
Trade or Mass-Market Paperback	50%	50%
Other Book Publication (including, but not limited to, hardcover, large-type editions, mail order, calendar, premium and other special editions and schoolbook and book fair editions licenses)	50%	50%
British Hardcover and/or Paperback (which may include the right of *GigantaMegaCorp* House's licensee to further sublicense any of the rights granted elsewhere in this Agreement, including first serial if available)	20%	80%
Translation (which may include the right of the licensee to sublicense any of the rights granted elsewhere in this Agreement, including first serial if available)	25%	75%

Electronic Book and storage and retrieval of the text (including any visual material) in whole or in part in complete, condensed or abridged form, including microfilm, microfiche, digital media or other electronic text format	50%	50%
Electronic Versions	50%	50%
Audio Recording	See subparagraph 11 (q)	
Videocassettes (not dramatized)	50%	50%
Commercial and Merchandising (derivative products such as the use of a title or character for greeting cards or clothing)	50%	50%
Performance (television, radio, dramatic, musical, motion picture and video rights and allied merchandising rights derived therefrom), subject to the Author's prior consent	10%	90%

If *GigantaMegaCorp* House exercises any of the rights specified above itself in lieu of sublicensing them, the royalty rates, unless specified in Paragraph 11, shall be subject to agreement between the parties. Further, if any right specified in Paragraph 12 is sublicensed by *GigantaMegaCorp* House to a company that is affiliated with *GigantaMega-Corp* House, it is understood that such license will be negotiated at arm's length and on terms similar to the terms of current agreements for similar licenses between *GigantaMegaCorp* House and unaffiliated companies.

This next clause says that even if the author has retained a right, say an audio right, if the publisher has an audio division, then they should be given the right of first refusal if the author decides to sell the audio rights. It makes a bit of sense, in terms of maximizing the sales potential of a book, but it is cracking an egg with a sledgehammer and could limit an author's ability to maximize earnings potential from a successful book by going with a more eager and better paying audio book specialty company. Such circumstances are usually negotiable, however.

Similarly, the publisher is trying to maximize its profit margins by insisting that it be allowed to be the publisher of the authorized film or TV version of the book, by agreeing to help get stills from the movie or TV show that could be used to promote the book in some form.

If the Author has retained any rights in the Work which any division of *GigantaMegaCorp* House, Inc., has the capacity to exercise itself, the Author shall give *GigantaMegaCorp* House the right of first opportunity for the acquisition of these rights before licensing them elsewhere.

If the Author disposes of performance rights, *GigantaMegaCorp* House shall grant the purchaser of those rights the privilege to publish excerpts and summaries of the Work in the aggregate not to exceed 7,500 words (or ten percent [10%] of the total Work, which-ever is less), for advertising, publicizing and promoting such rights, provided, however, that the Author's grant shall require the purchaser to take all steps necessary to protect the copyright of the Work. The Author will use best efforts to secure the agreement of the purchaser of performance rights to grant *GigantaMegaCorp* House the right to use photographic stills and the title of the performance in connection with any *GigantaMega-Corp* House tie-in edition of the Work in any format.

#13. This talks about royalty statements and when they will be sent to the author. The dates here are not reflective of when the author will see the state-ment. Instead, they are rather about when the company will conduct its semian-nual inventory check. The royalty statement usually arrives a couple of months after this date. So a June statement may not arrive until August or September, and a December statement may not arrive until the following March. The last sentence of this paragraph ("under this or any other agreement...") introduces the concept of "joint accounting." Joint accounting means that any book that loses money for a company can have its debt made up from royalties owed to the author for the next book she writes for the company.

It also has a clause about a work earning less than $25 within six months not being paid (assuming the royalty has been earned out) until the earnings reach $25. Many agents ask that regardless of whether or not the royalty is paid until the $25 limit is reached, a royalty statement still be rendered, or drawn up and sent to the agent.

---

13. GigantaMegaCorp House shall prepare a statement of account semiannually as of the 30th day of June and the 1st day of December for all six-month periods during which copies are sold, and shall send these statements, together with payment of the amount due, if any, within four (4) months following the end of the period. The Author's share of amounts received from the disposition of licenses granted under this Agreement shall be computed after deduction of any foreign taxes withheld. Bank charges and any of *GigantaMegaCorp* House's share of amounts received from the disposition of licenses granted under this Agreement shall be computed after deduction of any foreign taxes withheld, bank charges and any of *GigantaMegaCorp* House's sub-agent commissions. If the Author has received any overpayment or is otherwise indebted to *GigantaMegaCorp* House, *GigantaMegaCorp* House may deduct the amount due from any sum due or to become due to the Author under this or any other agreement between the parties.

If, after two (2) full accounting periods following initial publication of the Work, in any six month period the total income generated is less than Twenty-five Dollars ($25), *GigantaMegaCorp* House may defer rendering payment until such time as Twenty-five Dollars ($25) or more have been generated.

The Author shall have the right, upon reasonable written notice, to examine the books and records of *GigantaMegaCorp* House as available insofar as they relate to the Work at Author's own expense, and provided that the examination is conducted during usual business hours and in accordance with customary accounting procedures, and occurs no more than once a year.

This clause basically says that an author will not write a book for another publisher on the same subject that so closely resembles this book as to be a competitor in the marketplace that may damage the sales of this book. Under normal circumstances no one would do this. However, if you had a falling out with your publisher, this clause would prevent you from redoing the book and selling it to someone else while the original version of the book was still on sale in the stores.

14. Competitive Works.

(i) The Author will not, without *GigantaMegaCorp* House's prior written consent, publish or authorize publication by anyone other than *GigantaMegaCorp* House of any edition, adaptation, abridgment or condensation of the Work, or of any derivative work (including, but not limited to, any dramatic play, screenplay, television script, novelization, or photonovel) based on the Work or bearing a like title;

(ii) if the Author has licensed any territories to @@@ Publishing House on a non-exclusive basis, the Author shall not license or otherwise authorize the publication of any other English language edition of the Work in such non-exclusive territories earlier than the date of first publication of *GigantaMegaCorp* House's edition of the Work in the same format (e.g., hardcover, trade paperback, mass-market paperback or audio);

(iii) This part would seem to mean that the Author can publish the book in the English language abroad only once. What happens if you sell it in Australia as well as Great Britain? It is unclear, and you should get the publishing company to clarify what they mean here.

(iii) if Paragraph 3 is modified to reserve to the Author any English language publishing rights in the Work, the Author shall not permit the publication or licensing of more than one hardcover and one paperback English language edition of the Work in addition to editions published or licensed by *GigantaMegaCorp* House,

(iv) if the Author has retained audio recording rights and/or videocassette rights, the

Author will not authorize publication of an audio recording of the Work and/or a (non-dramatized) videocassette of the Work earlier than *GigantaMegaCorp* House's first publication of the Work;

(v) if the Author has retained Electronic Version rights, the Author will not publish or authorize publication of more than one-third ($\frac{1}{3}$) of the text (including visual material) of the Work in any electronic format without *GigantaMegaCorp* House's prior written consent;

(vi) if the Author has retained first serial rights, the Author will not license such rights without consulting *GigantaMegaCorp* House to coordinate publication of the first serial and *GigantaMegaCorp* House's edition of the Work;

(vii) If you write on one topic regularly, say you're an expert on beauty treatments, you should insert exceptions to this rule, say, if you have existing contracts to do another book in the genre for another Publishing House that hasn't been published yet.

(vii) if the Work is one of nonfiction, the Author will not publish or authorize publication of any similar material in a book or article which, in *GigantaMegaCorp* House's judgment, is likely to conflict with the sale of the Work; and

(viii) This means that it could be a year or more after you've submitted an acceptable manuscript before you could have another novel published, even if it's with another publishing company.

(viii) if the Work is one of fiction, the Author will not publish or authorize publication of any other novel by the Author within six (6) months of first publication of the Work.

15. Warranties and Indemnities. (a) The Author warrants and represents (i) that he or she is the sole author of the Work; that he or she has the full power to enter into this Agreement; that he or she is the sole owner of all rights granted to *GigantaMegaCorp*

House; that no material in the Work violates any contract of the Author express or implied; that he or she has not previously assigned, pledged or otherwise encumbered the Work; that no material in the Work discloses any information given to the Author in confidence or on the understanding that it would not be disclosed or published; and (ii) that except for any previously published or unpublished materials created by others and Related Materials for which permissions have been granted, the Work is original, has not been published before, and is not in the public domain; that it does not contain any unlawful matter and that all information in the Work has been lawfully obtained, that the Work does not contain any libelous matter, does not invade any right of privacy nor infringe upon any trademark, right of publicity, statutory or common law copyright and that any recipe, formula, or instruction contained in the Work is accurate and is not injurious to the user.

(b) In the following, you should add the phrase "the author has the right to choose his/her own counsel at his/her own expense." There is an inherent conflict of interest when an author and a publisher have to defend a book in a court case brought by a third party. While the publisher and the author may have _parallel interests_, at some point the publisher may decide to settle a case or not settle a case because of circumstances that have nothing to do with the author. (Perhaps they are running low on money and want to settle to save themselves the further cost of defending a breach of copyright or libel case.) The author, however, may be well advised for any number of reasons to want to fight on. If they share the same lawyer, the author is now at a disadvantage. If the author has her own legal counsel, however, she is protected. So the addition of the phrase guarantees the author the right to hire her own counsel at her own expense in case these events should take place.

(b) In the event of any asserted claim or legal proceeding ("Claims") based on an alleged violation of any of these warranties, _GigantaMegaCorp_ House shall have the right to defend the Claims by counsel of its own choosing. The Author shall indemnify

GigantaMegaCorp House and any seller violation or any of these warranties, *Giganta-MegaCorp* House shall have the right to defend the claims, by counsel of its own choosing, The Author shall indemnify *GigantaMegaCorp* House and any seller or licensee of rights in the Work against any damages or losses incurred including any amounts paid in settlement, as well as against the cost of defending any Claims (collectively "Losses").

(c) It's important you know the limits of the insurance policy, as mentioned but not defined in (iii). According to (iv), the Author may be required to pay most if not all of the cost of a lawsuit. These clauses are not usually worth trying to negotiate because the publishing company won't usually budge from its standard position.

(c) *GigantaMegaCorp* House shall include the Author as an "insured" in any publishing liability insurance that is in effect at the time of publication of the Work (the "Policy"). *GigantaMegaCorp* House shall look to the proceeds of that insurance, subject to the terms and conditions of the Policy and as set forth below, for payment of sums that may become due from the Author by reason of the indemnities undertaken by the Author pursuant to subparagraph 15(a)(ii). The parties agree that:

(i) the Author shall not be responsible for any premiums due under the Policy;

(ii) the Author shall be an insured only with respect to the Work which is the subject of this Agreement;

(iii) coverage is for Losses under the Policy for amounts in excess of the deductible but not greater than the Policy limits; and

(iv) the Author shall be responsible for the deductible as follows:

for Loss due to any Claims for libel or any violation of any right of privacy, ten percent (10%) of the total advance payable under this Agreement; and

for Loss due to Claims for infringement of any common law or statutory trademark or copyright, or right of publicity, injurious recipe, formula or instruction or any other claim covered by the Policy, twenty percent (20%) of the total advance payable under this Agreement.

(d) If any Claims are received by *GigantaMegaCorp* House or the Author, the recipient shall promptly notify the other party. The Author and *GigantaMegaCorp* House shall fully cooperate with each other in the defense of any Claims. *GigantaMegaCorp* House may, in addition to any other remedies, withhold payments due the Author under this or any other agreement between the parties to cover the Author's indemnity obligations under this Paragraph 15. The Author's failure to cooperate with *GigantaMegaCorp* House in the defense of any Claims shall be deemed a breach of this Agreement and could result in the loss of the insurance coverage. The Author's warranties and indemnities shall survive the termination of this Agreement.

#16. This next clause says that it is the author's responsibility to keep an original copy of the manuscript at home in case something happens to the manuscript. The publisher will only be responsible if they lose the manuscript or are otherwise responsible for its destruction. Once the book has been published, if the author so asks, the publisher will return to the author all materials supplied by the author for use in the book in an "as-is" condition. If the author doesn't ask for these materials, they may be destroyed by the company.

16. Original Work. The Author shall retain an original copy of the Work and *GigantaMegaCorp* House shall not be responsible for the loss of or damage to the Work or any materials supplied by the Author except in the event of *GigantaMegaCorp* House's negligence. *GigantaMegaCorp* House shall, upon the Author's written request, made within the first three (3) months after first publication of the Work, return the original Work and any original visual material supplied by the Author in its then "as-is" condition. *GigantaMegaCorp* House shall not be required to retain the original Work or visual material after three (3) months and may dispose of the original manuscript and proofs after that time.

#17. This next clause is fairly self-explanatory. The publisher undertakes not to put any adverts for other books by other authors in the back of your book, although they may advertise other books you've written.

17. Inserts, Back-of-Book Advertising. No advertising shall appear in *GigantaMega-Corp* House's editions of the Work except that, with respect to the hardcover edition of the Work, *GigantaMegaCorp* House may publish a listing of Author's other titles. With respect to the softcover or audio edition of the Work, *GigantaMegaCorp* House or its licensees may publish their own "Publishing House ads." Other advertisements will not be inserted or printed in any edition of the Work without the Author's prior written consent, such consent not to be unreasonably withheld or delayed.

#18. This next clause states that the Author cannot contract for his next book until after delivery of the one under contract here.

18. Next Publication of Author's Work. The Work will be the Author's next published work (whether under the Author's own name or under a pseudonym or in collaboration with anyone else) and the Author will not, prior to delivery of the complete manuscript of the Work, write or contract with any other publisher to write any other work for publication in book form without the written permission of *GigantaMegaCorp* House.

#19. *GigantaMegaCorp* House claims it should have an exclusive option to negotiate on the Author's next book for the same terms as this book, regardless of how successful this book may be. Additionally, they want to wait until publication of the first book *before* considering the option work. There's no mention of whether the next work should be fiction or nonfiction. Such a distinction should be made.

The time period for exclusive consideration should be thirty days, not sixty, following the acceptance of the current manuscript under contract. The phrase "solicit any third party offers, directly or indirectly" should also be struck out if possible as being too broad. "Reasonable period of exclusive negotiations" should be broadly defined as not longer than, say, a month after the initial indication of interest in the book.

The last sentence is particularly onerous for any coauthors who may be

working with other celebrity authors or well-established names who are not writers and should be carefully considered in light of the writer's career plans and other works.

19. Option. The Author grants *GigantaMegaCorp* House the exclusive option to acquire the same rights as have been granted in this Agreement to the next full-length work to be written by the Author. *GigantaMegaCorp* House shall be entitled to a period of sixty (60) days after submission of a proposal and sample chapters for the next work in which to make an offer for that work, during which time the Author agrees not to solicit any third-party offers, directly or indirectly. If *GigantaMegaCorp* House wishes to acquire the next work, the Author and *GigantaMegaCorp* House will attempt to reach an agreement as to terms during a reasonable period of exclusive negotiations. If they cannot reach an agreement, the Author shall be free to Submit the next work elsewhere, but the Author may not accept an offer from any other publisher on terms equal to or less favorable than those offered by *GigantaMegaCorp* House. *GigantaMegaCorp* House shall not be required to consider the Author's next work until publication of the Work which is the subject of this Agreement. The *GigantaMegaCorp* House option shall also apply to the next book-length Work by each party to this Agreement included in the term "Author," whether such manuscript is written alone or together with another coauthor.

20. *Remainders.* At any time after one year of initial publication of the Work, if, in the opinion of *GigantaMegaCorp* House, the continued sale of the Work is no longer profitable, *GigantaMegaCorp* House may dispose of any copies remaining on hand as "remainders" at any price as it may see fit. The royalty payable on all copies sold as "remainders" shall be ten percent (10%) of the amount received less manufacturing costs, not to exceed any other royalty rate specified in this Agreement and subject to Paragraph 11 (s). *GigantaMegaCorp* House shall notify the Author before the Work is remaindered and shall offer the Author the opportunity to purchase copies of the Work at the remainder price; any inadvertent failure by *GigantaMegaCorp* House to do so, however, shall not be deemed a breach of this Agreement.

#21. With the increasing popularity of the technology which can keep books in print indefinitely, the term in the next section "available for sale" is very

vague. A book could be considered in print if it's simply available for downloading from a Web site. This needs to be much more distinctly defined. A possible way to establish a more detailed definition could be the use of "thresholds" based on the number of sales made (say 250 books sold) or amount of money received in a defined period, usually two consecutive royalty periods, which is more or less a year.

21. Out-of-Print. If, after the expiration of three (3) years from the date of *GigantaMegaCorp* House's first publication of the Work, the Work is out-of-print, the Author may make written demand to *GigantaMegaCorp* House to reissue or license rights in the Work. *GigantaMegaCorp* House shall notify the Author in writing within ninety (90) days after its receipt of a demand whether it intends to comply. If *GigantaMegaCorp* House does not respond or if, within six (6) months of its notice that it intends to comply, *GigantaMegaCorp* House has not complied by reissuing the Work or entering into a sublicense for a new edition, then this Agreement shall terminate and all rights granted to *GigantaMegaCorp* House shall revert to the Author.

What this next clause means is that if the book is declared "out-of-print," the author has thirty days to buy the plates and film that were used by the publisher to print the book. Because the author has the rights back to the book, they can take these purchased plates and film and have the book reprinted elsewhere if they want.

Note that this clause also defines what "in print" means, which is an important consideration in getting back your rights.

Upon termination, the Author shall have the right for thirty (30) days to purchase the plates or film, if any, at one-fourth (¼) of the cost (including typesetting). For the purposes of this paragraph, the Work shall be considered in print if it is available for sale in the United States in a full length English language edition or if a contract for its publication by a sublicensee of *GigantaMegaCorp* Publishing House for publication within eighteen (18) months is outstanding.

22. Governing Law. Regardless of the place of its actual execution and performance, this Agreement shall be treated as though executed within the State of New York, and shall be governed by New York laws. Any action or proceeding regarding this Agreement or the Work shall be brought solely in the New York courts (state or federal) in New York County.

23. Assignment. This Agreement, including the provision of Paragraph 24, is binding upon the assigns, heirs, executors, or administrators of the Author and upon the successors and assigns of *GigantaMegaCorp* House but no assignment shall be binding upon either of the parties without the written consent of the other, except that *GigantaMegaCorp* House shall have the right to authorize or sublicense publication or use of the Work in the Territories to its parent or any subsidiary or affiliated company, or to any company which acquires all or substantially all of its business or the business of one of its divisions. If there is more than one party constituting "the Author," each party shall be jointly and severally liable for the Author's obligations under this Agreement.

#24. Many agents delete this clause and substitute their own as a rider to the contract. (A rider means an additional clause to the contract.) If you compare this clause with the agency clause included at the end of the contract, you'll notice there are a number of things in the agent's version not in this version. That's because the agent's clause is also, in effect, the contract that the agent and the author enter into with regard to this book. It means the agent is the "agent of record" for this book, and all monies will pass through the agent to the author. The agent will take her commission and then pay the remainder to the author.

24. Agency. All statements and sums of money due and payable to the Author under this Agreement shall be rendered and paid to the Author's agency (the "Agency") which is authorized to collect and receive such monies and the Author declares that the receipt by the Agency shall be a valid discharge of *GigantaMegaCorp* House's obligations under this Agreement. The Agency is empowered to act in the Author's behalf in all matters arising out of this Agreement.

25. Reserved Rights. All rights not expressly granted to *GigantaMegaCorp* House pursuant to this Agreement are reserved to the Author, provided that the Author will neither exercise nor authorize others to exploit any of such reserved rights in a manner that will impair the value of any rights granted to *GigantaMegaCorp* House under this agreement.

26. Full Agreement. This Agreement contains the following additional paragraphs: Rider to Clause 24, which paragraphs together with Paragraphs 1-26 constitute the full understanding of the parties and supersedes all prior agreements, understandings and proposals whether written or oral. No modification of this Agreement shall be binding unless in writing and signed by all parties.

AUTHOR   *GigantaMegaCorp* House   TRADE PUBLISHING a division of
Worldwide GigantaMegaCorp Publishing Group, Inc.

By: _____   By: _____
Author President and Publisher

Payee's-Tax ID/Social Security Number:

_____

Rider to Clause 24.
Agency Clause

The Author hereby confirms that s/he has irrevocably appointed and designated the Peter Rubie Literary Agency (hereafter referred to as the "Agent") of 240 West 35th Street, Suite 500, New York NY 10001 as the Author's sole Agent throughout the world with respect to the Work and all rights herein. The Author hereby authorizes and directs the Publisher to pay and forward all statements and monies accruing from the Publisher to the Agent, and the Publisher agrees to do so. The Author hereby empowers the Agent to act on the Author's behalf in all matters arising from or pertaining to this Agreement and/or the Work. The Author hereby irrevocably agrees to pay the Agent, and the Author hereby irrevocably authorizes the Agent to receive and retain, and the Author hereby irrevocably assigns and transfers to the Agent an amount equal to fifteen percent (15%) of all monies accruing, payable, or paid to the Author under this Agreement and otherwise accruing from the Publisher or Author with respect to the Work, and the Publisher hereby accepts and agrees to honor said assignment and transfer. Any sum payable by the Publisher under this Agreement and paid to the Agent pursuant to this paragraph shall constitute a valid discharge of the Publisher with respect thereto. The Author warrants that he has secured the rights that he has given Agent clearance to represent on Author's behalf. The Author indemnifies the Agent and holds them harmless from any legal action that may result from the contents or presentation of the books.

chapter eight

? Subrights and Royalties

What's a subright, and why should I care about it?

Selling a book creates a whole body of rights to the work, called subrights or secondary rights, besides a publisher's right to print it in English and distribute it in the United States. For example, where else will the publisher print and distribute the book? Canada, Great Britain, Australia? Can they resell it for translation into a foreign language? What about movie rights, audio rights, electronic rights and so forth?

When you sell a book, what you're really doing is licensing certain aspects of that book. It's still yours, because eventually all the rights to the book will return to you. When you get them back, you can resell them (*i.e.*, relicense them) if you can find someone interested in taking them on again.

The more rights you license away, the less control you have over your work and the more money you should be paid as a result. Always be explicit about the rights that you're licensing. The more rights you keep for yourself, the more money you can potentially make through resale of a successful piece.

Perhaps this is the agent in me talking, but it seems publishers always want as much as they can get for as little money as possible, and they try hard to make you share everything. We once had a book about how to contact the dead, and the publisher asked for theme park rights. Somehow, "Contacting the Dead: the Theme Park," works better as a theoretical idea than an actual one.

If, after shopping the book around, all you have is one measly offer from a publisher and they insist, for example, on electronic rights and world rights, you have three choices: Negotiate and hope that good will and an editor's enthusiasm for the project will prevail enough to give you some negotiating room; or if they are recalcitrant, you must decide to take their offer as is; or, finally, tell them it is not acceptable and walk away from the deal.

Many authors who represent themselves to small publishing companies end up signing dreadful contracts that give away all sorts of rights they later regret. Once you've signed the contract, there's not much anyone can do to help you.

Am I allowed to use parts of my published book for other publications?

Most books are copyrighted in the name of the author, so if you own the copyright, the answer is yes. However, contractually you may only be allowed to use a certain amount of the book (often three hundred words) without getting the permission of the publishing company. Large chunks quoted in another book might be considered a "competing work," which would be a breach of your contract with the publisher. If in doubt, ask either your agent or your editor.

What are the typical subrights of a book?

Territory: North American Rights
This is the right to publish the book only in the United States, Canada and U.S. territories and dependencies.

World English Language
This allows the right to publish the book anywhere in the world where there is an English language market, such as the United Kingdom, Australia, South Africa, etc.

Translation and Foreign Rights

Some people rather clumsily refer to foreign rights when they mean translation. Translation rights are the exclusive right to publish the book, in translation, into a country's native tongue, e.g., German rights published in German in Germany, French rights published in French in France, etc.

Foreign Rights

Foreign rights are the right to publish the book outside of North America. It doesn't matter if it's in English or French (a translation), it's still a foreign right. However, you can license world English language and keep translation, but still not have all the foreign rights because you're allowing someone outside of the United States to publish the book into their market.

Open Market

When publishers license your book for printing and distribution, they are contracting to be the *exclusive* publishers and distributors of your book. (This means that they are the only people allowed to publish and distribute your book.)

Even if you retain foreign rights, a U.S. publisher usually retains the *open market* right, that is, the *nonexclusive* right, to sell *their* English language U.S. version of a book in a foreign market regardless of whether or not publishers in that country publish their own version. (A nonexclusive right means that other publishers besides your publisher have a right to publish your book.)

For example, in Germany it may be possible to buy the German language (translation) version of Tom Clancy's Op-Center books in translation (an *exclusive* right), as well as copies of the American edition and/ or the British edition, because the publishers have the right to sell *their version* of the book on the open market on a *nonexclusive* basis. Open market books are aimed at a perceived American audience stationed abroad (such as businessmen and women or serving members of the military) who would be interested in buying a copy.

World Rights

This allows the publisher to sell all foreign and translation rights to a book on behalf of an author and the company. There is an agreed upon split, usually 80/20 or 75/25 in favor of the author, although this split is negotiable at the time of signing the contract.

Hardcover Rights

These give the publisher the exclusive right to publish and sell the book in a hardcover edition, usually through outlets such as bookstores and libraries.

Paperback

There are two general kinds of paperback rights: trade and mass market.

Trade paperbacks are considered "quality" paperbacks (or paperback "hardcovers," if you like) and are the larger format paperbacks you generally find in bookstores. Mass markets are the smaller or pocket-size books and are the more common form of paperback. Genre books such as mysteries, romances, etc., would fall into this category. The books are distributed through bookstores, supermarkets, direct accounts, magazine retailers and the like.

These days most publishers retain these rights, which are split 50/50. In the past, publishing was thought of as "horizontal." That is, hardcover houses just did hardcover editions, and paperback houses did paperback editions. A hardcover house would sell the paperback rights to a paperback publisher. In rare instances, really successful books were sold to a hardcover house for a hardcover edition. (For example, Richard Matheson's *I Am Legend* started life as a Gold Star paperback in the early 1950s and became such a popular genre classic it was reprinted in hardcover by Walker & Co. in the 1960s. More recently, *Ghostwriter* by Noreen Wald was published in paperback by Berkeley and then reprinted in hardcover by the Detective Book of the Month Club.)

These days, with all the merging of publishing companies, publishing is considered "vertical." That is, the same company buys the right to publish a book in both hardcover and paperback. They later decide which format will be the most commercially successful.

Sometimes a house that has the license to publish a reprint in paperback decides to sell that right to another house to help recoup some of the money they have advanced on the book. Walker's surprise hit *Longitude*, by Dava Sobel, for example, was bought in paperback by Penguin USA.

Book Clubs

These are usually split 50/50. A book club has a specific consumer base and interest, and it will guarantee to sell a minimum number of copies because of its member base. The book may be acquired as a main selection or an alternate selection, depending on how successful it is seen to be.

Each month a club member is automatically sent a main selection unless the member decides to send it back. This is often a successful book that club members can buy at a reduced or discounted price. Members are also offered premier books each month at a discount called alternate selections.

When club members join the book club, they guarantee to buy a set number of books over the course of their membership, so the club, which may print up special club editions of the book and sell it at a special club discount, has a relatively known number of copies it will likely sell.

First Serial and Second Serial

Periodical rights to publish excerpts from a book are offered to magazines and newspapers, and they are broken into first serial and second serial. A territory, such as North America, can be added to specify a geographic limitation.

When an excerpt comes from a book that has yet to be published, it is known as first serial. This is often split 90/10 in favor of the author; once the book has been published, the right to publish an excerpt is called second serial. This is usually split 50/50.

Performance or Dramatic Rights

These include television, radio, theatrical (either dramatic and/or musical), motion picture, video rights and the like. It's not likely that anything more than an option will ever be made on your book; however, these rights are so potentially lucrative that you should think twice before sharing them with a publisher. Most publishers automatically assume an author will hang on to these rights. Unless the publisher is willing to pay substantially for their share, you should rarely give them up or share them with a publisher. If you must, the split should be 90/10 in favor of the author, and the author's Hollywood agent should handle the deal. "Substantial" should mean the very high six figures for a new writer and at least seven figures for a more established author.

Audio Recordings

Audio rights should be a part of dramatic rights but are often treated separately these days. Audio rights can be split up into dramatized readings; nondramatic (*i.e.*, one person reading the book's text into a microphone); abridged, which means a condensed version; unabridged, which is the whole book on tape; and digital audio, which is often a downloadable MP3 version. The most common version of an audio book will be nondramatic, abridged, but again, be specific about what you're licensing.

Electronic Rights

Electronic rights are contentious and evolving at present. More appropriately they should be called "digital rights." Any version of a book that can be digitized, or turned into computer-friendly material (that is, material that can be either read or listened to on a computer system), can be considered a digital right.

Electronic rights are also becoming tied to the concept of print on demand (or POD) because a publisher who has the digital rights to a book and who is allowed in perpetuity to produce only as many copies as the market demands will forever control the rights to a book, regardless of how many copies are sold, unless a minimum sale number or minimum demand number is inserted in the contract.

Everyone wants electronic rights, and often they form "deal breaker" points in contract negotiations. There are two basic types: verbatim electronic rights and electronic versions.

Verbatim electronic rights are the rights of a publisher to electronically reproduce the book they are in publishing in paper form. The only modifications are editing or condensing cuts, similar to what happens to audio books.

Electronic versions are adaptations of the published paper text that may include images, sound and other things. It becomes, in effect, a new and different version of the book, much as a movie or play is a different version of the original book.

The joke is that despite all the noise and the huffing and puffing, there really isn't much money to be made from electronic rights because not enough people are prepared to sit in front of a computer screen and read a book, and there is no electronic book reader of any serious commercial merit on the marketplace yet.

And that's the point. Publishers are heading inexorably to becoming clearing-houses and repositories for literature of all types, and they are working their hardest to ensure that they control the digital rights to as much of their material as possible. And if a publisher has the digital rights to your book, how will you ever get them back? How does a digital book go out of print? These questions are now being addressed in the industry.

On this new frontier, publishers and agents are dueling over who should retain control of these rights and how, exactly, these rights should be defined.

Verbatim Electronic Books

Most agents and editors agree it's fair that publishers should have the right to electronically reproduce a verbatim version of the book they published. The book can be edited, abridged, or the text amended or adapted in some form to make the book available in a visual form. Such verbatim rights should cover text versions on the Internet or on a CD-ROM or DVD. In effect, this would be any version in any format that could be a substitute for the printed book itself. These are often referred to as *electronic books*.

Electronic Versions

These are versions of the book that have been adapted by adding sound, images, additional text or graphics not contained in the original work. Publishers, particularly when they are part of a large media conglomerate that can create and market audio and electronic media as well as books, feel they have at the very least a right of first refusal to exploit the book electronically. (First refusal is the chance to look at material before anyone else and decide ahead of the game whether or not you want to buy the material in what amounts to a preemptive offer. Authors are not forced to take an offer, but they are not usually allowed, by contract, to take an equal or lesser offer from another company until the company with first refusal passes on the project.)

An example of an electronic version might be an adaptation of a book that is a game based on the book or its characters.

Unfortunately, because this is a volatile field, there is some overlap between definitions of verbatim electronic rights and electronic versions, depending on which company you are dealing with. This can cause confusion and problems.

In many cases, when deadlock is reached on who gets what with these rights, a way out is to grant the publisher the right to do something with the property for a fixed period, say, eighteen months. If nothing happens within that time, the author has the right to write to the publisher and demand back his electronic rights. The company then asks for a further six months to do something with the electronic rights before giving them up.

Commercial and Merchandising

These are basically toys, games, calendars, T-shirts, greeting cards and the like based around characters and situations in the book. Again, they can be terrifically lucrative, so retain them for yourself unless the publisher is willing to pay handsomely to share in them.

Other Rights

These rights include large-type editions, mail order, premium and other special editions, photocopying and facsimile, microfilm, direct-response marketing, theme park, etc. These rights are usually split 50/50.

Can I make more money keeping rights and selling them myself? Or should I let a publisher take a share and sell the rights?

If you have an agent with contacts abroad and in Hollywood, etc., your best bet is to have your agent sell the rights. You will keep all the money derived from any sales without having to share the advances with a publisher.

Next line of defense: If you have to give up some rights, have your agent sell them for both the publisher and the writer. The difference is, if you keep the rights and your agent sells them for you through their foreign subagents, you get to keep all the money. If the publishing company sells the rights, then you have to share the money from any foreign sale.

If a book's subrights are licensed to a publisher, they will be handled and sold by the subrights department. Just like the agent, the subrights director will use subagents in various foreign countries, and she may travel to book fairs in places such as Frankfurt, Milan and London in an effort to interest international publishers in her company's books.

If the rights are handled by the agent, she will also handle them through her subagents, in much the same way as the publisher's subrights department. In either case, the agents in the various foreign countries are considered the experts on the publishing industry in their locations. They know their markets as well as the agents in the United States know the North American market. If the U.S. agent doesn't attend one of the various international book fairs, one of her subagents almost certainly will on her behalf.

What this means to the writer is that they end up being represented (through their affiliation with the U.S. agent) by publishing professionals in other countries who know their markets and the publishers' likes and dislikes very well and can most effectively sell the author's work into that market.

My agent is charging me more for selling foreign rights than for U.S. rights. Is that fair?

An agent's standard commission fee for foreign rights is usually 20 percent of all monies earned because another agent and extra expense is involved. The higher commission is generally split 50/50 between the agents.

What's a book scout?

Book scouts, based mainly in New York, work on retainer for various foreign publishers (usually one per country) to keep an eye on new books published in the United States that might be of interest to their clients.

When they spot one, they contact the agent (or the publisher, if they happen to control those particular foreign rights) and have them send a copy of the book, which is then forwarded to the foreign publisher they are working for with a view to being published. A U.S. scout for Hiyakowa, a Japanese publisher, for example, may want to see *Hirohito and the Making of Modern Japan* by Herbert P. Bix, published in English in the United States for possible translation and publication in Japan.

This is another reason why writers and agents should retain as many rights as possible. As a book starts to generate a buzz, people who work in foreign book markets (as well as Hollywood, audio companies and so forth) will contact the rights holder of the book. If they like what they read, they will offer an advance against royalties (just like the original deal signed in the United States for the book), which is extra earned money for the writer.

Scouts are a way for a foreign publisher to get an edge on their competitors and snag big books just as the buzz is starting. Many foreign publishers are already aware of big books or interesting books before they've even hit the bookshelves.

Am I being ripped off? Why is it that my book has sold in three countries, we have an audio edition as well as a paperback sale, and I've still not seen a dime beyond my initial royalty advance?

If a book doesn't sell, the publisher is out of pocket for the money advanced to you (or royalty advance). The only way a publisher can recoup a royalty advance (also called just "an advance") against expected royalties paid to you is to sell books and/or licenses they've acquired to reprint the book in various formats and venues. (Royalties are agreed-upon percentages of the net sale price of the book that are paid to an author twice a year. The more books you sell, the more royalties you earn. You can tell how much you should be paid because a royalty statement is always enclosed along with any check.)

Any money earned by you and divided between you and the publisher will go toward paying off the outstanding royalty advance "debt" that needs to be earned out or recouped before you start earning royalties. (I mean debt here only in the sense that it is money that has been paid out. You don't have to pay back a royalty advance unless you fail to produce a manuscript that the publisher thinks is publishable.)

For example, say you were advanced $100,000 and the paperback rights are sold for $100,000. You'd think you'd see some of that money, but you'd be wrong. Given a 50/50 split between you and the publisher (the norm, in the case of a paperback sale), you'll get $50,000 and $50,000 will go to the publisher. However, because you need to earn out your royalty advance of $100,000 before you see any money from subrights sales, your $50,000 share of the paperback deal will go toward paying off your royalty advance. You still have to earn back $50,000 before you see royalties.

Let's say we now discover that the book is sold in Germany and France. The rights split is 80/20 in your favor. So on a $20,000 German deal, your share is $16,000. You now have to earn $34,000 ($50,000 − $16,000). The French sale is $10,000, of which your share is $8,000. Now you have to earn back only $26,000 ($34,000 − $8,000).

So you can make foreign sales and paperback sales and still not see a dime of extra money. With those kinds of sales, however, the odds are strong that you will. You can begin to see why your agent wants to retain and sell as many of these rights as possible for you. If he sells them, they generate an income for you that is not tied to your "debt" to the publisher.

How do I keep track of the money my books earn with all these potential sales?

Royalties earned by a book, including subrights sales, are detailed in your twice yearly royalty statement and, when appropriate, accompanied by a check.

While the contract may say that the statements will come in, say, July and December, the reality is that you probably won't see your copy until about two months after these dates. It can take that long for the warehouse to complete its inventories and the royalty department to churn out statements for every author published by the publishing house. If the company owes you money, a check will accompany the statement, which is first sent to your agent. The agent takes her 15 percent and then forwards the rest to you.

Royalty statements are stunningly complicated things to read (many editors have trouble understanding them) and vary greatly in form from publisher to publisher. Sometimes they contain accumulative figures of books sold, and sometimes they only include figures for that six-month period.

The statements usually take into account sales to bookstores, retailers, wholesalers, book clubs, foreign rights sales (if applicable), discount premium sales and so on.

What happens if my book doesn't sell very many copies? Do I have to return any of the advance royalties the publisher paid me?

The short answer is no, you don't owe the publisher any money. The publisher takes the risk, and if the book doesn't sell, it's their problem, not yours.

What do publishers mean when they talk about "returns"?

Returns are books that have been sent back to the publisher by a bookstore. Publishers ship copies of a book to a bookstore (or bookstore chain), who take them on consignment, hang on to them for a couple of months, then ship them back to the publisher for a refund, saying they don't sell. Whereupon the publisher then ships the bookstore another consignment of books by another author.

These days it isn't uncommon for publishers to suffer high returns of 50 percent or more particularly with mass-market paperback books. In recent years it has been possible for bookstores to order just enough copies of an author's book and sell just enough that they pay very little to the publishing companies in cold, hard cash. Books in and books out began to become a paper transaction.

Meanwhile, because they were creating books that they never managed to "sell through" (that is, books that were sold "through the bookstore" to the public), publishing companies started to hemorrhage real money. This lack of cash flow contributed to the orgy of consolidations and mergers and the demise of small and midlevel publishing houses over the past few years.

What does "reserve against return" mean?

The most inventive thing on a royalty statement is a column tucked away in the corner called "reserve against returns."

Here's how it works: Publishing is perhaps the only retail industry that allows its customers to return the product they get from the manufacturer (*i.e.*, the publishing company) if they decide they don't want it or can't sell it and exchange it for new and different items.

What this practice means is that when your publisher initially "sells" thirty thousand copies of your book, you can't be sure this is an accurate figure. The publisher more accurately talks about "shipping" thirty thousand copies to bookstores that are either going to hang on to them or send some of them back and ask for a refund. You could end up "selling through" (i.e., having the bookstore sell) only fifteen thousand to twenty thousand copies.

So, for example, even though your December 31 royalty statement (which you'll likely receive in February or March) says you've sold thirty thousand copies, the publisher won't pay you royalties on all those copies until the end of the next royalty period, or perhaps the end of the next two royalty periods. Exactly when is up to them. They'll wait for the returns. And while they do, they hold back a certain percentage of the total money owed to you, often one-third (the actual amount is mentioned in your contract), as a "reserve against returns" until they're certain of the actual sales figures.

Since bookstores have the option of returning to the publisher books that don't sell, publishers maintain they are taking all the risk in publishing an author; they have no guarantee of a single copy of a book selling when they're shipped to bookstores.

Agents and authors have a different perspective. "If a copy of my book is sent to a bookstore, then you owe me an agreed-upon percentage, known as a royalty," they claim. "I have no control over the way you convince stores to take your books, so why should I be inconvenienced and my income held to ransom, as it were. Pay me as per our contract."

Publishers claim that because bookstores take books on consignment, they have to wait and see what happens with books before they can pay an author all the royalty money it seems they have earned. And, if publishers need some ready cash, they can go to the "reserve against returns fund," which can be used to help relieve a liquidity problem or earn some extra interest for the company before the money has to be handed over.

For agents and authors, "reserve against returns" is an insidious accounting trick that delays authors getting their just rewards for work done many months if not years earlier. But you agreed to it when you signed your contract.

How did the "reserve against returns" system get started?

It all began innocently enough, in an effort to sell more books. The reserve against returns policy was devised in the 1960s just as mass-market paperback books started to become big business. It was a sales and marketing technique to induce wary booksellers to stock books by little-known authors.

However, in a way that no one really understands, it's as though the "special offer" price became the "established price." This inducement (a sales ploy, in effect) to take paperbacks by unknown writers, backfired on publishers, who found themselves in a situation where the only way that the bigger bookstores (and bookstore chains like Barnes & Noble and Crown) would take books in larger numbers (every publisher's goal) was to give them this inducement full time on every book.

Before anyone knew what happened, the exception had become the rule and was applied to all authors regardless of their fame or track record or whether the book was in paperback or hardcover.

What does remaindering a book mean?

On average, about three to five years after your book is published, depending on the sales rate, your publisher will announce that sales of your book have slowed to such a degree that they intend to "remainder" it prior to putting it "out of print." You'll be able to buy copies at a deep discount.

The publisher will sell what you don't buy to a wholesaler who specializes in taking books off a publisher's hands on a "ten cents on the dollar" principle (the actual figure will vary, of course). He then sells them job lot back to the bookstore, who shovels them into large bins at the back of the store, for next to nothing.

The author is next tormented by seeing his book selling like hotcakes at a dollar a time and receiving no royalties from the sales.

E-Publishing and Other Routes

What is meant by "nontraditional publishing"?

Nontraditional publishing breaks down into self-publishing and subsidy publishing. Some of these books can be electronically published.

What should I consider when signing a contract with a nontraditional publisher?

Make sure you know:

1. Who owns the book? Subsidy houses not only charge for design, printing and distribution services, but also claim various rights to your book. Printers and book producers charge only for their services. All rights to your book remain with you.

2. If you are told you receive royalties, you're dealing with a subsidy house. Subsidy publishers pay authors a standard royalty of around 10 to 15 percent. When you self-publish, you receive all sales proceeds.

3. A subsidy publisher will retain all books except for a few "author copies." A printer or book producer will give you the option of storing the books yourself or paying for warehousing, but the books belong to you.

4. A book producer will offer you a menu of services; you pay only for those you need.

5. Whichever route you take, you'll be responsible for marketing the book.

Exactly what is electronic publishing?

Electronic publishing really should be broadly defined as digital publishing. It's a visual way of presenting a book page without using paper. The page is displayed on a computer screen by downloading the text from the Internet or by buying a CD-ROM disk or DVD.

As of this writing (Fall 2001), we are in the situation of having lots of people scrabbling for digital or e-rights in the forlorn hope that "thar's gold in them thar hills." In fact, despite all the hype of Gemstar, Palm Pilot technology and other makers of digital readers, there is no reader that remotely comes close to the ability of the plain printed page to reach thousands of people cheaply and swiftly.

E-publishers create and distribute original "books" (even the term "book" begins to become an anachronism here) that are appearing for the first time in an electronic format.

However, at present, the harsh fact is that relatively few people read books on their computer screens. It can be awkward, inconvenient and, even with the new software that Microsoft and Adobe have introduced, it can strain the eyes. What's more, none of the so-called electronic books, such as Rocket-Books, Palm Pilot, or Psion, make reading on screen a viable or even pleasant option at present for enough readers—and that's if you can find a book "published" in a format that will work on your computer. It's only a matter of time before an electronic reader really rivals the ease and scope of a book, but for the moment sales of electronic books are limited. At present, an e-book "bestseller" is under one thousand copies and an e-book can be a very poor cousin to the real thing.

Are there different types of e-publishing?

Electronic publishing can be divided into three basic categories: commercial, subsidy and self-publishing.

• **Commercial e-publishers** work a lot like traditional publishers. Manuscripts are accepted on the basis of quality and marketability and go through a similar process of review, editing and proofreading before publication. Writers pay no fee for publication and receive royalties.

Commercially published e-books are sold primarily through the publisher's Web site, but are also available from online bookstores (including Amazon.com and Barnes&Noble.com). Some are beginning to be available through stores in the form of handheld readers such as Rocket Editions downloadable for the RocketBook e-reader. As all e-books have ISBNs, they can be ordered through any bookstore.

• **Subsidy e-publishers** produce and distribute books for a fee, usually about $500 per manuscript, but authors receive a royalty comparable to that offered by commercial e-publishers.

Unlike commercial e-publishers, however, subsidy publishers provide little screening (except for offensive content such as pornography or hate material) and usually accept any manuscript, regardless of quality. Most subsidy publishers provide no editorial services or proofreading (though some offer these services for an extra fee), and books are posted exactly as submitted.

Like commercially published e-books, subsidy-published e-books are available through most online bookstores. They are less likely to be available in a downloadable RocketBook edition, however, and are rarely found in traditional bookstores. They also have ISBNs and can be ordered from any bookstore.

• **Self-published** e-books are produced entirely by the author and are usually posted and sold through the author's Web site rather than that of a publisher. All the expenses of publication and distribution are handled by the author, who also receives all revenues from book sales rather than royalties.

Is e-publishing a good idea?

One of the big problems with e-books is the wide range of formats the text can be created in. This, of course, affects the distribution of the e-book. E-books are available in a wide range of formats, including rich text, html or xtml for Windows and Windows CE; AportisDoc for Palm Pilots, RocketBooks, and Librius books; as well as PDF files, that can be read by Adobe Acrobat.

Some publishers still only offer Windows-compatible formats. In fact, one of the problems with e-books is that not many people are willing to spend $500 or more to buy a device just to read an electronic handheld version of a novella.

E-books fiction compares in price to paperbacks, *i.e.*, between $7 and $12, though shorter works, such as Diana Gabaldon and Bonnee Pierson's novella *Hellfire*, can be as cheap as $2. Stephen King was selling his novel *The Plant* on an honor system at $1 a download. The experiment, for one of the world's best-selling authors whose books usually sell in the millions, was a miserly forty thousand copies. Nonfiction titles, particularly self-published, can range up to $30 or more.

What is e-text publishing?

E-text is separate from e-publishing. It is a "bare bones" version of a book that is available in ASCII without any "bells and whistles" like underlining, fonts, boldface and so forth, but it is readable on almost any computer.

A good example of an e-text project is *Project Gutenberg*, which reproduces public domain and noncopyrighted material for ready access by anyone who has a computer and a modem.

Project Gutenberg was born after Michael Hart was given a grant of $1 million for research on a computer project. Developing a kind of proto-Napster philosophy, Hart realized that once a book (or any other item, such as pictures, sounds, etc.) is stored on a computer, any number of copies can and will be available.

Project Gutenberg e-texts are made available in "Plain Vanilla ASCII," meaning the low set of the American Standard Code for Information Interchange, so that italics, underlines and bolds are replaced by capitalization. The reason for this is that 99 percent of the hardware and software a person is likely to run into can read and search these files.

Should I sell the e-rights to my book first, then get a traditional publisher?

This is a tough question. It's certainly something to consider, but publishers are becoming wise to this ploy. It may seem to take off the table the contentious question of whether or not a traditional book publisher should share in electronic rights, but it may also handicap a book's chances of regular publication. Publishers are heading toward a concept of being repositories for literature. As a result they are striving to get as many rights to a book, including digital, as they can. Once they possess these rights, they are loath to give them up easily. The real battle in e-publishing is going to be over such things as print-on-demand books (POD) and out-of-print clauses.

Most e-publishers also only ask for electronic rights, leaving the author free to market print rights and subsidiary rights elsewhere. Most reputable e-publishers post their contracts online. Be cautious of any publisher that posts an incomplete contract, such as a contract that omits key details about royalties or rights.

Do e-publishers pay normal royalties?

E-publishers often pay 30 percent royalties, usually sent on a quarterly basis. Some traditional publishers are offering as much as 50 percent, while others, like iPublish, are willing to renegotiate royalty rates as the market changes over the next few years.

The royalty statements often break down sales by how many titles were sold on disk, by download, etc.

Many e-books pay no royalty advance, sell significantly less than traditional books and sell much slower. It can take years for a book to become a bestseller, and sales of five hundred copies are considered good.

The lack of a royalty advance can create other problems for authors. Several genre organizations consider a book commercially published only if an advance is paid, so an e-book may not qualify an author for membership or for an industry award.

What's a good e-book royalty?

Anywhere from 25 percent to 50 percent is considered good. Royalties are often accounted for every quarter, rather than twice a year as with traditional publishers.

What sells well in e-books?

Offbeat genre fiction, particularly cross-genre and nontraditional romance, science fiction and fantasy do well in the e-publishing market. The general philosophy of commercial e-publishing is that it fills the "holes" that traditional publishing is leaving in its wake. They're the publishers to go to when everyone tells you your book is great but . . .

Unlike print publishing, length is far less important in e-publishing. Best-selling author Diana Gabaldon offered her story, *Hellfire* (co-written with Bonnee Pierson and anthologized in Britain) to Dreams Unlimited because there was no traditional market for 11,000 word historical mystery stories.

What about the impact of the Internet on publishing?

The Internet is the Wild West of the book world at present. It's in its pioneering infancy and changing almost daily. Sites go up, sites go down, and finding stability and dependability is a challenge.

It's also developing in ways that are starting to leave behind traditional notions of publishing. Perhaps you've seen the adverts for *inside.com*, a digital magazine declaring that print magazines are dinosaurs. Is this the death knell of the book as we know it? Will printer's ink and paper be replaced by electronic ink on a digital screen? Will the book of the future be contained on a wafer-thin piece of plastic that you slide into an electronic reader in the shape of a book?

I don't believe so, but some would have you think otherwise. Despite electronic publishing's ardent supporters, will it ever be more than an intriguing fringe for a literary *avant-garde* and those who just can't "make it" in traditional publishing?

Currently, what the Internet really can do well is help target an audience for your traditional paper book and then help you reach that audience in order to increase the sales potential of the book. You can also put the complete text of your paper book in a downloadable form on the Web (as long as your publisher doesn't object), though this is not as effective a use of the Web as some would have you believe at present.

What if I put my book up on the Web and someone steals my idea?

The big author concern of piracy stops many authors from considering e-publishing, and the truth is there's not much to stop someone from making and distributing copies of your book. In a rather strange about-face, however, e-publishers say that the very limited nature of their market and operation means that there's not much reason to pirate copies.

What's the best way to choose an e-publisher?

Like anything else to do with publishing, do substantial research before committing to anything. Does the publisher offer books you like to read? Have you read any of them? If not, do so.

Visit each publisher to get a feel for what they publish.

Ask yourself, "Does the publisher have a good Web site?" Have they won awards or praise from worthwhile organizations?

Is the publisher asking for money up front? If so, be wary.

Who have they published, and what do they consider a sales success to be?

Does the publisher use a proprietary format, or do they port the book to different formats (such as Internet download using Acrobat's PDF format, print-on-demand, RocketBooks or Palm Pilot)? Do they offer only downloads, or disks as well? Do they offer the prospect of also publishing a traditional book if the e-book performs well? Does the publisher get reviews for their e-books and where? Do they advertise and where? What are the marketing plans for your book? Is the publisher a member of the Association of Electronic Publishers (http://members.tripod.com/~BestBooksCom/AEP/aep.html); the

Electronically Published Internet Connection (www.eclectics.com/epic/); the Electronic Publishers Coalition (www.epccentral.org/)?

Will you feel proud of the finished product?

Should I be concerned about signing a contract with an e-publisher?

Absolutely. Beware a demanding contract. Most e-publishers use time-limited contracts that enable either party to terminate the agreement easily after a period of one or two years. Reputable subsidy publishers do the same. Be very careful of anything else, and take advice before committing yourself. Watch out for a contract that asks for other rights (such as print, translation, dramatic, etc.). Give these away and you leave yourself open to sharing with a publisher a percentage of any money you earn from selling those rights later on.

Why is it that when I browse the Web I find almost no print publishers selling directly to the public?

The fact is that nearly all the book sites you'll go to online to get something to download and read will be run by someone other than a traditional publisher. These new sites are run by authors, bookstores or hardware-related companies such as Gemstar.com, stephenking.com, booksense.com, Amazon.com, Barnes &Noble.com, etc. The one obvious exception is iPublish, owned by Time Warner.

It brings us back to something I have mentioned elsewhere—distribution. Publishers are still in the dark ages when it comes to understanding, identifying and reaching target audiences through the Web. They still think of books as a mass-market medium like "cornflakes" or "toothpaste." In fact, of course, books do best when targeted at audiences interested in what they have to say. Look at the proliferation of special interest magazines, and then try translating that audience into the book world. The one thing the Web has proven is that whoever creates an effective database (i.e., list) of customers will win. Perhaps one day publishers will catch on, but for the moment the worlds of electronic books and traditional publishing are still miles apart, though slowly coming together. The best thing an author can do is create an effective Web site, target his audience and try to grow an effective database of readers.

What is self-publishing?

Self-publishing means publishing and distributing your own book; you, essentially, become the publisher. It is an expensive business project. If you want to do it successfully, you need to treat it as such.

The big problem with book publishing is distribution. The professionals solved that problem decades ago, although they continually try to refine and improve their distribution. Book publishing is about numbers of books sold. Nowhere will you be more starkly confronted with that fact than when you undertake to publish and distribute your own book.

For self-publishers, actually writing the book may be the smallest part of the process; so if that's what really interests you, self-publishing is probably not a good route to follow.

To self-publish well, you need to have enough money to pay someone else to manage and market your book for you on a professional basis or enjoy doing masses of that work yourself. You also need to figure out exactly who your target audience is and aggressively market to them.

Is self-publishing the same thing as vanity publishing?

Until a few years ago, self-publishing was considered vanity publishing. It was generally thought that if you had to pay to get your book published, it probably wasn't worth publishing in the first place.

However, recent self-published successes picked up later by major publishing houses, such as *The Celestine Prophecy, Mutant Message Down Under* and *The Christmas Box*, have made publishers look again at what individuals with determination, a focused message and a demonstrable audience have to say. Numbers of books sold speak for themselves, and big publishers listen if the author's work speaks a loud enough commercial message. Nearly all successful self-published books are nonfiction, however.

What's the difference between vanity press and self-publishing?

A commercial publisher purchases manuscripts from authors and handles the cost of producing those manuscripts: cover and interior design, typesetting, printing, marketing, distribution, etc. The author is not expected to pay any of these costs. The books are licensed by the publisher, who claims ownership of the book until the book goes out of print. The books remain in the publisher's possession until sold; the author receives a portion of sales in the form of royalties.

A subsidy publisher asks authors to pay for the cost of publication, so any publisher that requests a fee from the author is a subsidy publisher. There are two types of subsidy publishing: vanity press and self-publishing.

Vanity press publishers not only ask you to pay for the cost of producing the book, they claim ownership of the books through their contract with the author, and the authors receive royalties.

Self-publishing means that an author pays a printer to help professionally design, print and distribute his book. The author often invents and registers a publishing imprint. Most importantly, self-published books are the property of the author and all profits belong to the author.

How reputable are self-publishing companies?

Self-publishing companies are like any other group of professionals—some are good, and some are not so good. The question becomes, how do you tell the difference? The answer is: research. Look at the books the company has published. Ask yourself, first of all, do you like the look of them, and do they look like something you could sell in a store like Crown or Barnes & Noble?

Talk to other authors published by the company and get their opinion on their experience. Before you sign a contract or send money, make sure you know exactly what you're getting. Make sure you know the difference between a vanity press and a self-publishing printer.

If I self-publish, how do I distribute my books?

Self-published authors use a variety of techniques for distributing their books, such as the Internet, direct mail, specialty stores, conferences, seminars, adverts in trade magazines and newsletters, etc. Bookstores often come low on the list. Authors have been known to rack up significant sales figures by selling books out of the trunk of their car after giving a lecture.

Do I really need to keep track of how many books I sell?

All sales should be accounted for, first for the tax man and second because one day, if you're successful, one of the major publishing companies may well make you an offer and you'll need to substantiate your sales figures in order to ask for that six-figure advance.

Self-publishing means that you can control exactly what goes into your book and how it will look. These are not small things because authors fight with publishers about such things all the time.

One of the best reasons to self-publish is to have written material to sell at the end of seminars and lectures you give routinely.

You can also get out the product much faster than a traditional house and you can make money faster because you're taking all the profit once your expenses are taken care of.

How do the economics of self-publishing work?

The following math is obviously very generic but will give you some idea of what your income and expenses could be. If you're interested in self-publishing, read *The Publish-It-Yourself Handbook* by Bill Henderson, the owner and publisher of the prestigious Pushcart Press, and *How to Publish, Promote and Sell Your Own Book* by Robert Lawrence Holt.

You have to figure that publishing one thousand copies of a 250-page hardcover book will cost about $40,000. The more copies you print, the cheaper things become proportionally. However, you will also have to figure out what it will cost you to store a bunch of books for, say, a year or more.

If you sell two thousand books at $20 per book, you've made back your initial costs. Everything now is profit. If you sell ten thousand books . . . well, you do the math; ten thousand copies of a book sold is a modest but respectable number.

If a mainstream publisher were to publish this book, you might earn on average, say, $2 per book. So, to earn back a $40,000 royalty advance, you'd have to sell at least twenty thousand books, or ten times as many as if you published it yourself.

If a publishing company were to make you an offer for your book based on successful sales, if you can substantiate how many copies you've sold, you'll know how much money to ask for based on what you've already earned from those sales.

Financing your book can be a substantial expense, so unless you have money to burn, leave your ego out of it, and make decisions based on purely business considerations. However, if you've studied the market and developed a professional product, self-publishing can be effective and maybe even profitable.

Do people really care if the book is from Random House or Henry Holt?

Only professionals take an interest in the name of the company publishing a book. That's an advantage to the self-publisher. If a book looks and reads professionally produced and you can get it decent distribution; not even reviewers who are inundated with books will give you a hard time, and they may even review the book anyway, despite the hundreds of books they are sent all the time.

If you want to catch the attention of an agent with your next book, a self-published book that sold five thousand to ten thousand copies or more is impressive and will almost certainly get you noticed and probably picked up.

Is it a good idea to publish with a company like iUniverse or XLibris and then try to get a mainstream publisher to pick it up later?

Without specifically commenting on the publishing companies named in the question, if you're going to go the alternate publishing route, do it because you have a vision or plan that you can actuate.

The only way a mainstream publisher will take an interest in a self-published book is if you can substantiate sales of over twelve thousand to fifteen thousand copies. At that point you'll be able to figure out how much the book has cost, how much it has earned for you, and therefore what the book is worth in terms of selling it to a mainstream publisher who will be able to maximize its sales potential.

The problem with all subsidy publishers is one of control over your material. How much will you concede to get what you want?

How do self-publishers compete for bookstore shelf space when the competitors are such as Random House and Simon & Schuster?

The truth is that most don't. iUniverse has a relationship with Barnes & Noble, for example, but sales of alternately published material is really the responsibility of the publisher—that is, *you*. The biggest problems that publishers face is distribution, and if you self-publish your material in some fashion, that is the problem you will have to deal with most acutely. Be warned.

What is the best way to go about letting the world know that you have an electronically published book available?

Almost the only two ways to advertise books that are published, self-published, electronically published or otherwise is by a Web page and through newspapers, magazines, newsletters and e-mail. Target your audience and then do what you can to reach them.

What do I do when my print-on-demand publisher takes eight weeks or longer to fulfill an order?

I'm afraid the short answer to this question is "not much." The problems with print on demand include: (a) an onerous out-of-print clause that guarantees that the publisher will own the book as long as they want to because there is often no definition on how many orders constitute "in print" or "out of print" over a set period, such as two royalty periods (*i.e.*, a year); and (b) there is nothing to compel the publisher to respond quickly to the orders you *do* get.

Can you put an order-fulfilling deadline clause in the contract? Maybe, but you'll have real difficulty enforcing it if the publisher decides to carry on printing orders in their own sweet time.

What's a book packager?

A book packager is neither a publisher nor an agent, but a little bit of both. They are usually entrepreneurs who think up ideas for books and hire writers to work on a "for hire" basis. The writer generally gets a flat fee with no share of royalties once the book is published. The packager then sells the finished product to a publisher.

Packager projects are often design intensive. Kids' books with merchandising attached to the book might be an example, or a line of books connected to a single entity such as the Getty Museum in Los Angeles. They succeed because the books they deal with are appealing commercially but are too time intensive for publishing house staff to bother with.

Packagers do many different types of books, from cookbooks to dictionaries. Parachute Press, for example, specializes in children's books; while Byron Preiss Visuals, Inc., is more of a generalist, tending toward fiction and nonfiction based on successful copyrighted characters created in the comics world (e.g.,

Alfred Hitchcock as a detective) or other copyrighted material which they license from the creators (such as books based on the show *X-Men*).

Is it worth my while trying to work for a packager?

This is a tough question. In general, the answer is no. Only experienced writers can do the job and make money at it. Can you work as part of a team and put your ego aside? Can you work in someone else's world while they look over your shoulder? Can you accept someone else having the final say about what you're writing and getting no royalties for writing a book? If the answer is no, don't work for a packager.

What does a packager look for in a writer?

A packager is interested in how professional you are as a writer. That usually means showing examples of what you've already published. You need to be able to write quickly and well, be flexible and meet deadlines.

A packager is not interested in your ideas. They generate them themselves. What they want is someone who, with a minimum of fuss and a maximum of skill, can make those ideas come alive.

Writing and Editing Tips

How do I get started writing a book?

Writers are an idiosyncratic bunch—we're probably all a little nuts when push comes to shove. Who else would shut themselves away in a little room when everyone else is having a great time in the summer sun?

Plus, we're all a little obsessive. Once that vision comes into focus, you try to capture it, to grasp the idea behind the vision and wrestle with whatever demon is blocking your creativity or trying to seduce you into going somewhere else, distracting you from your vision.

No is a word you will hear a lot when you first start out as a writer. But it isn't a no about *you*; it's a no about *that particular piece of writing*. So learn from it. Keep trying and experimenting until you start hearing yes. Work at your craft long enough and you *will* hear that wonderful little word one day.

When you're starting out, it's useful to have someone say, "Do it this way," if only so that you can reject that way in favor of a better one that you've figured out for yourself. That's absolutely OK. Whatever works for you is what you should be doing. Just make sure you're doing it, not just talking about it or thinking about it. If you want to be a contender, you've got to get into the ring and take some punches.

I read that "real writing is editing," but I don't know what that means. Will you explain?

One of the analogies of writing I use is cabinetmaking. When all is said and done, cabinetmaking is just carpentry. It's about how mundane pieces of wood are shaped and connected to become something more than the sum of their parts, and it involves an appreciation of the aesthetics of wood (in the same way that writers love words and language). Carpentry, like writing, is about harmonizing the creative instinct with the mundane task of measuring, shaping and joining together pieces of wood.

Rewriting is about editing your words, shaping your language and your ideas the way you would use a chisel, a plane or sandpaper to smooth and sculpt those pieces of wood into a seamless, graceful whole. Writing is about shaping and polishing the images and scenes of that "movie" in your head until the words on the page convey *exactly* what you see when you close your eyes and watch and listen as your characters interact.

What's the most important thing I should concentrate on when I edit myself?

One of the hardest jobs when it comes to editing yourself is cutting. The best thing to remember is that if you are too stuck on your own writing and not on what you are writing *about*, you will be concentrating on form rather than substance. If you're working on fiction or narrative nonfiction, remind yourself that the higher calling is not to be a writer but to become a storyteller. Concentrate on what is important to your narrative, what moves it along, and you'll resolve a lot of writing-related problems such as what to cut out and what to keep.

Members of my writing group give me a hard time about how slowly I write. I feel I always have to get a page just right before I go on. Am I wrong?

The only rule is: Finish what you start.

Writing is about grace and clarity of vision. It's about making sure the image in your head is on the page exactly as you imagine it. It's about rewriting.

Some people overwrite on the first draft, getting down masses of words and images, and then they begin to pare away the garbage from the gold until the image shines through. Others put down a mere skeleton of their idea, then return to it, having gotten down on the page a suggestion of what they want, and start to put muscle and then flesh on that skeleton until the images in the scene stand firm and clear. Whatever works for you is what you should do.

It's very unlikely that you'll write a perfect first draft. Those initial words on the page are just a place from which to start. Now the work begins. Two drafts, three drafts, four, five, it doesn't matter. Take as long as it takes. Just remember it all has to be done by the time the manuscript is ready to be shipped off to an agent or an editor.

Sometimes when I sit down at the word processor it takes ages for an idea to emerge. How can I shorten this?

Not all your writing has to be done at the computer. Try to recall what it was like the first time you sat behind the wheel of a car and started to drive on the streets. Remember all the things you seemed to have to do at once? Look ahead, look behind, check the sides, watch your speed, watch the road, watch the other cars, watch the rearview mirror . . . it was endless, or so it seemed. Now you drive and do these things and don't think twice about them. They are things you do instinctively. Writing habits are the same.

Go for a walk, do the laundry, clean the house, do anything mundane and mull over your writing ideas. Train yourself not to sit down at the word processor until you have something to write. Force yourself to write something, even if it's only the opening hook of a piece.

People tell me to be original in my writing, but when I try, I keep getting rejected. What's wrong here?

One of the problems that authors of both fiction and nonfiction face is that they think that being original means flouting the expectations of what readers want in a certain type of book. If you write a romance novel with the title *Slasher Nun From Hell* or a nonfiction how-to called *The Agony of Zen Meditation*, you're going to have a problem.

Authors do this kind of thing more often than many realize. They mix third person with first person, violate point of view or unity of time and place, and so forth. What these writers are doing is confusing *what* the story is with *how* you tell it.

The story is not what happens, *but who it happens to.* In other words, focus on the characters and heightening the emotionality of the narrative, not on two-dimensional plot elements that should be thought of as what the characters do next.

How can I improve my writing style?

The best style comes from reading and absorbing the work of strong writers. Who is a strong writer? There are plenty of books, writing courses and book reviews that will give you suggestions about who would qualify.

Writers are like actors. Different actors can play the same character, for example, and yet bring to the role an individual interpretation that is distinctive. What's more, while that actor's voice and style singles him out in a role, both may well vary from character to character and role to role as needs fit.

A writer's voice on the page, her style, may well vary a little from story to story. Not only is that good, it is probably worth striving for in a subtle way. Try to fit the voice to the story if you can.

Use active words and say things in a positive way. Ask yourself, Is this sentence as powerful as it can be? Does every word carry its own weight? Am I saying what I mean simply and clearly? Can what I wrote be misunderstood? Does it have a literal meaning that is mocking the sense of what I'm trying to convey?

Know what's appropriate to the genre you're writing.

I'm struggling with my book at the moment. A writer friend said I have writer's block. What is it and how do I get rid of it?

I've always had a problem with people who talk about writer's block. It is usually a problem of viewpoint or lack of imagination brought on by boredom with the characters you're writing about or because you're writing about the wrong characters and should be telling your narrative through other eyes or over other shoulders.

Nearly all structural writing problems are in essence problems of character. This is true whether you're writing fiction or narrative nonfiction.

The answer, then, is to write from other perspectives. When that seems to free you up, trace it back to the beginning so that you have a continuity to your narrative perspective.

If you're really blocked, start stream-of-consciousness writing in a journal. It is almost certainly not going to be publishable, but it may help you get to where you want to be.

Writer's block can be thought of as a form of inhibition. If you really see that as the problem, then just let go. Take a deep breath and write the very worst that you can. Pack in every excess and problem you have and that you've seen others do. Confront your inner critic with the very worst that he or she is accusing you of, then silence the voice and go back to the task at hand. So what if it doesn't work? It's not life and death here; it's just writing.

Go for a walk or do something menial and mindless so that you can let your mind roam around the problem away from the computer. Finally, sit back, listen to some soothing music with a glass of wine and chill out.

How do I go about tackling rewriting? It looks fine to me.

Regardless of whether you're working on fiction or nonfiction, look at the beginning of your book.

Ask yourself, Have I begun with my main character in a situation, not with a lot of background, setup or description, but by plunging the reader straight into the story? Remember, we read to see how the main characters get out of the situation they find themselves in, how they solve the problem or the dilemma they are faced with. That's what catches us, makes us care and forces us to turn the page.

If it's a nonfiction piece that doesn't have a narrative, the equivalent question is, Have I stated my problem and the thesis I'm going to develop in this book?

In either case, grab the reader from the outset. Compel us to go on this journey with you by making us care about the people in your story and the situations they get themselves into and out of, or find a way to humanize the ideas you're writing about and trace how they affect us and what this means.

Once you've sorted out the beginning, check the ending. Look at the last chapter and ask yourself, Does this resolve something that was begun way back at the beginning of the book?

In terms of nonfiction, ask yourself, Have I made my case? Have I presented both pro and con equally, allowing the superiority of my ideas to stand up to the fire of opposition?

If you're still in trouble, go back and look at those first pages. Nearly all narratives have the seeds of their ending planted within the first chapter or so.

In your opening pages you should have created a problem, shown something about to upset the status quo, and that's exactly what you're trying to solve by the end of the book.

If it resolves something that was begun in a chapter or two before the end, then you're probably writing in an episodic way.

Make sure the ending of the book relates to the beginning of the book.

When you look at the scenes you've created in your narrative, make sure something happens. You don't want a bunch of talking heads and no action.

Make your characters *do*, not *say*, as much as possible. Is there a reason for the scene? Where does the conflict, the obstacle, the problem that has to be overcome, come from?

I'm criticized for making my narratives too expository. What does that mean?

The exposition of a narrative is the information we need to follow what's going on. What exposition fails to do is engage us emotionally and make us care.

Too many writers ignore the old adage, show (i.e., dramatize), don't tell (i.e., be too expository). Ask yourself repeatedly, Do I need this information? Is there a way of *showing* this information dramatically, instead, so I can get my reader involved? If not, can I cut it out?

If you *do* need exposition, that is, story information, then ask yourself, Do I need it right here? Can I move it somewhere where it won't interrupt the flow of the narrative? Don't give a reader information before it's needed. Instead, give the information to the reader just before she needs it for a better understanding of the coming scene.

Then ask, Can I shorten this? Is there a way I can work it into the scene rather than have an authorial voice "explain" what's about to happen or why it's happening?

I write description well, but my characters are weak. How can I get over this?

Look at your description and ask yourself, Is my description active? Does it move the story along? It should always be seen through a character's eyes, not the author's.

I've been trying to teach myself how to edit other people's work, and when I review my edits, I notice that I tend to excise the author's voice and try to replace it with my own. What suggestions can you provide?

This is an interesting problem because it plumbs several levels. First of all, why edit? The simple answer is that the material doesn't work. What I mean by that is that it is unclear or clumsily written.

Working on other people's material can be illuminating for writers interested in bettering their own style and technique.

The main question the editor needs to ask herself is: What is the heart of the piece? What is the author trying to say? Assuming that you and the author are in sync with these elements, then the editor's job is clear: It is to clarify and simplify, increasing the grace of the writing and crystallizing the meaning without deleting the author's voice. Indeed, good editing is invisible because it not only preserves the author's voice but finds ways to heighten it.

The editor's job is not to say, "I think this would sound better this way," but to say, "You intended to say this, and yet your language and meaning do not convey it well (whatever "it" happens to be). It might work better this way, by emphasizing *this*, or that way, by altering or deleting *that* (again, whatever *this* and *that* happen to be)."

Editing is an art and takes a long time to master—but it is the heart of good writing, whether you are editing you own work or someone else's.

What else should I look for in rewriting my manuscript?

Ask yourself, "Have I switched viewpoint too often? Have I used more viewpoints than I need?"

Keep your transitions short. All you need is one or two sentences to get you from A to B. "Meanwhile, back at the ranch . . . " "Later that day . . . " Keep it simple.

If there's no conflict, the reader's attention starts to drift from the page and the passage is not working.

Keep in mind, wood is malleable and so are words. You can destroy them, erase them, rework your images and scenes until they look exactly the way you want them to look and sound and feel. The key, of course, is to have a clear idea of where you are going and what you want from your creation.

What do people mean when they talk about structure in writing?

Nonfiction writing is very dependent on strong structure, and successful commercial fiction in particular also needs it. So what is it? Consider this: What's the difference between the building you live in and a big pile of wood, brick and shingles?

The answer is that your home was meticulously planned and put together so that every part of the building supported every other part. Someone thought about how to put together your building before they built it. They thought of where to put a foundation, the best place to put support walls so that they take the right amount of weight and stress, the best way to build a frame that would hold everything together, etc.

That's structure, and it applies to your book just as much as it applies to the building you live in.

The building blocks—beams, bricks, mortar—for your book are scenes, exposition, bridging passages, sequences, chapters, sections and so on.

A narrative, whether fiction or nonfiction, has two distinct kinds of structure: *what* it is and *how* it's put together.

What your narrative is begins with your synopsis. It includes the spark that lit the fire that sets your story in motion. It tells us the prize (or goal) your protagonist is ultimately striving for and the minor prizes he may win along the way; the conflict or opposition the protagonist must face and overcome and the strategy he uses to do this; and lastly, the stakes, in other words, what it costs the hero to achieve his goal. In nonfiction, the *what* includes the problem or history you're exploring and the benefits this exploration will offer the reader.

How it's all put together involves the invention of the kind of drama you create for your scenes, the action that you put in them, the kind of language you choose to use, the tone of the piece, and so on.

Without these elements working together and in deliberate harmony, your narrative will not have structure.

How does knowing structure help me edit my book?

Once you "see" structure, it's like a light that goes on and won't go off again. When you come to revise your first draft, being aware of structure will give you the tools you need to see the overall shape of how the narrative is building and how it should be shaped, shored up and polished.

Go through your draft and ask yourself, "Do these scenes relate to each other, or does this particular scene actually relate to a sequence I've put earlier or later in the book?"

You'll discover that you may well have written some scenes that are either out of place and should be moved around or can be discarded.

What's "creative nonfiction"?

Creative nonfiction is a much abused form. The basic difference between fiction and narrative nonfiction, which is really what is meant by creative nonfiction, is that fiction is an invention and nonfiction is not.

If one writes that Alexander the Great leaped from his boat as it crossed the Bosporous and threw down his spear, claiming Asia by right of conquest, this is a historical, established fact. However, if we embellish this fact by writing that "Alexander, his red cloak swirling around him in the breeze and his burnished breastplate glistening in the afternoon sun, leapt lithely from the lead boat and waded toward the shoreline . . . ," then we are embellishing with things that are not recorded fact.

Using written eyewitness accounts of what life was like at a particular point in history can allow us the flexibility of saying, "We don't know that it happened this way," but let us suppose, from records of others at the time, that as he leapt from the boat, Alexander's red cloak swirled around him in the breeze.

The trick is to balance the skills of the novelist to bring something alive, with the need for the historian or nonfiction chronicler to state just the facts and not choose them just to make a point with no regard for the accuracy of the end result. We read nonfiction to learn about the truth in terms of what, how and when. We read fiction to learn about the truth in terms of why and to discover, if we can, the real spirit of an event.

What do I do when I have some information I have to give the reader, but it will be too much to dramatize it?

There may come a time in your narrative when you have something that's important for the reader to know but not important enough to devote a whole scene to it. A half-scene is basically a transition with a little bit of dialogue, and the scene is made to come alive through the dramatization.

How do I know if my way is the right way to go?

Writing is not a religion. There are no real rules. We all learned what we do by *doing* it over and over again until we got it right. What does that mean? It means we kept writing and submitting and listening to what those who were published bothered to say about our work until we started to get published.

Until you're published, you're not the best judge of your own work.

If you find a way that works for you (and I mean that gets you published and published regularly), ignore everything else.

If writing fiction is an art, is that also true of nonfiction?

Writing nonfiction well is just as skillful as writing fiction. It just involves different skills and disciplines. A good example is the poet Andrew Motion's biography of Thomas Griffiths Wainewright, a little-known (today) gentleman criminal from the early nineteenth century.

A lot about what he did is no longer available, and Wainewright has been made into a legendary symbol of evil by other writers. However Motion creates a portrait of Wainewright based on fragments of information that do remain. He tells the story from Wainewright's point of view (in the form of a confession) and adds the known (sometimes contradictory) facts as notes at the end of each chapter. *Wainewright the Poisoner: The Confession of Thomas Griffiths Wainewright* becomes a fascinating and imaginative work that retains its nonfiction integrity.

Any idiot can paste up basic information and assume that this is writing. A real nonfiction writer has to make readers care, if only for a minute, about the subject matter. The real trick is to take something reasonably dry, ranging from quantum physics to ornithology, and make it sparkle.

I'm an expert in my field, and yet I keep getting rejections that when they comment at all on my material are close to being rude about how I write. What's going on here?

Poor grammar irritates huge numbers of readers, regardless of whether the subject is fiction or nonfiction. A writer whose grammar and spelling are poor is a writer who will be ignored more than he is read. The thinking is: "He can't be saying anything worth reading if he can't even write decent English!"

I'm sure what you have to say is worthwhile. You clearly need to work on how you say it. Writing isn't just about meaning. It's also about style and the enjoyment of a reader to bask in language well used.

Appendix:

Sample letter of agreement between agent and client

Many agents, often at the request of clients and potential clients, have a separate letter of agreement between the agency and the client that defines the relationship for both parties. It is different for each agency; this is the one that we currently use in our agency. I've been advised that for legal reasons it is important that such an agreement originate with the client and is sent to the agent.

Date: _____ 20—

LETTER OF AGREEMENT

TO: The Peter Rubie Literary Agency
240 West 35th Street
Suite 500
New York NY 10001

FROM: _____

Please regard this letter as the declaration of a business relationship between myself, _____ ("the Author"), and The Peter Rubie Literary Agency ("Agency").

Agreements

The Peter Rubie Literary Agency will exclusively represent my literary works of fiction and nonfiction, unless we mutually agree otherwise.

As the exclusive Agent of Record on all my works sold by the Agency to a Publisher or other media licensee, I accept that this Agreement will last for as long as any compensation is or can be derived from the exploitation of such works and their attendant subrights such as, but not limited to, all English language, translations, audio, electronic, dramatic, and TV and film rights, and/or the book is considered "in print."

You agree to make your best efforts to guide me and enthusiastically represent my work in the publishing and related industries (such as electronic, audio and other media) in North America and throughout the World through your foreign and subsidiary coagents; you also agree to put forth your best efforts to get my work representation by your motion picture and television associates if I do not already have an existing agreement with such an agent.

You further agree not to sign any contract or make any commitment on my behalf without my prior consent.

Authorization and Warranty

I authorize you to direct a Publisher to pay and forward all statements and monies accruing from the Publisher to me. I empower you to act on my behalf in all matters arising from or pertaining to any Agreement with a Publisher. I warrant that I have secured the rights that I have given you permission to represent on my behalf. I further indemnify you and hold you harmless from any legal action that may result from the contents or presentation of my books.

Compensation

For the responsibilities of managing and selling my work, I agree that The Peter Rubie Literary Agency will take 15% (fifteen percent) of any monies earned which shall be written into any publishing contract you are successful in making on my behalf. Any commission for a movie or TV deal you are successful in making for me through your coagent will be split between the coagent and your Agency. Foreign sales will be charged at 20% (10% for the foreign agent and 10% for The Peter Rubie Literary Agency).

Payment of Monies

After deducting Agency commission, The Peter Rubie Literary Agency will remit monies owing to me, no later than 21 days after monies have been received and deposited in the bank if paid in U.S. currency. The Agency will send me copies of all royalty statements and contracts received from the Publisher concerning a work.

Author Expenses

I agree to pay any and all mutually agreed upon expenses including, but not limited to, photocopying of manuscripts and postage to foreign agents (not to exceed $200 at any one time). Such reimbursement for expenses will be paid by me if I am presented with an itemized bill or deducted by the Agency from funds received for my account.

Term of Agreement and Termination

I understand and agree that this Agreement will run for the term of one year from the date above and will be automatically renewable. However, either party is free to notify the other that they wish to terminate this agreement, as long as it is done in writing and within one month's notice of the annual renewal date.

Arbitration of Disputes

Any controversy, claim or dispute between the Agency and myself that cannot be resolved will be taken to Arbitration and our differences resolved under the laws of the State of New York.

Sincerely,

_____

_____

SS# or Federal ID

ACCEPTED AND AGREED TO:

_____

The Peter Rubie Literary Agency

Glossary

AAP—Association of American Publishers, the national trade association of publishers of general, educational, trade, religious, reference, scientific, technical and medical books.

ABA—American Booksellers Association.

Acquisition—A work for which a publisher has signed a contract.

Acquisition editor—The editor who buys your book.

Advance—(*See* Royalty advance, Earned royalty and Unearned royalty.)

Advance dating—Use of future date on invoice, delaying requirement for payment.

Advance galley—An advance copy of a book reproduced from early galley proofs of a newly typeset work; galleys are submitted to reviewers and potential subsidiary rights clients.

Advertisement—Paid public announcement describing something for sale.

Advertising—Public announcement describing something for sale.

Agency plan—Marketing arrangement enabling bookseller or library to earn preferential discount on short-discount titles in return for commitment to stock or order a minimal title selection, often in preselected categories.

Agent of record—The agent who sold an author's book whose name and particulars appear in the agent's clause of the book contract.

ALA—American Library Association.

Assistants—The next generation of editors, laboring in the shadows, who answer phones, sort mail and make sure everything runs smoothly.

Auction—Simultaneous submission of manuscript to several publishers, with contract going to highest bidder. Common practice, particularly in area of subsidiary rights.

Author—Writer, especially of books.

Author tour—Promotional trip by author (usually arranged and paid for by publisher) to promote book's publication.

Author's questionnaire—A form that authors are asked to complete and return to the publisher to provide guidance or advice on marketing and promotion plans.

Autographing party—Author's visit to bookstore to inscribe copies and meet admirers.

Back end—Money earned after a book has been published, usually in earned royalties.

Back order—An unfilled order held for future delivery, generally caused when a book is out of stock.

Backlist—List of publisher's previous publications still in print and available for sale.

Berne Convention—Common name for the agreement establishing the International Union for the Protection of Literary and Artistic Works, to which more than seventy nations are signatory.

Best-seller—A term that refers to a book that has appeared on a best-seller list somewhere. Some of the more common lists are *The New York Times*, *Publisher's Weekly* and the *LA Times*.

Bind-in—Message printed on a two- to four-page insert bound in book's center or at the back; usually provides a response card.

Blockbuster—Enormous best-seller.

Blurb—Comment, usually from well-known person or authority, praising book, used in advertising or on book jacket (also known as endorsement).

Boilerplate contract—A publisher's standard contract before the author or agent gets the modifications they want.

Book auction—A situation where two or more editors bid against each other to buy a book from an agent. The agent sets the rules of the auction ahead of time. The highest bidder usually wins.

Book club rights—The rights purchased by a book club, allowing it to offer the book to its membership.

Book clubs—Book clubs sell by direct mail, offering hardcover and paperback books to members at special club discount prices. They achieve these prices by buying large numbers of the book from the publisher at a high discount, reducing the author's standard royalty, but also binding their club members to buying "X" number of books per year.

Some book clubs reprint their own editions of books; this will ensure the author of a higher than usual book club royalty rate. But this only happens if the book club thinks it can sell vast numbers of a title to its membership, say the new Stephen King or Danielle Steel. Such books are often called main selections and alternate selections. Book clubs often cater to specific tastes, such as history, gardening, cooking, religion, computers and so on.

Book jacket—Removable paper cover, usually highly decorative, that protects a book's binding and usually gives information about book and author. It is sometimes said that a jacket is often a book's only form of advertising.

Book packager—Packagers create finished product for publishers, who often just print and distribute them under their own name.

Book proposal—This describes the structure of your proposed book and includes a sample chapter to demonstrate the voice or tone of the piece.

Bookseller—Person in retail business of selling books.

Bookstore—Retail establishment that stocks and sells books.

Bounce-back—Offer of a book or additional titles in a coupon or on the cover of the inside pages of a premium book.

Bound galleys—Uncorrected galleys cut and bound in booklike form before final corrections and revisions. Sent to reviewers and subsidiary rights clients.

Breakeven point—The number of copies a book must sell in order for the publisher to recover its costs for acquiring, producing and marketing the book. In theory, money earned after the breakeven point is reached is profit.

Brochure—Folded leaflet with advertising message, usually illustrated.

Business-to-business—Designating communications or dealings by agencies or between companies.

Buzz—Word-of-mouth excitement about a book.

Byline—The line that states the name of the author on a published article or feature.

Camera ready—Material that is ready to be photographed, without any further alteration or modification.

Campaign—Total planned sales/marketing effort on behalf of specific client, usually multimedia and over a specific period of time.

Case—Hard cover for a book.

Cash discount—Discount given for prompt payment of bills.

Catalog—An illustrated list of books usually from a publisher, that is systematically arranged usually by author or subject or publication month with descriptive information, prepared for a specific market, selling season or other purpose.

Category fiction—(*See* Genre/category.)

Chain—National or regional network of bookstores owned by one company.

Chapter book—A category of children's books. Chapter books are written for intermediate readers (four to eight years old) and have longer stories than picture books.

Children's books—Books published for children from preschool age to mid-teenage.

Clips—Samples of an author's published work or reviews taken from newspapers or magazines.

Clothbound—Hardcover book with a cloth binding.

College store—Retailer, institutionally or privately owned, catering predominately to college faculty and students.

Commission—The percentage an agent or manager receives as his fee after selling your work to a publisher. Agents receive commission on any money the book earns. Publishers' commissioned sales representatives also earn commission when they sell a book to a book buyer.

Compose—To set type to be printed.

Compositor—The person who designs and typesets manuscripts.

Concept—General ideas behind a slogan, pitch or campaign.

Consumer—Private individual at whom advertisements are aimed.

Cooperative advertising—Ad run by bookseller, the cost of which is shared by publisher.

Copublication—A book produced for two or more publishers, usually from more than one nation, where costs are shared.

Copyright—Literary, dramatic, artistic and musical property protection as authorized by the U.S. Constitution (Article 1, Section 8).

Cost to net sales ratio—The relationship between the cost of promotion and the net sales realized from it, usually expressed as a percentage.

Counter display/prepack—A display unit, usually constructed of cardboard, large enough to hold a limited quantity of books but small enough to be placed on a retailer's counter, frequently near the cash register to promote impulse buying.

Cover letter—A short letter of introduction sent along with a manuscript. The letter is usually only one page long and is normally used to remind an editor that the manuscript was expected or requested. A cover letter also accompanies a book proposal. (*See also* Query letter. A cover letter is not the same as a query letter.)

Cover price—The retail price of a book suggested by the publisher and printed on the jacket or cover.

Custom book—A book assembled from a large variety of available materials specifically to the customer's order. Used to some extent now in higher education by a teacher who may choose a set of text materials and then have it manufactured as a textbook in very small quantities for classes. A special edition of a book or parts of a book with a special cover for a specific company or association.

Deadline—When your book is due to the editor. It will be stated in the contract.

Demographics—A term used by market researchers and marketers to describe the quantifiable characteristics of a market or audience, such as age, sex, educational level, income level, number of books bought during a certain period, number of books read and so on. Demographic statistics permit researchers to segment markets.

Direct mail—Marketing directly to the consumer exclusively by mail.

Direct mail testing—Testing a segment of the market with different variables in a promotion, such as formats (package vs. self-mailer), copy approaches, price offers, reply devices, ink color, etc.

Direct marketing—Marketing via leaflets, brochures, letters, catalogs or print ads mailed or distributed directly to potential consumers; any medium used to elicit responses directly from consumers.

Direct premium—Book given free with purchase.

Discount—A percentage deducted from the retail or list price of a book, which determines the cost of the book to the dealer or institution purchasing it from the publisher or the wholesaler. Trade discounts (also called long discounts), established for selling general books to retailers, range from 30 to 49 percent and upward. A trade discount is printed by the publisher to announce the variations in discount dependent on quantities ordered. Legally a publisher must offer the same variations in discount to all booksellers. Short discounts are smaller discounts, usually under 30 percent, offered on the types of books sold primarily to professional persons or institutions.

Drive time—Radio ads directed at commuters in cars especially during morning or late afternoon.

Dummy—Paper, folded to look like an unbound book (usually), which can function as an artist's showcase for sketches for a book or can show the size and appearance of a projected publication to help sell the book to subsidiary rights clients or to retailers.

Dump bin—Floor display holding an assortment of loose items. Often it forms an eye-catching display unit on the shop floor.

Earned royalty—Money that a book makes in sales once it is available in the stores and elsewhere. (*See* Unearned royalties.)

Easy readers—A form of children's book that features short, easy sentences for younger readers.

Editorial board—The group of people in a publishing house who decide whether or not an editor can acquire a book. Also called a "pub board."

Electronic submission—Manuscript or proposal submission to an editor through electronic means, usually by e-mail or on computer disk.

Examination copy—A free or on-approval sample of a book given to a prospective buyer (often an educator) who will, the publisher hopes, study the work, approve of it and then adopt the book, resulting in multiple orders for institutional use. Also called inspection copy or comp (for complimentary) copy.

Exclusive submission—If only one editor or agent has been sent a submission, it is considered "exclusive."

Exhibition—Public show or display; convention.

F&Gs—Folded and gathered sheets, which are the printed signatures of the book, collated in sequence but not sewn or bound. Used for advance sales and reviews.

Face out—Books that are placed on a shelf with the face out toward the customer, rather than the spine facing out.

Fair use—A use of copyrighted material not needing authorization of the copyright holder. There is no exact definition.

Fiction—This is an invention, usually in the form of a story, that may or may not be based on real things that happened to you or someone else. There are broadly three types of fiction formats: short stories, usually no longer than 30 double-spaced manuscript pages and often much shorter; novellas, which range from 30 pages to 150 manuscript pages; and novels, which start at about 250 manuscript pages and go up. In reality, a good length to aim for in a novel is between 250 and 450 manuscript pages. Usually novels are the only thing that book publishers are interested in looking at as far as fiction is concerned.

First printing—The number of books printed in an initial print run. (*See* Second printing.)

First serial—A book excerpt that appears before it is published. (*See also* Second serial.)

Floor—The minimum bid in an auction situation.

Floor display—A sales device used in retail bookstores, also called a floor dump or dump bin.

Foreign rights—The right to publish a book either in its own language or in translation outside the country of origin.

Freight pass-through—A system designed to help retail booksellers defray freight charges on books by passing most of these charges on to the public. The actual cover price may be 3 to 5 percent higher than the price the publisher uses to calculate the seller's discount.

Front matter—The pages preceding the main text of a book, including half title, title page, copyright page, dedication, table of contents, foreword, preface, introduction.

Frontlist—A frontlist book is any new book, particularly something with high expectations from the publisher, that is featured as an up-and-coming book in a publisher's latest catalog.

Fulfillment—Activities embracing order processing, invoicing, handling of accounts receivable, payments and collections, credit control, shipping and warehousing, and the maintenance of sales and inventory records.

Galleys—Proofs made from type before it has been arranged in page format. With modern printing techniques, even first proofs are paginated, but the term still remains.

Genre/category—A classification of a work by its content. Examples of genre include Western, horror, romance and science fiction. Fiction that fits into these classifications is often called category fiction.

Genre publishing—Producing books in specific, well-defined and marketable subject areas. Also called category publishing or special interest publishing.

Ghostwriter—Someone who writes a book under another person's name. Nearly all ghostwriters are professional writers hired by high-profile celebrities or businesspeople without the time or talent to write the book themselves.

Giveaway—Promotion involving free novelties or gifts with purchase.

Handle—A strong, concise summary of key selling features of a book that can be used by a sales representative on calls to booksellers and by the bookseller to promote the book to prospective buyers.

Hardcover or cloth—Publishers sell their books in a variety of formats, principally "cloth" or hardcover, and paperback.

Hardcover books usually sell for $22.95 on up and have cardboard covers.

They are paid the most attention, reviewed more than any other type of book and offer an author the most prestige.

There are also large-size books known as "coffee table" books, which are usually collectable and often heavily illustrated rather than text-based. Except in special circumstances, such as when the author hits a best-seller list, hardcovers also sell less than any other type of book sold. Depending on who markets it and how enthusiastically, an average hardcover novel sells between three thousand to ten thousand copies. Authors can earn as little as $1,000 or as much as several million.

High-concept ideas—A high-concept idea is an idea that can be stated in a short paragraph. It's often outrageous and compelling, but it doesn't have to be.

House—Publishing house.

Imprint—Publisher's name printed on book's title page; division within publishing house.

Impulse buying—Buying for momentary pleasure rather than out of genuine need; buying on the spur of the moment rather than planned; sometimes encouraged by advertising or displays.

Independent distributor—Frequently shortened to ID; a wholesaler who specializes in the distribution of magazines and paperbacks to newsstands, supermarkets and outlets other than bookstores. IDs are generally local or regional in coverage of markets.

Independent store—A single retail outlet; one unaffiliated with any regional or national chain. Although there are more independent stores in the United States than members of chains, independents often charge that chains are sometimes given preferential treatment by publishers because of their enormous volume of orders, which entitles them to a higher discount and thus a higher margin of profit.

Independent wholesaler—Local wholesaler of magazines and mass-market paperbacks; same as ID.

In-pack—Book enclosed in a product package.

In print—A book that is currently on a publisher's frontlist or backlist, that is, still available for sale. (*See also* Out of print.)

Insert—Printed sheet or sheets inserted into publication or enclosed with mailing.

Instant book—A book that appears on the book stands within weeks of an event that is the focus of the book.

Inventory—Total stock of materials, including bound books in a warehouse or at a printer or bindery, unbound books at printer or bindery, paper owned by publisher. Sometimes, used as a verb meaning to count these materials.

ISBN—Each book has a unique ISBN (International Standard Book Number) that identifies it.

Jobber—Large-volume buyers of hardcover and softcover trade titles for resale to retail bookstores and libraries. Jobbers are distinct from wholesalers in the inventory they carry and in the services they offer, although recent years have witnessed a blurring of distinctions.

Juvenile books—Another name for children's books.

Kill fee—An amount paid to an author when something they wrote (usually on assignment) has been cancelled. The amount varies depending on the publication and the length/research done on the piece.

Kirkus reviews—An advance book review service.

Launch (concept meeting)—The first presentation by an editor of forthcoming titles to the marketing and sales staff. The first step in defining the publisher's seasonal list, these meetings enable editorial, marketing, sales, art and production staff to discuss the marketing and production requirements for each title. Based on the launch meeting presentation and discussion, the marketing director will project a first printing and, at a later point, will develop the marketing plan through discussion with individual departments.

Layout—The working diagram of a page or spread of pages for a printer to follow. Marked to show placement, size and kind of type, illustrations, etc.

Lead title—The one (or more) major book on a publisher's seasonal list.

Leader—Book, especially paperback, expected to sell best during a particular season and receiving greatest attention and promotion from publisher. Books of outstanding importance, whether commercially or by virtue of literary accomplishment, on a publisher's list of new publications.

Legs—Means an author's successive books are getting more and more sales.

Libel—A written statement or visual representation that holds a person or organization up to contempt and ridicule or monetary loss. Slander is spoken libel.

Line editor—As opposed to an acquisition editor, who signs up manuscripts for publication and may or may not work with the author over the text, a line editor doesn't usually acquire books but does work very closely with author and text to make certain the manuscript is in the best shape for publication.

List—(*See* Publishing list.)

Literary agent—Sometimes called an author's representative, a person who acts on behalf of the author to find a publisher, negotiate the contract and handle the subsidiary rights not acquired by the publisher. The agent is paid on a commission basis by the author, typically 15 percent of the author's income derived from the book represented.

Logo—Publisher's trademark.

Long discount—40 or 50 percent discount given by publisher when selling books in multiple quantities, usually to retailers and wholesalers.

Mail-in—A book offered on a mail request; either a self-liquidator or a free offer based on proof of purchase.

Mail-order publishing—Book publication or distribution by mail, especially through book clubs.

Mailing list—List of prospective customers organized by location, income, association or other aspect of consumer profile.

Mailing list profile—The common characteristics of a mailing list.

Mailing list rental—The rental of a mailing list from its owner for one-time use only for a special fee.

Market—Prospective customers for a given product.

Market profile—Characteristics of group or area target for campaign.

Market research—Study of consumer groups and business competition used to define projected market.

Market share—Percentage of specific market reached or sold by given product, advertisement or agency.

Marketing—Strategy and specific techniques used in reaching consumers to sell a product.

Marketing plan—Prepared for each title on a publisher's seasonal list, this plan itemizes the projected advertising, promotion, publicity and sales activities and their associated costs. Included in the individual marketing plan are subsidiary rights and special sales transactions. Marketing plans are generally prepared after launch meetings for forthcoming titles and are subject to revision before and after sales conferences.

Mass market—(*See* Paperback.)

Media—Forms of mass communication that carry advertising, especially newspapers, magazines, television and radio.

Midlist books—Books that acquire modest advances, have modest print runs and have a relatively short (two to three years) shelf life.

Multiple submissions—Submitting more than one piece of work at a time. (*See also* Simultaneous submissions.)

National distributor—In mass-market book distribution, national distributors function as agents for publishers and other clients in soliciting orders from local or regional independent distributors (IDs) and handling shipping and fulfillment. Every paperback house engages the services of a national distributor, which may distribute for a number of houses or solely for its own publishing outlet.

Negative option—Book club marketing technique in which member receives selection automatically unless he notifies club to the contrary.

Net price—What a wholesaler or bookseller pays for a product after all discounts and allowances have been made.

Net pricing—A method of determining a wholesale price without reference to a suggested retail price. The publisher sets the price of a book to the bookseller or wholesaler, and each bookselling and wholesaling operation establishes its own resale price to the consumer, thus determining its own margin of profit.

Nonfiction—This is exactly what it means—anything that is not fiction. That is, it's all true and based on research and/or expert opinion. Pay attention to that last part—expert opinion, not just your opinion on something you think you have an insight into.

Novelization—A novel created as a tie-in with a movie or television program or series.

Novelties/chatchkas—Free items, such as matches, calendars, buttons bearing the advertiser's logo.

On consignment—Merchandise supplied to a dealer with the understanding that it need not be paid for until sold. If not sold, it can be returned to the supplier without penalty.

On spec—Something written after an editor has expressed an interest in the topic or idea but has not made a specific request or assignment for the piece. The editor has no obligation to accept the final work. Most book projects (whether fiction or nonfiction) fall into this category.

On-demand publishing—Method of publication that manufactures books only in response to specific purchase orders.

Option clause—The clause in an author's contract that requires an author to give his publisher an exclusive period (often thirty to sixty days) to buy his next book before other publishers get a chance to see it.

Orphan—A book that has lost its editor (because she's moved to another house or has been fired) and is being published with no in-house advocate.

Out of print—A book that is no longer for sale or available for sale is considered out of print. Author's contracts specifically define what "out of print" means.

Out of stock (OS)—A term used when the publisher's inventory on a specific title is temporarily exhausted and the new printing has not yet been received.

Over-the-transom—Manuscripts that have arrived unrequested at an editor's or publisher's office. (*See* Slush pile.)

P&L statement—A profit and loss statement is one that an editor uses to calculate whether or not he can afford to acquire a book and how much of an advance he will offer.

Page count—The number of pages in a book. In a book contract it is often calculated and defined by a word count.

Paperback—Paperback books break down into two main types: trade or hardcover-sized formats (usually 6″ × 4″), and mass market.

Trade format books fill the gap between mass market and hardcover and are often used for high-quality fiction or a certain type of practical nonfiction such as child-rearing advice, Zen Buddhism, commercial but intellectually stimulating titles, etc. On average they sell anywhere from ten thousand to twenty-five thousand copies and cost approximately $13 to $15 each.

Mass-market books are aimed at the lowest common denominator and the highest possible sales. In nonfiction it's often *National Inquirer* or *People* magazine type material, reprints of successful (or sometimes not so successful but nevertheless well-publicized) hardcovers. In fiction they are usually genre books (science fiction, mystery, romance, horror, Westerns, etc.) and are widely available in bookstores, supermarkets and so forth.

They are usually priced in the $6 range. Mass-market paperbacks were developed in the 1950s and boomed into the 1960s and 1970s. They sell from twenty-five thousand copies to upwards of one hundred thousand, though more copies are often returned to the publisher than are actually sold. A 40 percent sell-through is considered average for a mass-market paperback's print run.

Paperback original—A work published in paperback format without having been previously available as a hardcover. It may be a mass-market paperback or a trade paperback.

Paperback rights—The rights to publish a book in a mass-market or trade paperback format. The rights may be to a paperback original or to a paperback reprint. Rights to mass-market and trade paperback editions are usually negotiated separately, but they can be combined as a package deal.

Parody—A piece that pokes fun at a well-known book, film or TV show.

Payment on acceptance—Payment is sent to the author as soon as a piece is accepted by the editor.

Payment on publication—Payment for an accepted piece is delayed until the work appears in print.

Pen name/pseudonym—A name other than an author's legal name. Works are published under a pen name or pseudonym when the author wishes to remain anonymous.

Permission—The right to use someone else's material in your book. A writer must usually get a permission form signed by the copyright holder.

Platform—The author's proven ability to promote and sell books through public speaking, a TV or radio show or newspaper column.

Print run—The number of books printed each time a book goes to press.

Public domain—A work whose copyright has expired.

Public relations (PR)—Business of producing goodwill and acceptance in public toward an individual, cause, company or product.

Publication date—Date on which a published book is first available for sale, often called pub date.

Publicist—Person responsible for informing media and public of book's publication.

Publicity—Exposure and promotion of new book in the electronic media and the press.

***Publisher's Weekly* (PW)**—News magazine of the publishing industry.

Publishing—Business and practice of reproducing and issuing for sale books or periodicals.

Publishing house—Company engaged in acquiring, editing, producing, marketing and selling books and/or periodicals.

Publishing list—Publishers generally have two major seasons when they announce with as much fanfare as they can muster the publication of their author's latest books.

These are the spring list, roughly from April to September, and the fall list, roughly from October to the following March. The actual months covered vary from publisher to publisher.

Some publishers have rejigged their seasons, introducing a third season that covers the summer months, in an effort to attract booksellers' attention when no major books are due to be launched.

Query letter—A letter sent to ask an editor if s/he is interested in seeing your project. The query introduces the nonfiction proposal or novel, outlines the writer's qualifications for writing it and lists previous publications. (*See also* Cover letter. A query letter is not the same as a cover letter.)

Rack—A unit commonly made of wire designed to display magazines or mass-market paperback books. A rack may be massive and permanent, but it is usually light enough to be portable, and it may even revolve.

Rack size—Describing typical format of mass-market paperback books.

Readers—People who are paid to read manuscripts for editors and write reader's reports on the manuscript.

Reader's report—A one- or two-page summary of a book that also points up its strengths and weaknesses.

Reissue—Newly printed edition of previously published book. Books are often reissued when a national event or a movie based on the book or late-breaking publicity calls for a new edition and new promotion and publicity.

Rejection letter—A letter that says "no thanks" from an editor or agent.

Religious books—Bibles, testaments, hymnals, prayer books and other works of specifically religious or inspirational content.

Remaindered books—Books that have been sold by a publisher to a discounter (also called a "jobber") for a fraction of their cover price value and end up on remainder tables in bookstores.

Reprint—1. New printing in original format. 2. Reissue in new format.

Returns—Copies of a book that are returned to the publisher by the bookstore once the store clears its shelves to make way for copies of new books to be sold. Publishers hate them.

The intricacies of selling books involve sell-through rates, returns, discount rates to bookstore chains and less favorable discounts to small independent bookstores, etc. If an author has heavy returns on his books, it can affect his ability to publish future books with that or any other publishing company.

Review—Published critical assessment of new book.

Review copies—Copies of a book that are sent to reviewers ahead of the publication date.

Rights—Rights to a literary property include the following: prepublication serial;

book publication, including book club; postpublication serial; book reprint; dramatization; musical adaptation; amateur leasing; motion picture, television and radio; electronic; condensation and abridgment; anthology; translation; quotation; merchandising and other commercial exploitation. Most of these are also commonly referred to as subsidiary rights and are governed by the prevailing copyright law.

Rights and permissions—Rights to reprint, excerpt, condense or otherwise exploit published matter in some form, negotiated by the subsidiary rights and permissions department of publishing company or literary agent.

Royalty—(*See* Royalty rate.)

Royalty advance—This is the money that an author is paid by a publisher for the license to print and sell the author's book. It is more accurately called an advance against royalties and is often paid in two or more payments: after the signing of the publishing contract and after the acceptance by an editor of the finished manuscript. Some publishing companies try to delay the second payment until after the book is published, but this is an old-fashioned practice that authors and their agents fight tooth and nail.

However, because the number of competing publishing companies is shrinking, creating a bias in favor of the buyer not the seller, and advances for certain authors can be so high, some companies are now splitting advances of over $100,000 into thirds or more, which includes a last payment on publication.

The money is not a gift to the author, however. It is a calculated "best guess" by the publishing company as to what the author's book is worth in terms of royalties earned through "X" number of copies sold.

Royalty rate—The author's fee or royalty advance for writing is "guesstimated" by the editor and included in the total costs of producing the book.

For each copy sold, the author earns at a predetermined royalty rate, which can escalate after a certain number of the books have been sold. (It can be, for example, 10 percent of the net price of the book for the first five thousand copies sold.) That earned income, collected like drops of water accumulating in a barrel, pays down the deficit of money already advanced to the author. The advance is not really a debt, though, because if the book does not earn back its royalty advance, the author does not owe the publishing company any money or have to pay back anything. The company took a gamble, rolled the dice, lost and takes its financial beating like a man—almost.

The author of books that regularly fall into the red will quickly get smaller and smaller advances, and within a short space of time have trouble getting anything he wrote published, regardless of its quality.

Sales conference—Meeting where new books are presented to publisher's sales-people, who then solicit orders; usually convened twice or three times a year and brings together sales, marketing and editorial staff.

Sales force—Publishing house employees involved with selling books to bookstores, wholesalers and others. Sometimes publishers use a commissioned sales force, that is, a company not employed directly by them.

SASE—A self-addressed, stamped envelope. SASEs are required if the author wishes to receive an answer from an editor. The SASE should be large enough and carry enough postage to return the manuscript if it is rejected. If the author doesn't want the manuscript returned, a note to that effect should be included, but a letter-sized SASE is still required for the editor's response. If the author requests any information from the editor, such as writer's guidelines, an SASE should be enclosed.

Scholarly publishing—Publication of books and periodicals on academic, research or scholarly topics. Not usually of interest to the general public.

Second printing—(*See also* First printing.) When a first print run sells through and the demand for the book continues, the publisher will go back to press and produce another print run of the book. This is a second printing. If these sell out and the demand is still high, they will do a third and perhaps a fourth printing until demand dies down.

Second serial—An excerpt from a book that appears after it has been published. (*See also* First serial.)

Self-publishing—Books published and financed by the author. There are notable cases where the rights to successful self-published books were acquired by a publishing house and became highly successful on a national level.

Sell-through—The number of copies actually sold of a particular title. Publishers take "orders" from bookstores, who get books sent to them on consignment. The bookstore guesses how many copies of a particular title they will sell and then orders that number of books. They keep the title on the shelf for perhaps a month; then if demand dries up, they ship the remainder back to the publisher.

All the sales figures are dutifully recorded on the bookstore's computers, and the next time a book by that author comes up, say when the sales rep comes back to the store trying to sell the author's latest book, the bookstore buyers will check their records and only order the number of books the last title by that author sold, regardless of how different or how much more potentially successful the new book is viewed.

Serial rights—Commercial rights to publication of parts of a work in a magazine or newspaper, either before or after publication.

Serialization—Publication of a book in installments by a periodical, either before or after publication.

Shelf life—Duration for which books are stocked by bookstores before being returned to publisher.

Shelf talker—Cardboard display piece designed to fit in bookshelf under books and that calls attention to the books. Helps compensate for spine-out display.

Short discount—Discount given by publishers to libraries, colleges and other institutions who do not resell the books.

Simultaneous submissions—Submitting a work to several publishers at the same time. Some publishers accept simultaneous submissions; others will refuse to even look at them. The author should always state when a work is being submitted to more than one publisher. (*See also* Multiple submissions.)

Slit card—A poster slit so as to fit into or around a book for display purposes.

Slush pile—Slush pile is what the sackloads of unsolicited manuscripts at a publishing house are called.

Small press—Publishing house with limited output, sometimes in a specialized field.

Special sales—Sales of books through other than normal wholesale and retail channels; *i.e.*, through catalogs, museum shops, to corporations or other organizations.

Spot advertising—Advertising in selected locales rather than nationally.

Standard Advertising Unit (SAU)—System of standard dimensions for print advertising based on six columns, each $2\frac{1}{16}''$ wide.

Stet—The term used to reinstate material marked as a deletion.

Streamer—Long, narrow sign with message in bold type hung across open area, window or doorway.

Subscription agent—An organization that handles the entering and renewal of subscriptions or by mail.

Subsidiary rights—These break down into a variety of potential moneymaking extras for a fortunate author from translations, to dramatic and film, audio and magazine reprints, especially if the author has managed to retain these rights for herself when the book was originally sold to the publisher.

If the publishing company has a share of these rights, an agreed-upon percentage of the money earned from the sale of these rights (say, 50/50 or 75/25 in favor of the author) will be split between the author and the company. If the royalty advance has not yet been fully paid back, the author's share of these sales will go toward paying off that royalty advance. Once the advance has been paid back, if the book continues to sell, the author will receive twice yearly royalty statements accompanied by checks.

Subsidy publisher—A publisher that requires an author to pay for the publication of his or her work. Often the subsidy publisher will retain the rights, paying the author a royalty on copies sold, even though the author is the one who must do most of the distribution and selling.

Synopsis—A brief summary of a work. Depending on the length of the piece, the synopsis may be from one paragraph to thirty pages long. The synopsis is not the same as an outline, as it rarely carries elements such as chapter headings and is generally in a narrative form.

Table topper—Exhibit arranged on table rather than floor.

Target audience—Consumer groups most likely to buy product, identified by region, age, demographics or economic status; target market.

Telemarketing—Selling, advertising or market research done by telephone.

Test market—Consumer group interviewed to determine target audience.

Textbook—Book created predominantly for use in formal educational settings and often equipped with educational apparatus such as summaries and test questions.

Tie-in—A book that exists because of a movie, dramatic performance or television program that inspired it. Sometimes a book is the original work, but a reissue is published that ties in with movie, etc., through new photographs, artwork and so on.

Title page—A page at the beginning of the book, usually on the right, giving the title, author and publisher, often with place and date of publications. The copyright page usually is on the reverse of the title page.

Trade book—Book for the general market, distributed largely through bookstores and libraries.

Trade paperback—A paperback book that is often like a hardcover book in size and quality, but with a paper cover instead of a cardboard cover.

Trade publishing—Publication of hardcover and paperback books of interest to the general public and distributed largely through bookstores and libraries.

Trade show—Convention at which advertising agencies or related companies show and compare products and ideas.

Translation—Text rendered in language other than original language in which it was written and published.

Typo—A misspelled word in a book, manuscript or page proof.

Unearned royalty—(*See* Royalty advance; Earned royalties.)

Universal product code (UPC)—A preprinted product and price code consisting of vertical bars that appears on the outside or inside cover or jacket of books and other consumer goods. UPCs are electronically scanned for sales price and inventory control.

University press—A publishing house attached to a college or institution that is not primarily for commercial purposes.

Unsolicited manuscript—A manuscript sent to an editor or publisher without its being requested. Unsolicited manuscripts normally end up on the slush pile.

Vertical publishing—A large number of publishing companies have converged and become part of groups and conglomerates. In the last twenty years, publishing has moved from a structure of individual hardcover houses and individual paperback houses, known as "horizontal" publishing, to companies that buy books that they can publish first as hardcovers and then as a paperback, known as "vertical" publishing. Doubleday and Dell are such an oak tree and ivy team, for example, as are New American Library and Dutton, or Simon & Schuster and Pocket Books to mention but a small number. However, many companies also publish both hardcover and mass market under the same name, such as Warner Books or Bantam.

Wholesaler—A large-volume buyer of primarily mass-market books for distribution to book racks in newsstands, drugstores, discount stores and similar outlets.

Word count—The number of words that make up a manuscript, usually calculated on a 12-point Roman or Courier font and 200 to 250 words to a page.

Work-for-hire—A piece of writing that is written to an editor's or publisher's request and all rights to the work belong to the publication. The writer gives up the copyright to this work and can never receive additional income from it, even if it is resold.

World rights—Publication rights to a particular work throughout the world.

Young adult books—Books written primarily for children twelve and up. Occasionally books published originally for adults become the province of the young adult market, *i.e., The Catcher in the Rye* by J.D. Salinger.

Index

More Great Books for Writers!

The Writer's Market Companion—Joe Feiertag and Mary Carmen Cupito. In today's information age there are more books, magazines and written communications being produced than ever before. *The Writer's Market Companion* helps you get in on the action, so you can get published and paid for your work, whether you write articles, screenplays, novels or newsletters. It's packed with sound information on professional writing issues, focusing on everything from contracts to creativity.
ISBN 0-89879-930-9 ✳ paperback ✳ 344 pages ✳ 10653-K

Formatting & Submitting Your Manuscript—Jack and Glenda Neff, Don Prues, and the editors of Writer's Market. Increase your odds of getting published! *Formatting & Submitting Your Manuscript* makes it easy by featuring full-size examples of how to present your manuscript. Covering every part of the manuscript submission package— from query letters and proposals to synopses and follow-up correspondence—this guide shows you the dos and don'ts for creating a persuasive and professional first impression.
ISBN 0-89879-921-X ✳ paperback ✳ 248 pages ✳ 10618-K

Guerrilla Marketing for Writers—Jay Conrad Levinson, Rick Frishman and Michael Larsen. Packed with proven insights and advice, *Guerrilla Marketing for Writers* details one hundred "classified secrets" that will help you sell your work before and after it's published. This wide range of weapons—practical low-cost and no-cost marketing techniques—will help you design a powerful strategy for strengthening your proposals, promoting your books and maximizing your sales.
ISBN 0-89879-983-X ✳ hardcover ✳ 292 pages ✳ 10667-K

Too Lazy to Work, Too Nervous to Steal—John Clausen provides all the information you need to turn your love of writing into a moneymaking business. Learn how to develop a realistic business plan, market your services and more. Clausen's friendly, funny style—a cross between a pep rally, a writer's workshop, stand-up comedy and good old-fashioned storytelling—will enable you to live your dream and succeed.
ISBN 0-89879-997-X ✳ hardcover ✳ 256 pages ✳ #10732-K

The Writer's Idea Book—Jack Heffron, Editorial Director at Writer's Digest Books, helps jump-start your creativity with over four hundred idea-generating prompts and exercises. He'll show you how to determine which ideas engage you the most, ensuring that the ones you choose are the ones you'll develop into something extraordinary. Heffron's encouraging insights and advice gets and keeps your words flowing.
ISBN 0-89879-873-6 ✳ hardcover ✳ 272 pages ✳ #10594-K

Get Organized, Get Published—Don Aslett and Carol Cartaino. This lively, inspirational and browsable book provides tips for living the writer's life simply and efficiently. You'll find page after page of useful advice, covering everything from organizing your desk to tracking submissions. By following this advice, you'll generate more ideas, complete more projects, and systematically submit your work to editors and agents.
ISBN 1-58297-003-3 ✳ hardcover ✳ 240 pages ✳ #10689-K

These books and other fine Writer's Digest titles are available from your local bookstore, online supplier or by calling 1-800-289-0963.